The Sea of Memories

David Gatward ■ Dynamo

OXFORD
UNIVERSITY PRESS

TEAM X

Max, Cat, Ant and Tiger are four ordinary children with four extraordinary watches. When activated, their watches allow them to shrink to micro-size.

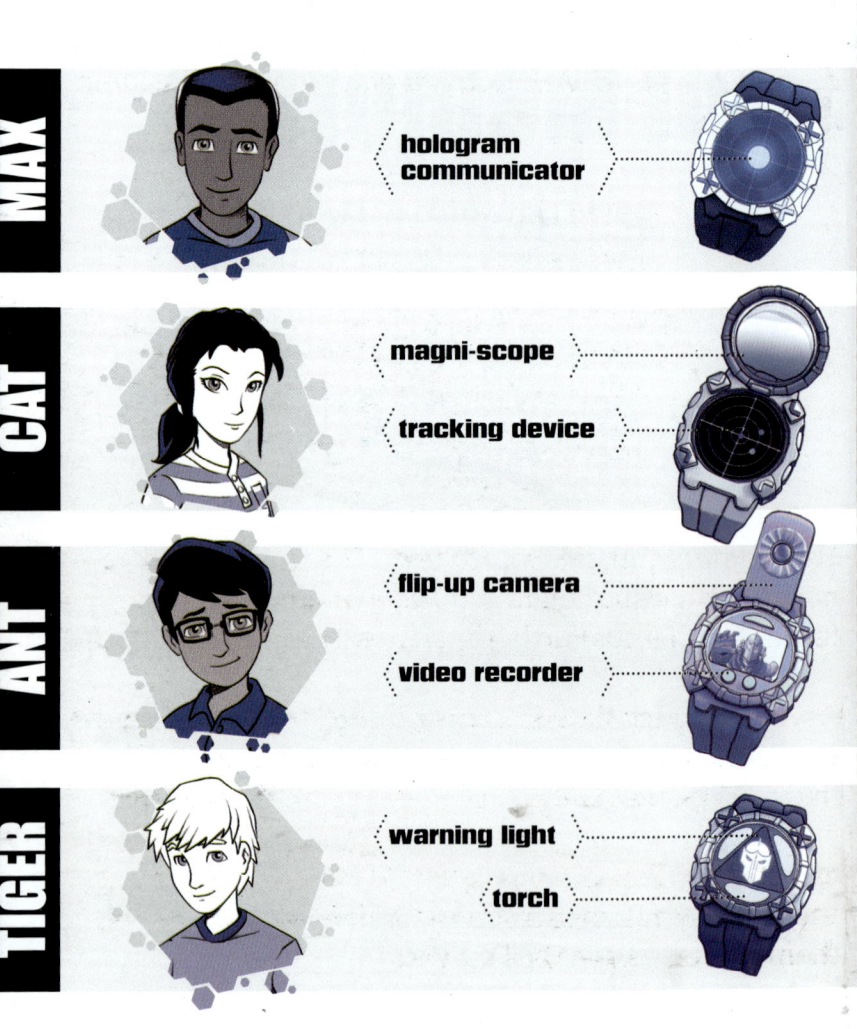

MAX — hologram communicator

CAT — magni-scope, tracking device

ANT — flip-up camera, video recorder

TIGER — warning light, torch

Previously ...

The watches were running low on power. Ant tried to recharge them using a machine that he had invented. However, during this process, something in the watches changed irrevocably.

When all the watches are synchronized, the micro-friends can travel through a rip in the fabric of space and time to other dimensions. Max, Cat, Ant and Tiger have become *rip-jumpers*.

Unfortunately, there is a problem. The rip has become permanently stuck open ... in Tiger's wardrobe! This leaves Earth – our Earth – open to attack.

A woman called **Perlest** came through the rip saying she wanted to help. She told the children that they need to find the **Weaver**. Only he can seal the rip shut forever.

Now the children are trying to find Perlest's hidden thoughts – contained in **thought vials** – which will help them to track down the Weaver.

Chapter 1 – Strange memories

Cat landed with a splash. She instinctively held her breath as she sank under the water. Above her, she saw sunlight glimmering on the surface. Then, with a kick of her legs, she burst upwards and out into fresh air. Nearby, her friends Max, Ant and Tiger were already treading water.

Only moments before, the friends had been in Tiger's bedroom.

'I didn't think we'd be dropped right into the sea,' Cat spluttered. She didn't mind swimming; she just wished she'd brought her goggles. Although she was soaking wet, her hair was already drying thanks to the bright, warm sun.

Tiger twisted his body in the waves, kicking round in a circle. He stared at the horizon. 'I can't see land anywhere,' he said, straining his eyes to see if he had missed anything. 'How are we supposed to find anything here? It's impossible!'

Perlest had sent the friends to this watery dimension in search of another of her lost memories, or, perhaps, news of the Weaver himself.

Max stared into the middle distance for a moment. His eyes glazed over. Then he said softly, 'We need to go to the underwater city.'

'What underwater city?' asked Ant, swivelling round to stare at Max.

'Yeah, Max, what are you talking ab–' Tiger stopped mid-flow. His eyes glazed like Max's had done. 'Yes. The underwater city. We can have a look at the crystal flower forest, too.'

Cat, who was as confused as Ant, asked, 'What are they talking about? What city? What forest? Did they knock their heads when they went through the rip?'

Ant scooped up some of the seawater in his hand and let it run out between his fingers. 'Of course!' Ant exclaimed. 'It's obvious!'

'Er, not to me!' Cat snapped.

'Perlest said this was a dimension of memories, right?' Ant said to his friends.

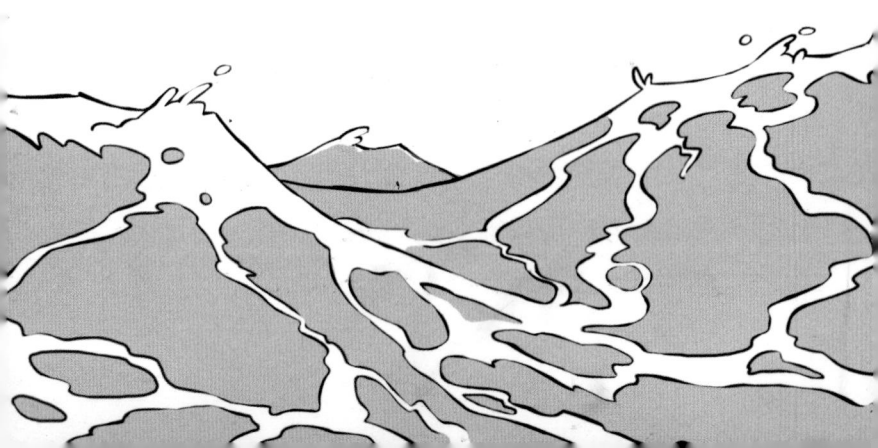

'And?' said Cat.

'Well, I don't think that this is just normal seawater,' Ant went on to explain. 'I think it conducts the thoughts and memories of those who live here!'

Max, who seemed to be back to normal now, nodded slowly. 'So what you're saying is, because we're in the sea, we have absorbed some of those memories?' he said. 'That's how we know about the underwater city and the forest?'

'That's it!' said Ant.

Tiger was lying on his back, as though he was relaxing on a bed. He gazed up at the sky. 'It could be worse,' he said. 'The sea could be filled with huge and terrifying sea monsters!'

'That isn't funny,' said Cat.

'Oh, come on, it's a little bit funny!' Tiger said with a smirk. 'It's not like sea monsters actually exist, is it?'

Cat opened her mouth to say something, then froze. Her eyes glazed over.

Max saw her face twist with fear. 'Cat? What's up?'

'Monsters are real …'

At that very moment, there was a disturbance in the water beside them. The friends watched, horrified, as something sinuous and slimy emerged from the waves.

It was a tentacle covered in a mottled pattern of browns, greens and reds that seemed to change colour and swirl together in the sunlight. Underneath, it was a mass of huge, pulsating suckers. The tentacle stretched high up into the air to tower above them, arching like a cobra.

'I've got an idea,' said Max.

The others looked at him, wide-eyed with terror.

'SWIM!'

Chapter 2 – **Tentacle trap**

The giant tentacle smashed down with a tremendous force where the friends had been only seconds before. Great waves exploded upwards, high into the sky. Water spewed out in every direction as though it was desperate to escape from whatever horror the tentacle was attached to beneath the surface. Then another tentacle appeared, bursting up and out of the sea with ferocious speed. The tentacles twisted together; slime dripped from them in great globs into the water below. Then the tentacles uncurled and began to reach in the friends' direction.

'Split up!' Max shouted. 'It can't chase all of us at the same time.'

Max, Cat, Ant and Tiger swam in different directions as the tentacles shot towards them.

Cat jabbed her arms out in front of her body, her hands cutting through the water to pull her forwards as her legs kicked hard. She was a strong, fast swimmer. Only she wasn't fast enough. One of the tentacles struck the surface next to her, and the force shot her and the others into the air in a fountain of water.

Cat could hear Max, Ant and Tiger yelling and screaming. Then all four of them landed back in the water.

Cat tried to paddle forward but, as she pushed into a stroke, her hands found nothing but air. She realized that, somehow, she was above the sea!

'Help!' she cried.

Ant's eyes almost popped out of his skull as he watched a tentacle rise from the water under Cat and bounce her high into the air. She shot upwards like a cork from a bottle. Then another tentacle caught her as she plummeted back down to the sea below. With a mighty splash, the tentacle pulled Cat down into the water, dragging her under the surface.

Ant's head snapped left and right, as he desperately tried to see where Cat had gone. As panic gripped him, Cat burst out of the water, a tentacle wrapped tightly round her waist.

'Help!' she called again, water spluttering from her mouth. Suddenly she was submerged, pulled downwards again by an irresistible force.

Ant felt something whip around his feet. Suckers gripped at his legs. He tried to kick them away, but it was useless.

Max had stopped swimming and was staring in horror at the spot where Cat had disappeared. The sea monster had her ... and it was coming for the rest of them, too. For once, he didn't know what to do. Panic was twisting his stomach into knots. How were they going to save Cat? How were they going to save themselves?

Nearby, Tiger called out, 'What are we going to do?'

Max wasn't given time to answer. He didn't even *have* an answer. The full awfulness of the creature was now breaking through the waves.

The sea monster strongly resembled an octopus – only much bigger and a lot more terrifying. Its eight gigantic tentacles were each as long as a cruise liner. The tentacles were twisting and entwining; the hundreds of suckers pulsated horribly. The slimy knots of squishy muscle reached out for the friends, churning the water into a milky white froth.

The once-calm sea was now broken by towering, crashing waves as the creature rose even further out of the water. Max had a split-second to hold his breath before a wave washed over him. He tried to swim, but another wave swept him backwards into Ant and Tiger. Then a tentacle grabbed Max. One of the suckers clamped on to his head. The rest of the tentacle wrapped round him and he couldn't move. The stench of the creature close up was unbearable.

Then Max heard the yells of his friends and, moments later, was suddenly face-to-face with Ant and Tiger, high above the water.

'Now what?' asked Tiger, gasping as the tentacle wrapped tighter and tighter around his body. Every time he breathed out, the tentacle crushed him a little more. He knew that soon he wouldn't be able to draw breath at all. The life was, quite literally, being squeezed out of him.

They were all completely helpless, held up in the air by the creature. The friends could see a bulbous, palpitating head with enormous hungry eyes staring up at them greedily. At the base of the body, where it joined the tentacles, was a hole big enough to swallow a yacht. Hundreds of teeth lined the giant mouth and, as they crunched and ground together, the creature's breath hissed out, sounding like shingle cast up on a beach.

'Any ideas?' Ant asked Max.

'Hold your breath,' Max answered just before the octopus dived under the water, pulling Max, Ant and Tiger after it and sucking them down into a watery whirlpool of darkness.

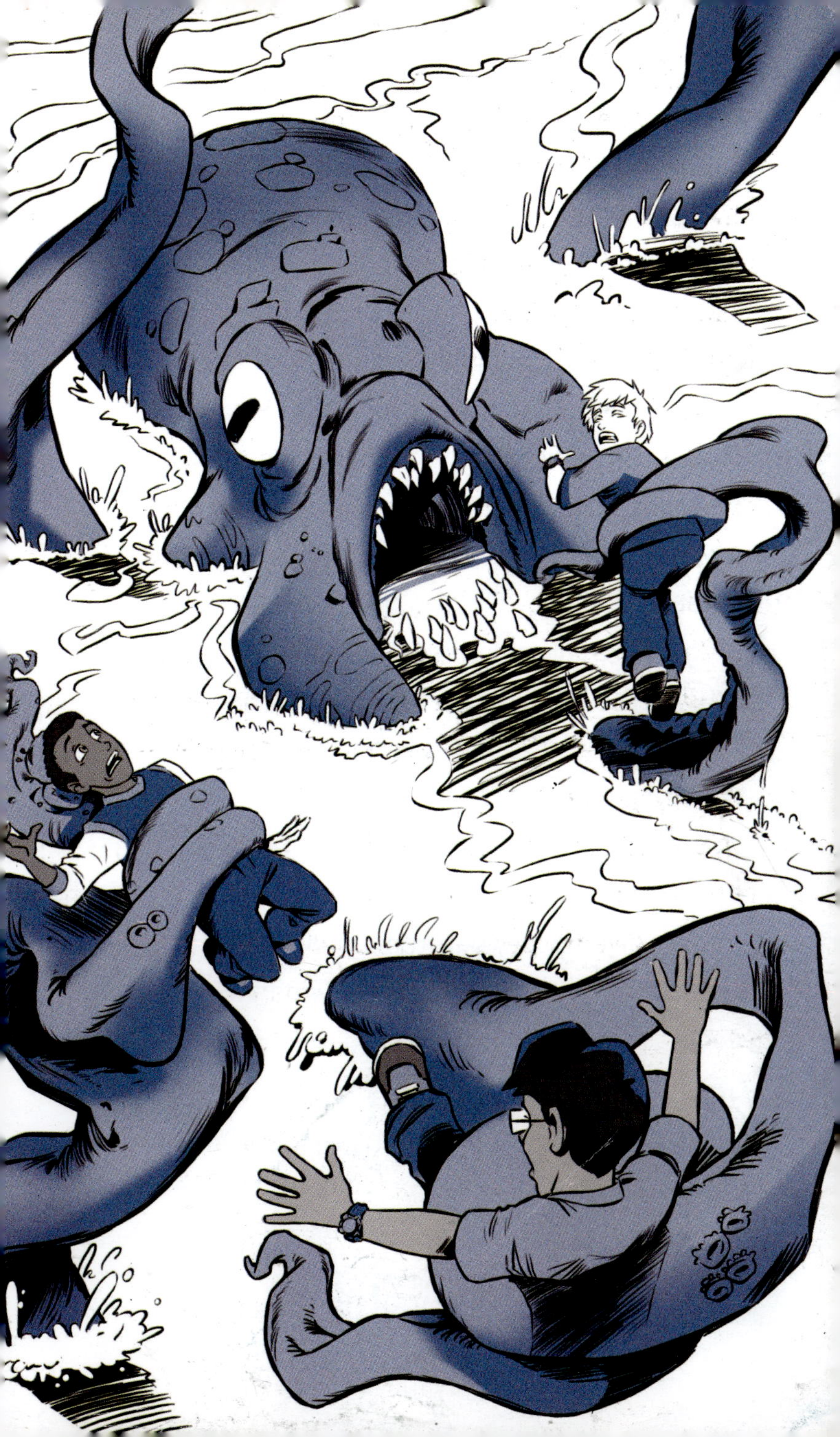

Chapter 3 – What's for dinner?

Tiger's eyes were stinging in the salty water. He closed them tightly. They were descending fast, the octopus pinioning them in its tentacles as it raced downwards. Tiger's lungs were hurting, too. He didn't know how much longer he could hold his breath. At home, he had once managed to swim a whole length of the local pool underwater, but at least then he'd known he could pop up for more air at any moment. There was no chance of that now.

Tiger held on for as long as he could. Then suddenly, it was no good. He had to open his mouth. He had to breathe!

Tiger's ears popped. It reminded him of being on a plane during take-off. Then he noticed something very peculiar indeed. He was still breathing!

But that's impossible, thought Tiger. He was underwater – and if there was one thing he knew about water, it was that being able to breathe in it involved being a fish and having gills. He wasn't and he didn't. So what was going on?

Slowly, Tiger opened one eye, then the other.

'I know, it's weird, right?' said Cat, her voice sounding muffled and distant.

Tiger's eyes were wide open now. Still wrapped in tentacles, he saw Cat and Ant. They each had what looked like a near-transparent space helmet over their heads. Tiger watched as the creature held Max with one tentacle while another tentacle released a helmet-shaped air bubble from its suckers and positioned it over Max's head, sealing it with a *plop*.

Tiger took another deep breath and managed to wriggle one of his hands free, reaching it out to touch his own air bubble. It was soft, springy and sticky.

'This is impossible!' he cried. 'In fact, it's even more than that; I don't think there's a word to describe it!'

'You could try *inconceivable*,' said Ant. 'But even that doesn't really do it justice.'

'Well, apparently it isn't impossible *or* inconceivable,' said Max, cutting in. 'Not in this dimension, anyway.'

The friend's voices were muffled but, amazingly, they could all hear each other well enough. The octopus-creature was now speeding through the ocean, dragging them along behind.

'I'm still trying to work out how the octopus has made the air bubbles,' Ant said.

'Who cares?' asked Tiger.

'I think it's the slime,' Ant continued, his brow furrowed deep with thought. 'Somehow the octopus can use its tentacles to trap air and create the bubbles … a bit like a balloon, really.'

'So I'm wearing a slime helmet?' Cat screwed up her face in disgust.

'Cool!' exclaimed Tiger.

'I don't know,' said Max. 'That hideous thing isn't keeping us alive just for fun.'

'How do you mean?' asked Tiger, wishing immediately he hadn't asked the question, because he knew what answer was coming.

'It probably prefers fresh meat,' said Max, shivering at the macabre truth. 'That's the only reason I can think of for keeping us alive.'

The octopus changed course, bumping the four friends so that their air bubbles knocked against the sides of their heads.

'Gross!' groaned Cat, as slimy mucus stuck to her face. Then she realized the octopus was slowing down. They were now drifting rather than speeding through the sea, and she was able to look around. Shoals of fish in all sorts of shapes and sizes swam above and below them.

'I think we're getting close to wherever it's taking us,' said Tiger.

'I agree,' Ant said. 'And that could be good. But then, it could also be *seriously* bad.'

'Then let's focus on the good,' countered Max. 'We're alive, because it wants us to stay that way. So we still have a chance to escape.'

'I think it's heading for those rocks on the seabed,' observed Cat, peering down through the water.

Max, Ant and Tiger looked to where Cat was pointing. Huge dark rocks, covered in coral, rose from a rippled sandy floor.

'Those rocks seem to form a cave,' said Max. 'Maybe we're going in there.'

The octopus slowed still further until it came to a dead stop near the rocks, then the creature wrenched them all downwards on to the sandy ocean floor. Using its tentacles, the octopus tied each of the friends to a rock with long pieces of viscous, sticky seaweed. The friends were bound so tightly they couldn't move their arms or their legs.

'What is that revolting smell?' asked Cat.

'That,' said Max, nodding. 'Look …'

Cat, Ant and Tiger stared. It was a whale. A very dead one.

Tiger grimaced. 'It reeks!'

The ground around the whale was dotted with the bones of other sea creatures.

'I think you're right, Max,' said Ant. 'The octopus has brought us to its feeding place!'

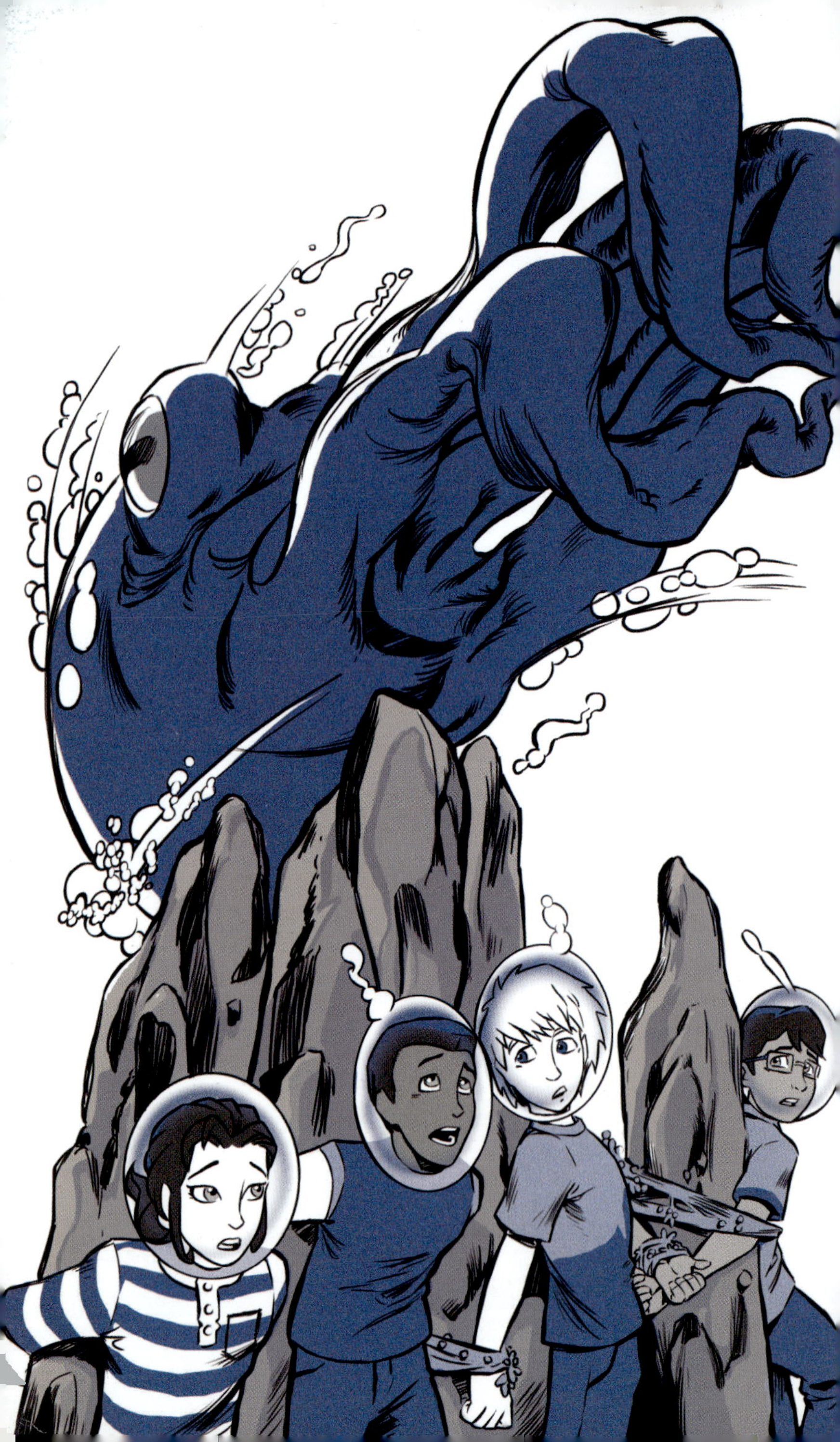

Chapter 4 – Rescue?

The friends watched in horror as the creature wrapped a tentacle around the smelly, rotting whale carcass and started to rip the last chunks of meat off the dead whale with its suckered tentacles. One by one, it pushed the pieces into its mouth, chewing with ease. When it had finished, the octopus drifted closer to the friends again, its mouth dripping with goo and whale blubber.

The creature's huge eyes loomed over them, staring down hungrily.

Cat screwed her eyes shut and twisted her face as far away from the octopus's mouth as she could, trying to escape the rancid stench emitting from it.

Max tugged desperately at the seaweed binding him. 'We need to escape!'

No one disagreed – but they couldn't move their hands and feet either. They couldn't even move their hands close enough to their watches to shrink.

A tentacle reached out towards the friends …

'What's that?' cried Tiger.

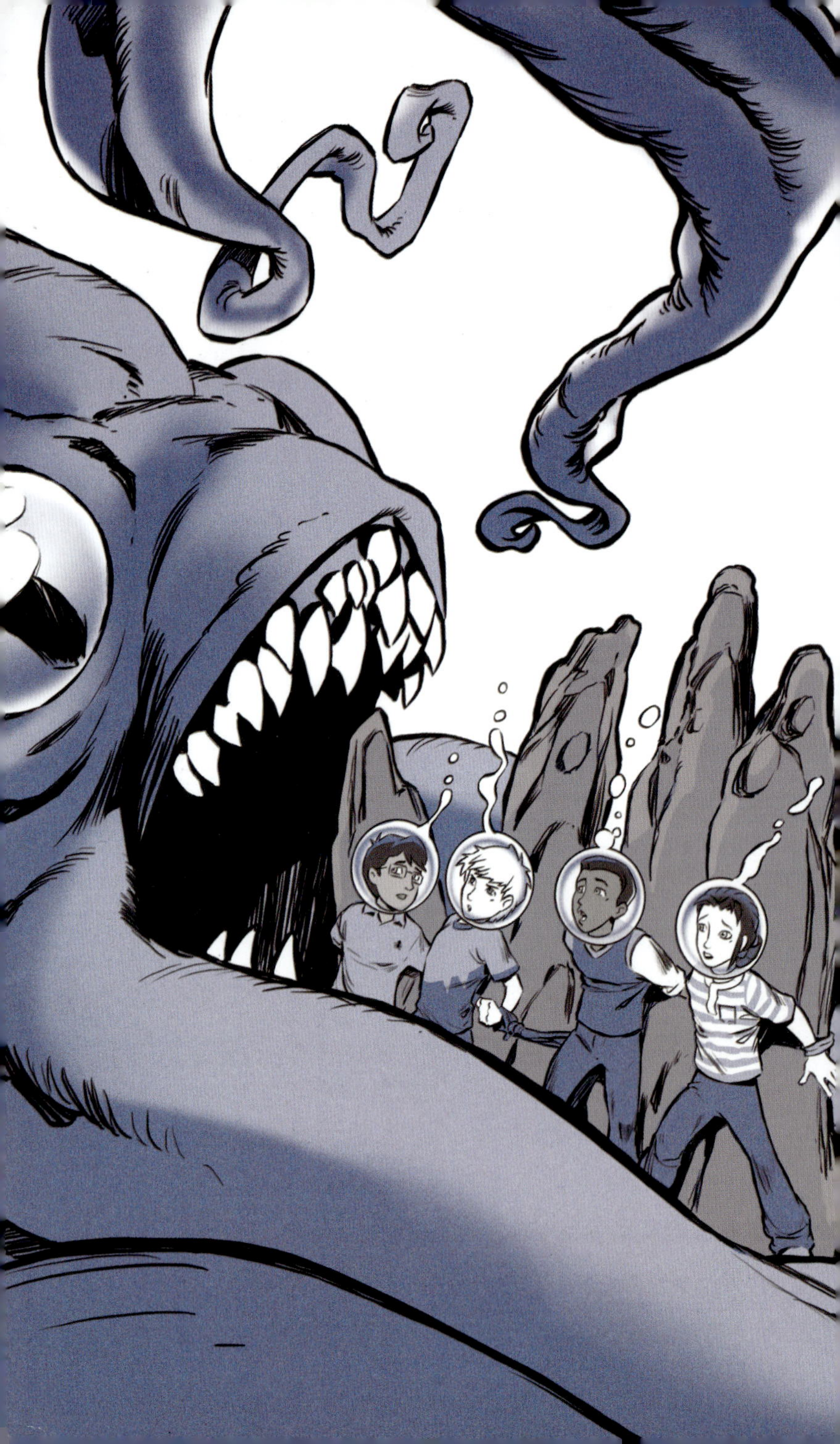

'It's a giant octopus monster thing, remember?' yelled Cat, staring at the tentacle that was beginning to untie her bonds. 'The one trying to eat us!'

'No, not that!' said Tiger, urgently. 'THAT!'

Cat looked again. Something was approaching behind the octopus. It was difficult to see what it was at first, but as it drew closer she could make out a group of creatures walking along the sea floor.

Ant had seen them, too. 'They look humanoid,' he said.

Suddenly, a sound like distant thunder echoed through the water.

'What was that?' asked Cat.

Ant winced. 'It sounded like some kind of sonic pulse.'

'It came from those creatures,' said Max. 'Or rather, from whatever it is they're pointing at the octopus.'

The creatures levelled their fearsome-looking spears at the octopus. The ends of the spears glowed menacingly.

There was another thunderous noise, and this time shockwaves rippled out from the spears and undulated towards the octopus.

The octopus tried to move out of the way, but it wasn't quick enough; the shockwaves caught it full on. Its great, bulbous body shielded the friends from the force of the blast. The creature tumbled through the sea as though it was caught in a whirlpool.

The octopus backed towards a jagged pile of rocks as the humanoid creatures approached it.

'It's retreating!' said Cat.

Then the octopus squeezed itself into a massive hole and, with an angry squirt of thick, oily ink, it disappeared.

'So long, sucker!' called Tiger. 'Get it ... *sucker* because of all its ...' Tiger saw the expression on his friends' faces. 'Never mind.'

Max turned his attention to the humanoid creatures as they started to move towards the four friends. The creatures had large shells on their backs. From the shells, a pipe led round to another shell on their heads, with a transparent area in front of the face.

'Amazing!' exclaimed Ant. 'They've got diving gear made from seashells and crystal. How cool is that?'

'The question is,' said Max, 'are they friendly?'

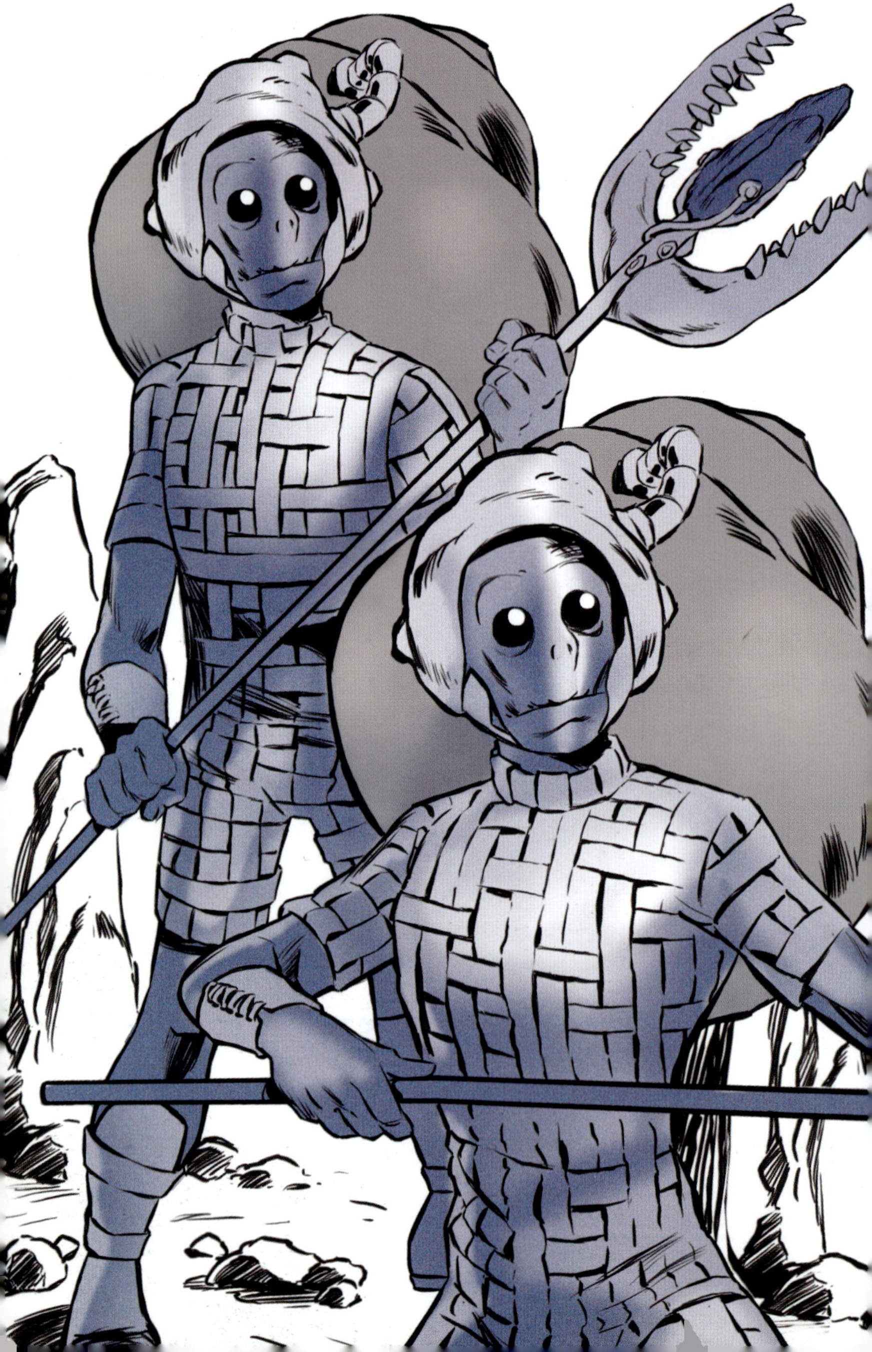

The friends stared in amazement as the creatures approached. Tall and slim, their skin was aqua blue, and they seemed to blend in with the water around them. They were clothed in suits made from seaweed. Behind the transparent, crystal masks, their faces were smooth, with huge bulbous eyes, thin, wide mouths, and only a small bump where a nose would be. The creatures did not smile or speak.

Cat began to wonder if this was a rescue mission at all. 'They don't look all that friendly,' she whispered, glancing over at Max.

The creatures quickly surrounded the friends. Then one of them slipped forward and spoke; its voice was like a warbling flute. 'We are marinians,' it said. 'We heard your distress calls through the water.'

DIMENSION 4455
THE MARINIANS

Many thousands of years ago, the Dimension of Memories was a dry wasteland. Then an apocalyptic rainfall changed the landscape forever. Rain fell for hundreds of years; the sea level rose until there was no dry land left at all.

EVOLUTION:

Early land-dwelling humans were almost all wiped out by the floods. Those that survived evolved into a species able to live under water: the marinians. Marinians breathe air from air-shells on their backs. Air flows from the back air-shell to the head air-shell, via a pipe. The face is protected by a crystal mask. Baby marinians are born without shells, which do not grow until the young marinian reaches two years of age. Until then, babies live inside air balls.

Head air-shell

Crystal face mask

Back air-shell

Marinian eyes are round and bulbous to enable them to see in the underwater gloom.

The marinians replenish their air-shells at natural air pockets that float close to the surface of the ocean. The city is built under several giant air pockets.

'Thanks for rescuing us,' said Max. 'That creature was terrifying … it wa–'

'There is no time for talking,' interrupted the lead marinian. 'You must come with us immediately. We will not hurt you. Well, maybe a little bit, but not yet. We'll have to see …'

'Oh great!' whispered Tiger.

'Hush!' ordered the marinian.

With spidery, nimble fingers, the creatures quickly untied the friends' bonds. As the long chains of seaweed fell away, the friends stretched their arms and legs in relief. Tiger took a few experimental paces along the sandy seabed; it was soft and crunched underfoot. He found he had to use high, slow steps.

Ant was grinning. 'Isn't it amazing to be walking on the bottom of the ocean?'

'It's incredible,' replied Tiger. 'Though it's a bit slow going – like how I imagine walking on the moon would feel!'

'It just feels good not to be tied up anymore,' said Cat, trailing her hands through the water.

'Be quiet and follow us,' the lead marinian said firmly. 'We haven't got much time.'

'Hang on a second.' Max frowned. 'What do you want from us?'

'You will find out when we take you to our great and wonderful city,' the creature replied. 'We must hurry! The sea is dangerous and the slimy multi-legs will not be put off for long. Also, there are even worse things swimming in our waters than the slimy multi-legs … Look! A sharp-tooth!'

The marinian pointed up at a massive shark that displayed a terrifying array of teeth. The shark glided towards the group so the marinians aimed their spears at it and blasted it with sonic pulses so that it swam away.

'Quickly,' the lead marinian commanded.

Walking across the seabed, the friends appreciated for the first time just how beautiful the ocean was. Everywhere they looked, brightly coloured fish danced in the water, chasing after food and dodging between beams of sunlight streaming down from above.

In the distance, Max thought he could see the octopus. Was it waiting for another opportunity to grab them? Max shuddered.

When at last they came upon the marinian's city, the friends were all wide-eyed with wonder. Standing at the top of an undersea cliff, they stared down at the vast city situated in a deep-sea trench below. Huge towers pointed up from the ocean floor – great shards of volcanic glass carved into living quarters. Giant flowers of crystal studded the cliff edge and around the towers; their semi-transparent petals reflected light into the city, causing it to glow with a soft radiance.

Beyond the city, the seabed was like a patchwork of farmland with crops of multi-coloured seaweed as well as plants the friends did not recognize.

The marinians led Max, Cat, Ant and Tiger along a path that was cut deep into the cliff, which took them down into the city. At the bottom, they were then taken through a tunnel of fluorescent blue crystal and into a dome-shaped room. A door slid shut behind them. A female marinian was waiting for their group.

'Welcome,' she said. 'The Memory Guardian is ready for you.'

Chapter 5 – The Memory Guardian

'Awesome!' exclaimed Tiger.

The room they were now standing in was like a cathedral but built entirely from coral, with a domed crystal roof. The sea outside the room caused light to spin and swirl around inside, dancing on the walls.

At the end of the room, Max could see an unusual-looking marinian sitting on top of a crystal throne inlaid with beautiful, fragile shells. *It must be the Memory Guardian*, he thought.

The Memory Guardian had his eyes closed and his legs crossed. Max wondered if the creature was asleep or perhaps meditating. He had the same slim, blue body as the other marinians but his head was different: his thin face was topped by an enormous swelling brain. Max thought it looked like any normal brain he'd seen pictures of in science books, except for its size and for the fact that this brain was fed by pipes that led up to the crystal roof and out into the sea. The pipes were transparent and had seawater rushing through them.

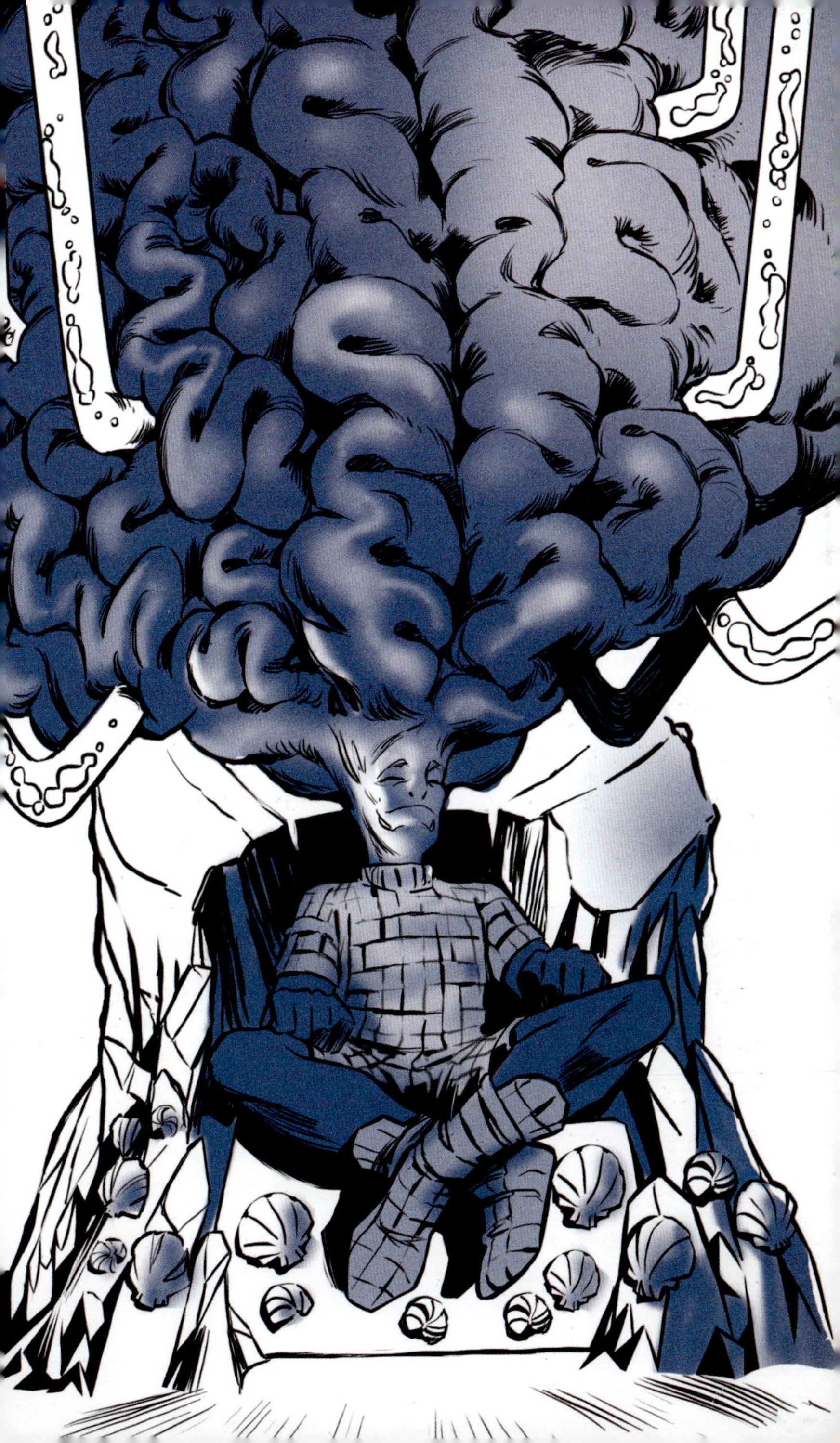

The marinians bowed low as they approached him. Max felt pressure on his back as his guard put a hand on it. It was clear he wanted Max to bow, too.

One of the creatures stepped forwards. 'Your Great and Mighty Pulsatingness!' it cried, bowing low. 'These are the owners of the thoughts you heard in the sea. The slimy multi-legs had imprisoned them.'

The Memory Guardian blinked slowly, then stared down at Max, Cat, Ant and Tiger.

'I heard your cries,' the Guardian said. His voice was deep and echoing. It was neither kind nor threatening and seemed to roll around the room as though it was trying to shut them off from the outside world. 'But they were jumbled up and confused. It took me some time to sort them out and to find you.'

'Those must be Tiger's thoughts,' said Cat. 'I'm never confused.'

'At first I could not comprehend the thoughts,' continued the Memory Guardian, slowly. 'They were new voices to me, ones I did not understand.'

Max saw the huge brain pulse. He had a horrible feeling that the Memory Guardian wasn't exactly pleased to see them. 'So why did you rescue us?' Max asked. He was beginning to wonder if being in the hands of the marinians was any better than being in the grip of the tentacles of the giant octopus.

'Two reasons. First, your screams were so loud, they were giving me a headache,' replied the Memory Guardian, his rumbling voice sounding annoyed.

'And the other?' asked Cat.

The Memory Guardian turned his full attention to her. 'You are strangers to our world,' he said. 'Your thoughts are new to me. They're difficult for me to understand because your voices are so strange and whiny, but they are, nevertheless, new.'

Max let the insult about their voices go. Instead he said, 'That still doesn't explain why you saved us.'

The leader yawned. 'I have lived for a long time. A long, long time. I have heard all the thoughts and memories in this world so many times they have become boring. New things interest me.' He uncrossed his legs. 'Now it's my turn to ask the questions.' His wide eyes narrowed a fraction. 'Why have you come here?'

Cat stepped forward. 'We are looking for a very special thought.'

The Memory Guardian's brain pulsed more violently now, changing colour like a kaleidoscope. When he spoke next, his voice was even louder. 'You are looking for a *thought*? You mean you have come to our sea to actually find *thoughts*?'

'Yes.' Cat nodded. 'Can you help us?'

'Help you? Help you steal our THOUGHTS? Our MEMORIES?'

Max stepped in. 'It's not like that,' he explained. 'It's not *your* people's thoughts that we want. It's someone else's. This thought belongs to a woman called Perlest.'

But the Memory Guardian was clearly unconvinced.

'You are in league with the Doom!' he bellowed, the colours flickering across his brain, changing so quickly they were almost a blur. 'You have come to aid the destruction of our sea!'

'I'm sorry ... what?' said Max. 'What's the Doom?'

A screen slid up from the floor of the room. On the screen were images of the Sea of Memories.

'You mean to say that you are denying any knowledge of this?' demanded the Memory Guardian.

On the screen, floating on the water, was what looked like a huge ship, similar to an oil tanker. Hanging over the sides of the ship were large funnels. Steam was rising from the sea beneath them.

'What's that?' Tiger asked.

'That is the Doom!' shouted the Memory Guardian. 'It is drying up our sea! It's destroying our greatest treasures – our thoughts and memories!'

'We've never seen it before!' cried Cat.

Ant noticed something walking around on the deck of the ship.

'Can you give us a closer look at the ship?' he asked.

The screen changed to a close-up. Soon the friends could see the figures that were controlling the ship. And they recognized them immediately.

'I thought so!' said Ant. 'It's the Krush!'

'What are they doing here?' Cat asked.

'Maybe the same thing as us,' replied Max, his voice low and secretive. 'Searching for other people's thoughts …'

The Memory Guardian interrupted. 'See?' he roared, the surface of his huge brain swirling with colours. 'You do recognize it! You are in league with the Doom!' His voice was growing louder with each word. 'You are here for our thoughts! Our precious memories!' The Memory Guardian let out a horrible gurgling, spluttering cry. 'Arrest them!'

'But you're wrong!' Tiger shouted. 'We didn't know anything about it!'

The marinians weren't listening. With the Memory Guardian watching, they moved towards Max, Cat, Ant and Tiger.

'Could this get any worse?' groaned Ant.

It was then that a mighty crack echoed through the water, and the whole city shuddered.

Chapter 6 – The Doom

'The Doom is attacking our city!' gurgled the Memory Guardian. 'We will all perish!'

'You're not … correction, *we're* not doomed – yet,' said Max to the Memory Guardian. 'I'm sure there's something we can do. And if we help you, will you help us?'

'The Doom!' bellowed the Memory Guardian again, as another shudder rattled through the city. Then the marinians joined in. 'The Doom! The Doom!'

'I have an idea, a way we can help fight the Krush, I mean, Doom,' said Ant urgently.

The Memory Guardian and the marinians were not listening; they just kept shouting 'Doom' incessantly.

'What's your idea?' Max asked.

Ant beckoned his friends to huddle in close, then he pointed at the image on the screen.

'You see that heat wave shimmering off the sea by the ship?'

'Just about,' said Max, staring at the screen.

'Well, I think those funnels hanging over the side of

the Krush ship are trying to steal the marinians' thoughts using an ultra-hot beam and some sort of distillation process … At least, that's my theory anyway.'

Max had learned to trust Ant's theories. 'OK. So what's next?'

'We need to locate the ship,' said Ant. 'Then we use the petals from some of those crystal flowers we've seen around the city to form a large, reflective surface, bounce the beam back towards the ship and *BOOM!*'

'Boom?' repeated Max.

'Well, I'm not exactly sure what sound it will make,' Ant admitted. 'But boom's probably close enough. Max, I'll need you and Tiger to stay here and help the marinians reflect that beam back at the Krush ship.'

'What will you be doing?' Tiger asked.

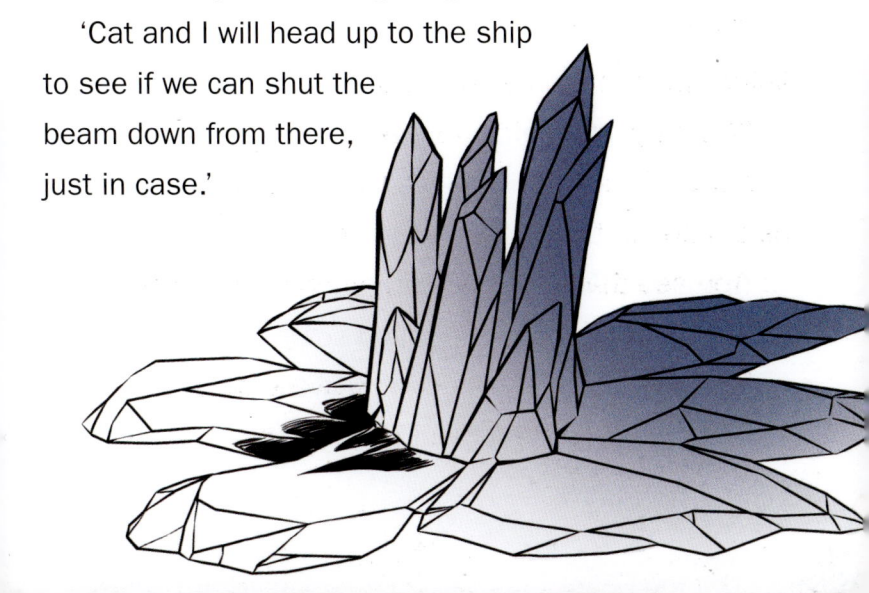

'Cat and I will head up to the ship to see if we can shut the beam down from there, just in case.'

'What if you and Cat are still on the ship when the beam reflects back?' asked Max.

Ant smiled. 'Don't worry about us.'

Cat's brow was furrowed as she thought hard about Ant's plan. 'But won't the crystal flowers melt?'

'I don't think so,' Ant replied. 'The heat from the beams would have to be many thousands of degrees hotter to melt crystal. I think this plan will work. Actually, I *know* it will.'

Max turned back to the Memory Guardian. 'We need some of your crystal flowers,' he said.

Another shudder hit the city, and this time bits of coral from the walls started to fall to the floor.

'And the sooner the better,' added Cat.

'What will you do with these precious things?' the Memory Guardian asked.

Ant explained his plan again. 'If everything goes to plan, then you should all be safe,' he concluded.

The Memory Guardian was silent for a moment. Then he said, 'We will get what you request. And if you can save us, then we will help you.'

'It's a deal!' exclaimed Ant. 'Let's go!'

The Memory Guardian issued some orders to the marinians nearby, and the friends were led quickly from the large room and out into the city.

Several minutes later, a squad of marinians ran up to them.

'We have found the ship,' one said. 'And we have collected a stockpile of crystal petals. We await your orders!'

'Well,' said Max, turning to Ant and giving him a quick salute, 'what next?'

Ant turned to one of the marinians. 'Can you help Max and Tiger to set up the petals?' Then he turned to another, 'And can you please show Cat and me the best way to swim to that ship?'

The friends split up. One of the marinians led Max and Tiger up several flights of rocky steps. About twenty marinians followed, carrying huge piles of crystal petals between them. The group made its way down a long corridor and into another large room.

The city shook again. This time they saw through the high window exactly where the beam was coming from.

'We'll need some seaweed rope,' said Max, talking to the marinians. 'We can use it to tie the petals together to make a large mirror. Then we'll float it outside to get in the way of the beam, and bounce the beam back.'

The marinians got to work immediately.

Meanwhile, two marinians swam up to the surface with Cat and Ant.

'I've got a bad feeling about this,' muttered Cat, as she and Ant broke through the surface near the side of the large boat. It was made of thick, grey metal.

'We need to shrink,' she told Ant. 'It's the only way that we can be sure the Krush won't spot us.'

Ant agreed. 'But let's climb on board first,' he said.

* * * * * *

Back in the underwater city, Max and Tiger helped the marinians lay out the huge crystal petals. Then they lashed them together using luminous seaweed rope. When it was eventually finished, the huge mirror looked more like a wonderful treasure: light reflected off the petals and danced around them, and the incandescent seaweed ropes made it seem as though the mirror itself was alive.

'Are you sure this will work?' asked Tiger.

'If Ant says it will, then it will,' Max replied. 'He's never wrong about things like this.'

'I'm surprised his brain isn't as big as the Memory Guardian's,' said Tiger, with a grin.

Another beam hit the city from above and the building they were in shook violently, bits of crystal falling around them.

'We need to do this now!' shouted Max, staggering to keep on his feet. 'Get the mirror outside!'

The marinians carried the precious crystal reflector outside. Max and Tiger followed quickly. The sea creatures spread out the mirror and began to swim up towards where the beam last struck.

'Fingers crossed,' said Max.

'But you said it would work!' said Tiger.

* * * * * *

Back on the ship, Cat and Ant had used their watches to shrink. They hid behind a coil of wire as one of the Krush guards thumped past.

'Let's see if there's some kind of control room,' suggested Ant. 'If we can find that, we might be able to shut the beam down.'

'We might even find Perlest's thought about the Weaver,' said Cat. She ran forward, with Ant following. 'There's a door ahead,' she called back to him. 'And it's open. Let's see what's inside!'

'Wait!' hissed Ant. 'We'd better check for Krush first. They could still sense us at micro-size.'

The friends gingerly crept forwards, but there was no sign of any more Krush warriors. Ant let out a sigh of relief and indicated to enter the open room.

Beyond the door they found themselves inside a room filled with tubes, pipes and steam.

'This must be the thought processing plant,' whispered Ant, trying not to choke on the oil fumes. 'So there has to be a control panel somewhere that will switch the beam off.'

'I'll look for it,' said Cat. 'You see if you can find where the thoughts are distilled.'

Ant moved through a doorway. 'This looks promising.'

* * * * * *

In the underwater city, Max and the others had floated the mirror outside of the building. They had just moved it to the highest point in the city when another beam from the Krush ship blasted through the sea. This time it hit the mirror. Some of the petals cracked, but the structure held strong.

For a few moments, all the mirror did was absorb the beam. Then, with a crackle like static electricity, the beam fizzed and shot back up the way it came.

Everything fell silent.

'Do you think it worked?' asked Tiger.

* * * * * *

On the ship, both Cat and Ant tumbled to the floor as the reflected beam hit the boat. Pipes and tubes burst all around them.

Cat stood up shakily and ran to Ant in the next room. 'I don't think I need to find the "off" button, do you?' She smiled. 'Your plan obviously worked. Did you find anything?'

Ant pointed to a machine above them. It was a huge tank and water was swirling through it.

'This looks like the distillation unit,' he said. 'But I can't see how to shut it down.'

'We could put a spanner in the works,' said Cat.

'I don't have a spanner,' Ant replied, slightly perplexed at Cat's suggestion.

'No, but I do have this.' Cat pulled from her pocket a piece of petal from one of the crystal flowers. 'All I need to do is get it into the tank.'

The friends grew back to normal size. Cat looked up; the top of the tank was open. She pulled her arm back and threw the piece of crystal as hard as she could. It soared through the air, bounced on the edge of the tank, then dropped inside.

For a moment, nothing happened.

Then the crystal started to spin and dance in the

whirl of the water in the tank. It flashed and glinted like a star.

'What's happening?' asked Cat.

'The crystal is reflecting the thoughts in the water!' said Ant. The water started to spin violently in the tank, forming a powerful whirlpool. 'It wouldn't happen underwater because the sea is so massive, but in a contained space like this …'

'Er, I think we can do without the explanation now, Ant,' Cat interrupted him, heading for the door. 'It looks like it's going to blow. Let's get out of here!'

The tank started to glow. The crystal fragment was spinning even more wildly.

'Move!' Ant yelled.

Cat raced out of a door leading to the outer deck with Ant right behind her. They scrambled across the deck and both leapt over the side of the Krush ship. The last thing they saw before they hit the water was light and smoke bursting from the door.

Chapter 7 – The lost thought

The Memory Guardian asked to speak again to Max, Cat, Ant and Tiger.

'Thank you,' he said. 'You saved us from the Doom! And now we shall help you. This Perlest whose thoughts you seek. If she has visited us, I will know …' The Memory Guardian sat back in his seat. He looked at the friends one by one. Then, with a gentle nod, he slowly closed his eyes.

'He's going to sleep,' hissed Tiger. 'Bit rude.'

'He's concentrating!' sighed Cat. 'Something you wouldn't know much about, I realize.'

Max was first to notice a strange buzzing sound in the room. 'Can you hear that, too?' he asked.

The others nodded.

The Memory Guardian's brain was glowing a deep purple colour. White lines were now visible, criss-crossing the brain's surface like tiny rivers of white light. Then the brain started to throb, its surface pulsing as though something inside it was trying to escape.

'That looks disgusting,' whispered Cat.

The brain continued to pulse, but now the colour had changed to a deep red. The rivers of light began to fizz and sparkle, causing tiny lightning storms to chase each other across the brain's surface.

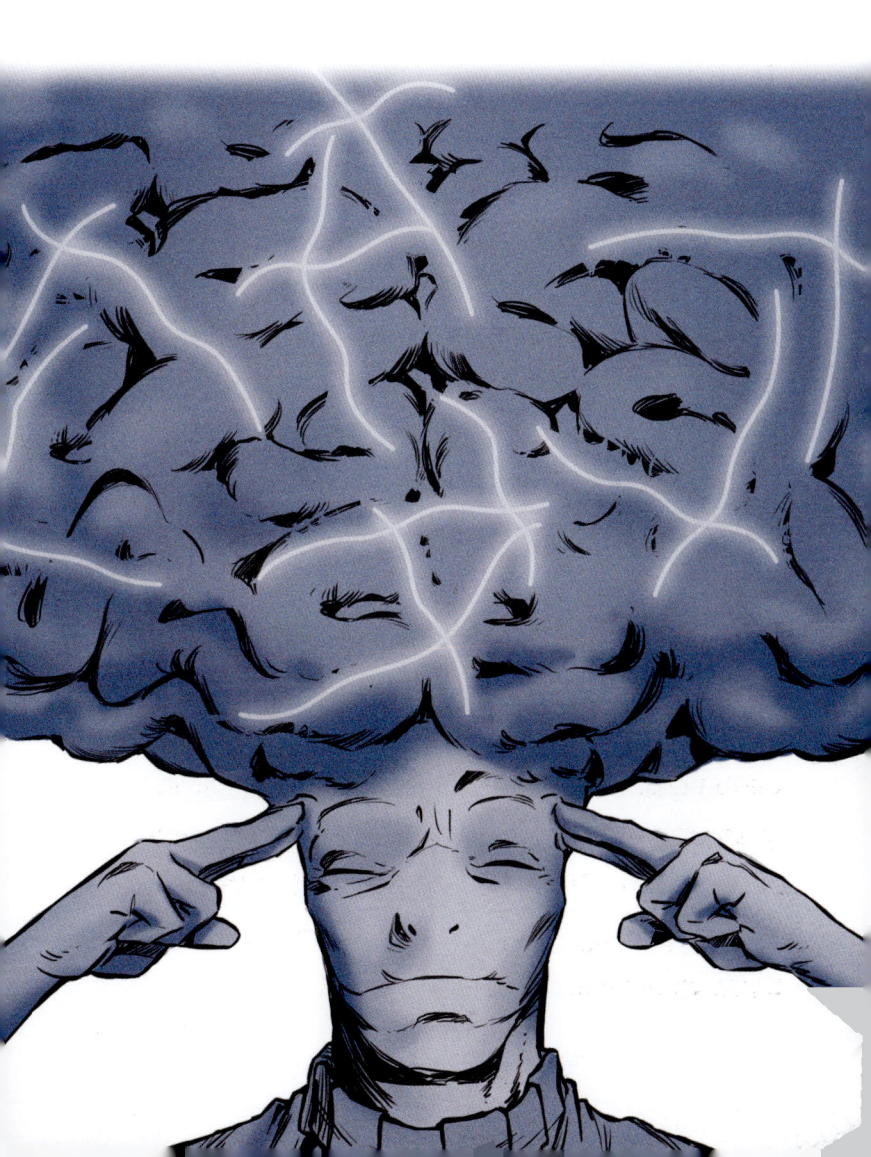

The Memory Guardian opened his eyes.

'Are you sure that this Perlest of whom you speak has been here?'

'Yes,' said Max, 'but it might have been a long time ago.'

'I will have to search further back.' At this, the Memory Guardian snapped his eyes shut once more. Immediately, the brain changed colour again – but this time, it kept changing colour, like a dark cloud torn apart by lightning. The buzzing was getting louder, too, filling the air with the crackle of static electricity.

'What are we going to do if he can't find a thought?' asked Cat.

Max didn't have an answer. But, as time went on, he started to wonder if Perlest had sent them to the right dimension. Perhaps her thought wasn't here at all?

Then the buzzing stopped. The Memory Guardian snapped his eyes open. 'I have found that of which you speak!'

The Guardian snapped his skinny fingers. 'A thought vial!' he called. 'Quickly!'

One of the marinians ran over to the Memory Guardian with a small glass tube that had a brass stopper stuck in the top. The Memory Guardian sat very, very still as the marinian opened the vial, then screwed the end deep into one of the tubes in the Guardian's brain.

'That's totally gross!' cried Tiger. 'Excellent!'

After a few moments, the marinian pulled the vial back out of the Guardian's brain. When he put the stopper back on the vial, Max could see that inside was a strange, grey, misty cloud, just like the mist in the thought vial they had previously given to Perlest.

'Behold!' announced the Memory Guardian. 'This is the thought you seek!'

The marinians all clapped loudly, clearly impressed.

Ant walked over to retrieve the thought vial. He reached up for it, but the Memory Guardian did not immediately let it go.

'Be careful with this. Thoughts are like doors. They could take you anywhere.'

'Doors?' said Ant. 'Now that's something we *do* know all about.'

At last the Guardian handed Ant the thought vial.

'So we've done it, then?' asked Cat.

'Yes,' said Max in a low voice. 'All we have to do now is open a rip to get back to Perlest. But we need to do that where no one can see us. We can't risk someone following us back to our own dimension!'

'Then the best place is back at the ocean's surface,' said Ant, putting the vial in his pocket.

Tiger raised his eyebrows. 'You mean where the octopus is probably waiting for us?'

Max looked at the Memory Guardian and then at the marinians. 'We need to get back to the surface safely,' he said.

'We shall take you,' said one of the marinians. 'But we cannot stay at the surface long, as our skin will dry out. And that is not nice at all.'

'Fare thee well!' called the Memory Guardian, as the friends were led from the room.

* * * * * *

It wasn't long before Max, Cat, Ant and Tiger were swimming up through the water with several marinians. They soon reached the sun-lit surface and burst through the waves.

'Time to get rid of these,' Tiger said, grinning and poking his finger deep inside his slime bubble helmet. His helmet popped like a balloon and Tiger gulped in the fresh sea air.

The others followed suit, their helmets bursting, leaving them covered in a slimy mask.

'Ughhh!' Cat exclaimed, as she peeled the octopus gunk from her face.

Two marinians surfaced nearby, dragging a raft made of seaweed. They floated it towards the friends. Grabbing on to the edges of the raft, the friends heaved themselves up and out of the water. Then, before they knew it, the marinians slipped beneath the waves and were gone.

'Now we just need to open the rip,' said Max.

Tiger looked at his watch and turned the dial. Just as he did so, a blast of hot air, followed by the sound of a screaming siren, shook the raft.

Tiger stared at his watch. 'Well, it's never done that before,' he said.

Max tapped Tiger on his shoulder and pointed behind him. 'I don't think it was your watch,' he said. 'Look ...'

Behind them was the Krush ship.

Chapter 8 – **Krush attack**

'It looks like we didn't stop them after all!' cried Cat.

'The Krush must have fixed their ship somehow,' said Ant in dismay. He could see black smoke pouring out of the back of the ship. 'Well, partly fixed it anyway.'

The ship slid through the water towards them. One of the funnels hanging over the side swung round to face them.

'This doesn't look good,' said Max. 'We need to get out of here!'

A beam exploded from the funnel. As it hit the sea around them, the water started to steam. Soon, the steam began to combine with the black smoke. A thick mist formed. The Krush ship was no longer visible.

'Well, at least now we can open a rip without the Krush seeing us,' said Tiger.

'But what about the marinians ... and our deal?' asked Cat.

'I don't think we can beat the Krush this time ... My plan didn't really work very well after all, did it?' said Ant sadly.

'Ant's right. I'm not sure there's any more we can do right now,' said Max. 'And remember our own dimension is in danger, too. I think we need to get back to Perlest – maybe she'll think of a way to help the marinians.'

The mist began to clear very slightly.

'Quick! Open the rip before the mist clears!' cried Max. 'Now!'

The friends turned the dials on their watches. Blue light sparked from each of the watches and the rip opened in the middle of the seaweed raft. Then there was a sudden gust of wind, the mist swirled and the imposing bow of the Krush ship became visible again.

'Do you think they've seen the rip?' shouted Cat in alarm. 'They might try to enter our dimension again!'

As if in answer, the Krush ship began racing through the water towards them.

'Close the rip!' Max cried. Frantically, the friends turned back the dials on their watches. The rip fizzed … Then, thankfully, it disappeared.

The beam from the Krush ship seemed to intensify and the steam hissed more ferociously, the nearer the ship got to the friends.

'If we can't use the rip, how are we going to get out of here?' Ant yelled.

Cat pushed up the sleeves of her already damp top. 'I've an idea,' she said, and with that she jumped over the side of the raft.

'Cat! what are you doing?' shouted Max.

Cat coughed up a mouthful of water. 'Well, someone's got to do something!' She began to swim backwards, kicking hard, dragging the seaweed raft with her.

There was a splash next to her and Tiger surfaced a couple of metres away. 'Looks like you could do with a hand!' He grabbed the other corner of the raft and began to tug it out of the path of the larger vessel.

Max jumped in too and began to push from the other end. But despite their best efforts, progress was slow, and the Krush ship was getting closer.

'It's no good!' said Cat, panting. 'We'll never get out of its way.'

'There might be another way,' said Ant, from on board the raft. He had been desperately trying to think of a plan as the others were paddling.

'Well, what is it?' asked Tiger. His legs were beginning to tire.

'The octopus ...' said Ant.

'What about it?' Max asked.

'It would make mincemeat of that ship. All we need to do is get its attention.'

'And how do we do that?' asked Cat.

'The last time it appeared, we were talking about sea monsters,' Ant carried on. 'I think our thoughts must have conducted through the sea, like the memories do.'

'You mean it heard us?' Cat had stopped trying to drag the raft and was now treading water.

'Yes.'

'So all we have to do is think about monsters?' asked Max.

'Yes,' replied Ant. 'Everyone, picture the octopus in your minds.'

'Easy,' said Tiger. 'It's not like I'll forget those suckers in a hurry.'

'Or the slime!' added Cat.

All four friends concentrated hard. Tiger imagined the creature wrapping its tentacles round the Krush ship. Max thought about its huge eyes and Cat pictured its massive, sharp teeth.

Soon, the water near them started to bubble.

'It's the octopus!' shouted Max. 'Yes! You were right, Ant!'

'I can't believe I'm actually happy to see something that tried to eat me,' said Cat.

One tentacle curled up out of the water, then the others followed until finally the whole octopus was visible. For a moment it stared at the friends with hunger in its eyes. Then it spotted something much bigger: the Krush ship!

'It's seen it!' said Max. 'Look!'

The octopus whipped out all of its tentacles and quickly wrapped itself around the Krush ship. The beam shut down immediately. The friends could see Krush warriors abandoning their boat as it began to sink. Then, with a mighty yank, the octopus dragged the ship beneath the surface.

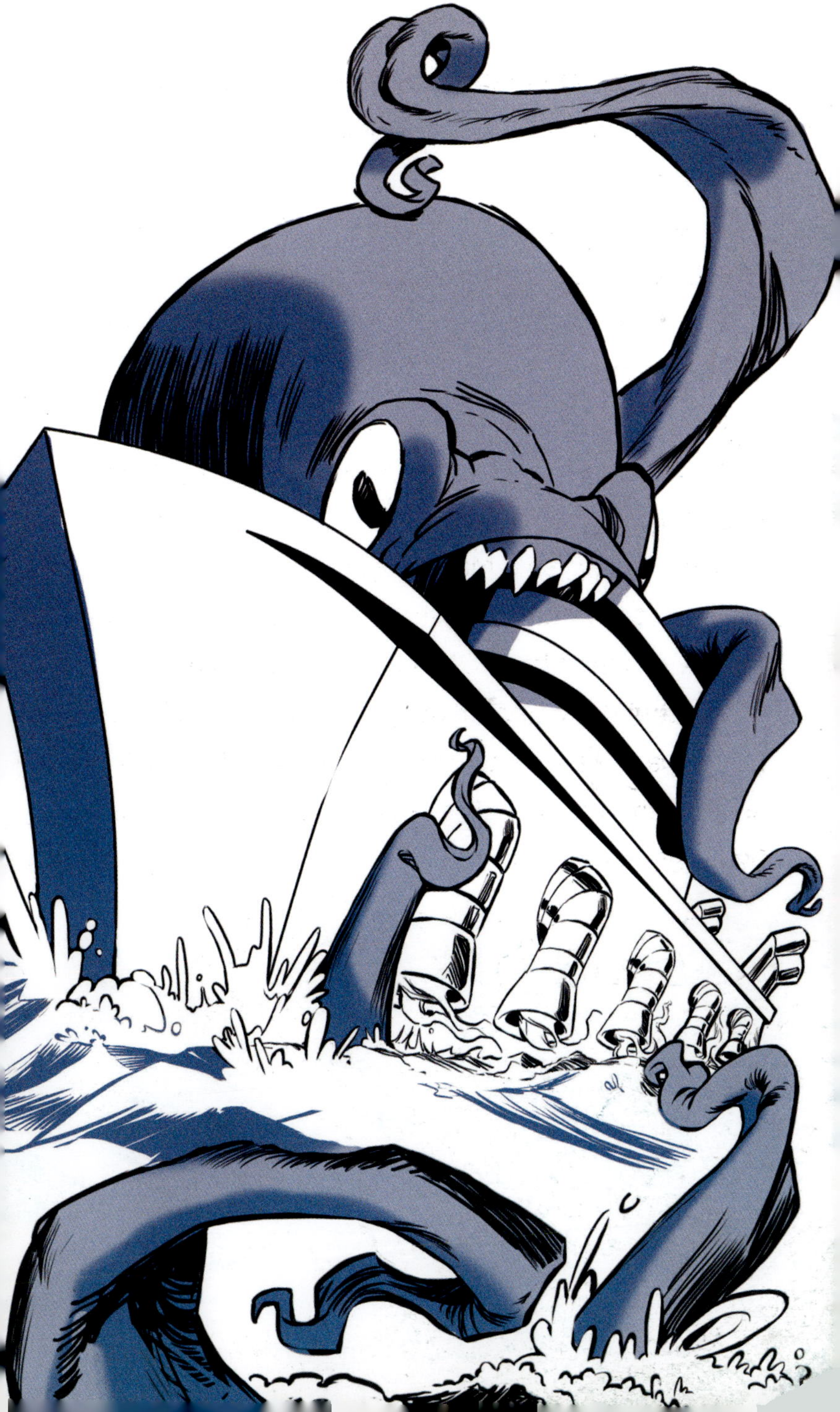

'That was your best idea ever, Ant,' said Tiger, as he clambered back on to the raft. 'Maybe even better than my one about making a chocolate spread and mayonnaise sandwich!'

Cat rolled her eyes. 'I think it's time to go.'

Chapter 9 – Perlest's request

Back in Tiger's bedroom, Perlest was smiling. Ant had just given her the vial. 'You found one of my missing thoughts!' she said. 'Wonderful work! Are you sure there were no more?'

'Yes,' said Max. 'The Memory Guardian found only that one.'

Perlest's cheeks flushed. 'But didn't you look for yourselves?' she asked sharply.

'Er … We were in the middle of the sea!' Cat pointed out, wondering why Perlest suddenly seemed cross. It was almost as though she had become someone else entirely. 'There was no way we could have found even that one without the help of the Memory Guardian.'

Perlest didn't answer. Instead she held up the memory vial to her eyes. Inside, the grey swirling mist seemed to grow agitated to be so close to her. She opened the vial. The memory slipped out of the glass tube and swirled in the air for a moment. Pictures flickered rapidly in the air, almost too quick for the friends to focus on. Max thought he caught sight of a village, a wood, men and women working in the fields, then nothing ... The memory was gone.

Perlest was silent, her eyes closed. When she opened her eyes, she didn't look happy.

'It's not enough!' she complained. 'The information ... I need more information!'

Max asked, 'What did the thought tell you?'

'That there are more fragments of my thoughts to collect,' said Perlest. 'And I do not know how many!'

The friends stood back. Perlest was angry and it was a little frightening.

Perlest breathed deeply. Then she visibly relaxed and, at last, smiled.

'I'm sorry children. It's just so … frustrating. Will you continue to help me?' she asked. 'Help me find my other lost thoughts so we can find a way to the Weaver?'

Max articulated what they were all thinking. 'We said we'd help. We wouldn't go back on our word.'

'Besides,' Ant added, 'it's our dimension that's in serious trouble, isn't it?'

Perlest nodded. 'Yes. Remember, the Weaver is the only one who can seal the rip shut forever.'

The four friends glanced at each other. They knew they had to carry on, despite the danger it could bring them.

'So, what next?' asked Cat.

'It is time to open another rip,' Perlest answered. 'You are now going to Dimension **8458**!'

NEXT ... Powerless

A Farmer in
East Lothian

Margaret S. Cannon

Copyright © 2024 by Margaret S. Cannon
ISBN: 978-1-3999-8068-5

The right of Margaret S. Cannon to be identified as Author and Publisher of this Work has been asserted in accordance with the Copyright, Designs and Patents Act 1988.

All rights reserved. No part of this publication may be reproduced, stored in a retrieval system, or transmitted in any form or by any means without prior permission from the Author, nor be circulated in any binding or cover other than that in which it was published, and without a similar condition being imposed on any subsequent purchaser.

Contents

Acknowledgements 4
Preface 5
Foreword 6
Chapter 1: Hugh Miller of West Fortune 10
Chapter 2: History of Agriculture in East Lothian 21
Chapter 3: The Manure Man 26
Chapter 4: Potatoes 35
Chapter 5: Grain, Hay and Straw 47
Chapter 6: Livestock and Keeping Them Fed 59
Chapter 7: Horses 76
Chapter 8: Miller's Mill 92
Chapter 9: Farm Management 104
Chapter 10: Lawyers' Letters 121
Chapter 11: Employer's Insurance 133
Chapter 12: Brother George the Banker 144
Chapter 13: Finance, Bank Managers and Accountants 154
Chapter 14: The Arbiter 163
Chapter 15: Life at Drem Station 173
Chapter 16: The Impact of the 1914–1918 War 179
Chapter 17: Mission Outreach 194
Chapter 18: Dear John 208
Chapter 19: Family Correspondence 229
Chapter 20: Politics / Miscellany 246
Chapter 21: Family Tributes 255
Explanatory Notes 267
Family trees 273

Acknowledgements:

I am grateful for the help and support of many people who have contributed to this production – to those who had done research on the Miller family in recent years, as well as various members of our wider family who have contributed photos, memories or answers to my many questions, especially over farming matters. Professor Donald E. Meek and Professor Alvin Jackson have also offered background knowledge from their areas of expertise.

Having started the challenging but pleasurable task of deciphering the letters during Covid lockdown, it has been a long drawn-out process, and I owe especial thanks to Kenneth Veitch of the European Ethnological Research Centre, University of Edinburgh for his encouragement. He is also enabling on-line access to the full collection of letters at:

https://www.regionalethnologyscotland.llc.ed.ac.uk

I acknowledge my particular debt to our daughter, Heather, for her support and efforts in moving the project forward.

I hope that interest and enjoyment will be the outcome for all who read.

Preface

Hugh Miller was my grandfather and following his move from Ayrshire to East Lothian in the early years of the 20th century, his four adult children and then his 15 grandchildren spent most of their childhood in the local area. During the Second World War my two older brothers had to be 'smuggled' into East Lothian via Haddington and then by pony and trap, as the area around Drem had been made a protected zone and the boys' registered address was in Ayrshire at that time. Our parents were permitted to visit their own parents at West Fortune, and as I was under five years old I was allowed to travel with them.

The extended family remained close and at family gatherings games were often played. One of Uncle Jim's specialities involved a bag of Scrabble type letters out of which the caller had to produce one, having already made known the required topic. Jim's specialist topic was 'A farm in East Lothian' which gave him a monumental advantage over the rest of the company. The game became familiar to me as 'A Farm in East Lothian' and when Grandpa Miller's Letter Book came to light and I explored its contents, a more in-depth picture of 'A Farmer in East Lothian' emerged.

Foreword

When I was growing up on a croft in the Hebridean island of Tiree, I often listened to stories about islanders who had ventured to the mainland as seasonal workers on large farms, particularly at harvest time. They usually went to a place known in Gaelic as 'Lobhdaidh' ('Lowdie'), a shortened form of 'Lothian'. I realised that, in practice, this meant East Lothian, and I often wondered how the farms of East Lothian functioned. Were they like our 60-acre croft, but on a much bigger scale? Did they carry the same kind of stock? Did they grow the same crops? How were they managed? Who owned them?

Academic studies, such as those by the late Professor Sandy Fenton, provided excellent technical overviews of such farms in Scotland. However, until I read 'A Farmer in East Lothian', I had not heard what might be termed 'the story from the horse's mouth'.

I was therefore delighted to peruse this revealing range of letters from the pen of Hugh Miller. I was captivated by their concise but highly informative style, as Mr Miller dealt with demands of the day-to-day business of West Fortune – selling and buying cattle and crops, negotiating with commercial interests, transport companies (and especially the railway managers), dealing with problems and 'problem people', challenging misunderstandings, and chiding those whose business practices were not always of as high a standard as he himself maintained.

The letters thus provide a multi-faceted set of insights into the life and work of a large East Lothian farm, but they also illumine the many strands in the make-up of Hugh Miller, the farmer himself. Here we find a man who could be absolutely 'straight', if not bluntly to the point, when tackling difficulties, a man who was not afraid to say what he thought, sometimes in a way that was laced with a very sharp, dry humour. In the unlikely context of buying manure, for example, he chided the supplier for supposedly believing that he (Miller) was even 'simpler' than himself. Mr Miller was not always right, of course, and he had the good grace to admit his mistakes.

Hugh Miller's business ethic was informed by his deeply-held Christian faith. His family roots lay in Ayrshire, where he had been brought up in a Christian Brethren context. Although he and Mrs Miller attended the local parish church, they were not entirely comfortable with its minister or with his teaching. So Hugh Miller compensated for the deficits which he perceived in parish ministry by providing a weekly Sunday-evening service in his barn, maintained by himself or by visiting preachers. His correspondence with these preachers is more personal, more revealing of the internal 'person' than his farming missives, and therefore different in tone and idiom. Nevertheless, his dead-pan humour and amusingly idiosyncratic turns of phrase, seasoned with Scottish salt, add a lively sparkle to his pen, perhaps unintentionally.

Hugh Miller was blessed with a long life, overcoming serious illness, and guiding his family with a firm hand into productive life-choices, including farming. His strong personality is woven into the texture of these illuminating letters. He lives on in their lines, thanks to the survival of his letterbook, and the diligence of his grand-daughter, Mrs Margaret Cannon, in reproducing it in this very enjoyable publication.

(Professor Emeritus) Donald E. Meek, PhD, DLitt, LittD
Falkirk and Tiree

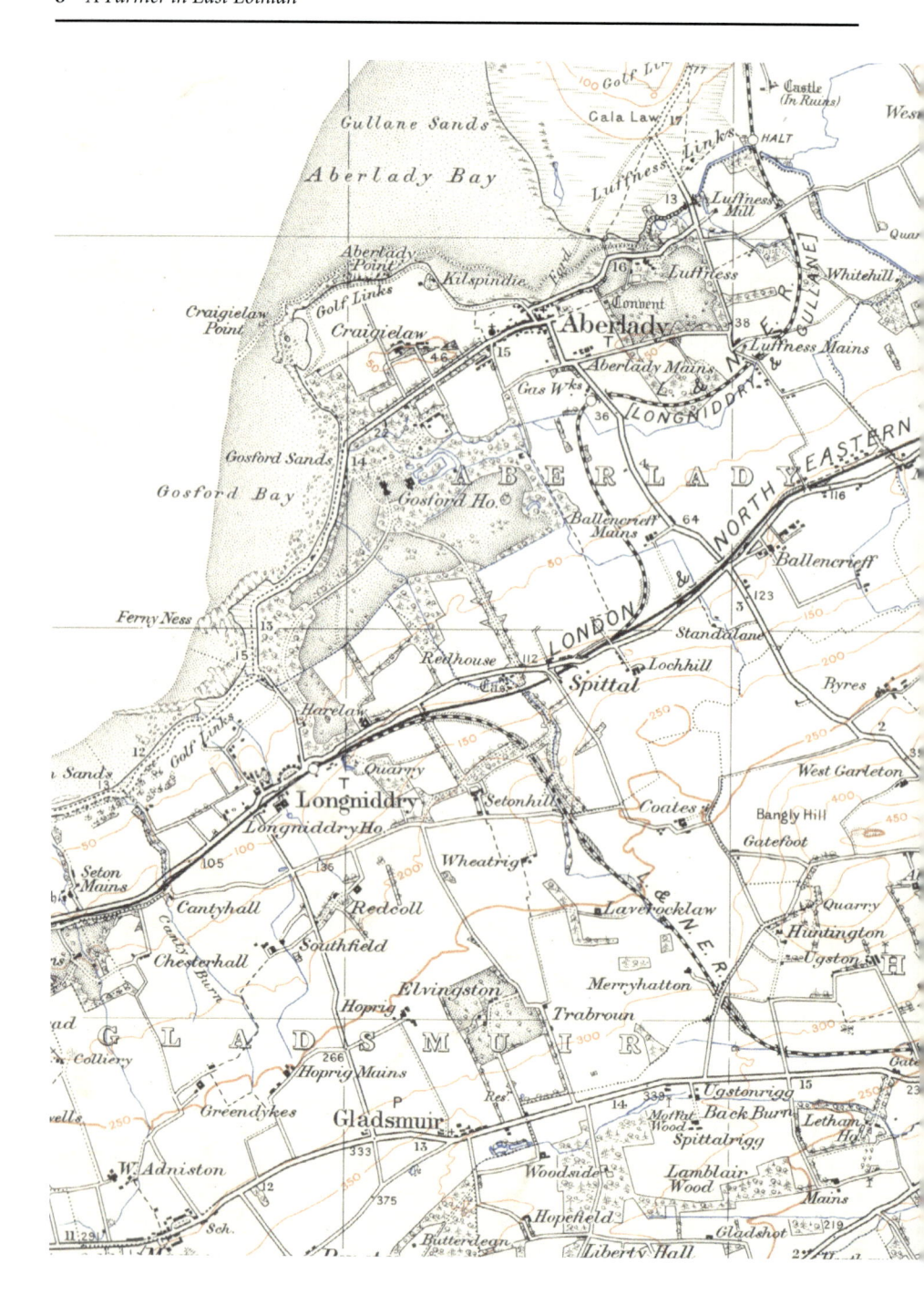

8   *A Farmer in East Lothian*

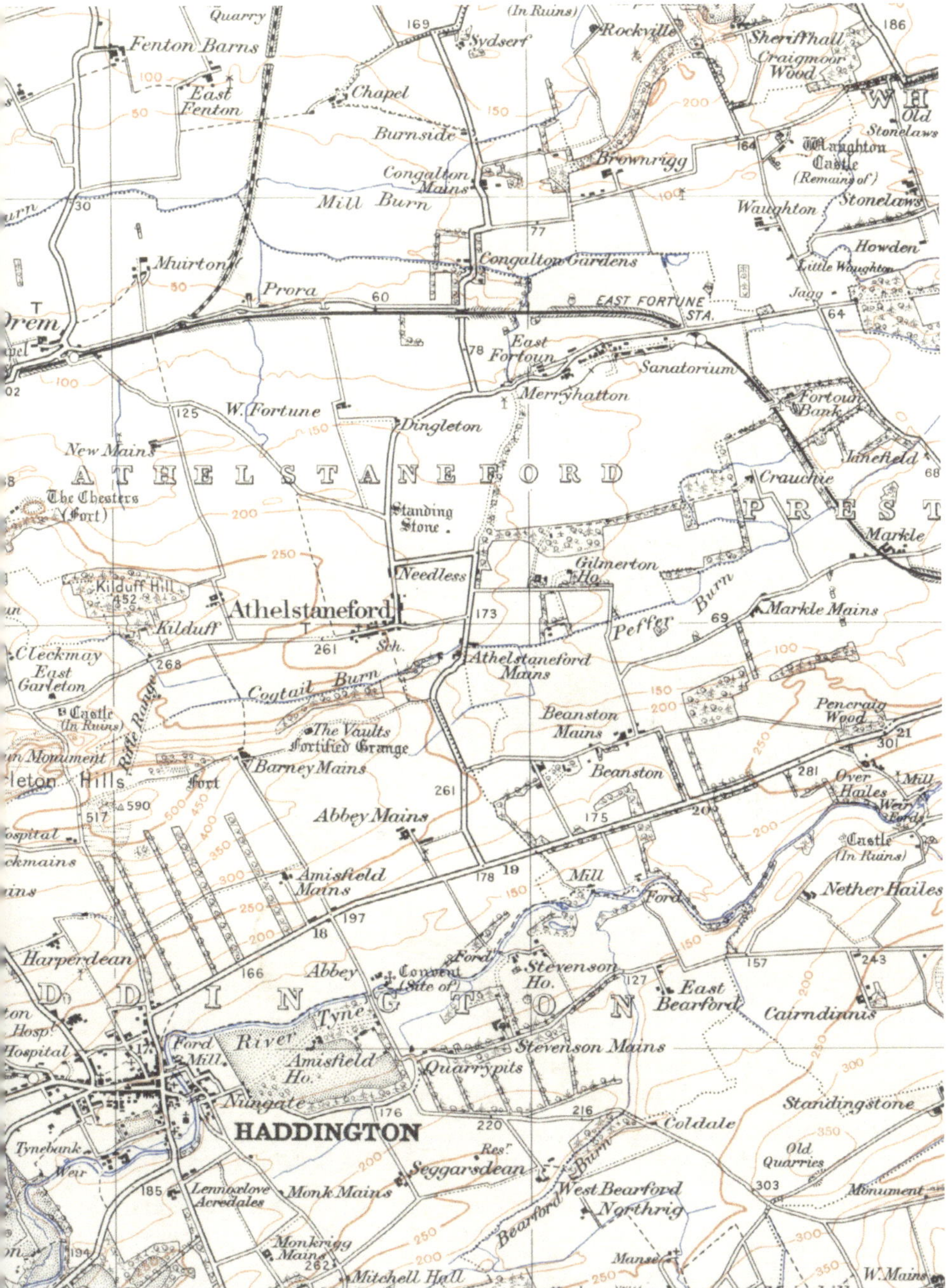
Quarry
Fenton Barns
East Fenton
Chapel
Burnside
Sydserf
(In Ruins)
Rockville
Sheriffhall
Craigmoor Wood
Old Stonelaws
Waughton Castle (Remains of)
Brownrigg
Congalton Mains
Mill Burn
Waughton
Stonelaws
Howden
Little Waughton
Muirton
Congalton Gardens
Prora
Drem
EAST FORTUNE STA.
Jagg
East Fortoun
Sanatorium
Merryhatton
W. Fortune
Dingleton
Fortoun Bank
New Mains
Janefield
ATHELSTANEFORD
Crauchie
The Chesters (Fort)
Standing Stone
PREST
Markle
Needless
Gilmerton Ho.
Kilduff Hill
Athelstaneford
Kilduff
Peffer Burn
Markle Mains
Cleckmay
East Garleton
Athelstaneford Mains
Cogtail Burn
Castle (In Ruins)
Rifle Range
Beanston Mains
Pencraig Wood
The Vaults Fortified Grange
Monument
Barney Mains
Beanston
Over Hailes
Mill
Garleton Hills
Fort
Weir
Fords
Abbey Mains
Castle (In Ruins)
Amisfield Mains
Mill
Ford
Nether Hailes
Harperdean
Abbey
Convent (Site of)
Ford
Stevenson Ho.
East Bearford
Cairndinnis
River Tyne
Stevenson Mains
Ford Mill
Amisfield Ho.
Quarrypits
Nungate
HADDINGTON
Coldale
Standingstone
Tynebank
Weir
Res.
Seggarsdean
Old Quarries
Lennoxlove
Acredales
Monk Mains
West Bearford
Northrig
Monument
Bearford Burn
Monkrigg Mains
Manse
Mitchell Hall
Monkrigg
Morham Village
Mainshill
W. Mains

Hugh Miller of West Fortune

West Fortune from the air.

Early in the 20th Century developments in farming and technology brought about social and economic changes across Scotland. Several farmers can be identified as moving from Ayrshire to East Lothian, including my grandfather, Hugh Miller. Members of his family continue to farm in East Lothian and recently his letterbook, containing over 700 copies of his correspondence, came to light in one of the farmhouses. The resource offers glimpses, albeit one-sided, into many aspects of farming, the community and his personal life. This edition includes many of these letters and additional background information on both local and farming history in addition to personal anecdotes of the Miller family.

A letterbook predates the use of carbon paper to keep a copy of correspondence. Ink-written letters were pressed between tissue-paper thin

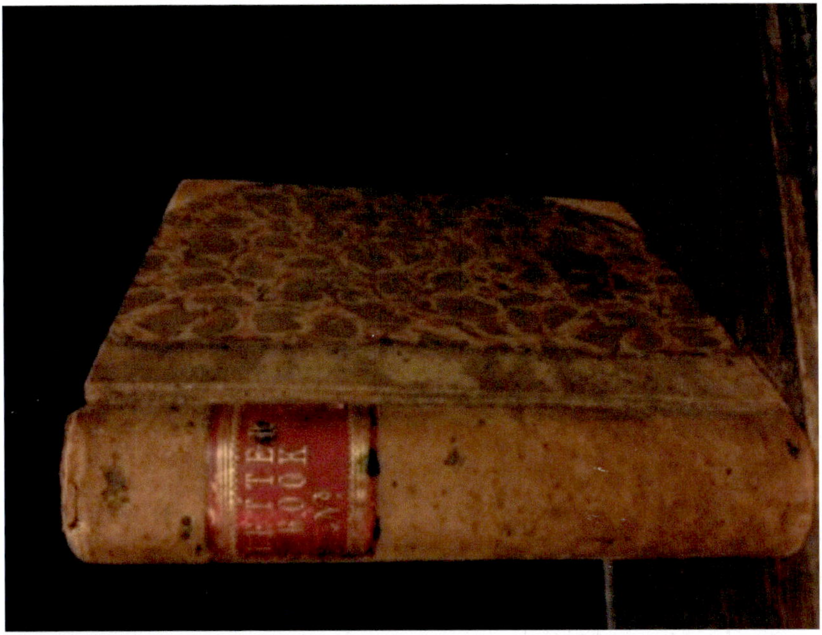

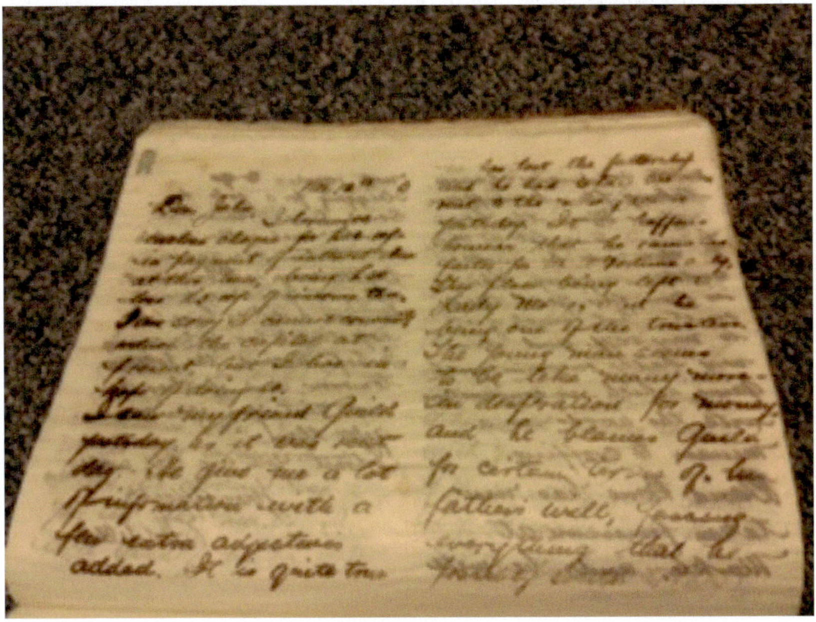

pages, the book then being placed in a press and copies made which could be read through the page. The letters were written in the period 1910 – 1934 and though they often leave us wondering the outcome, they open a window into his way of life in that period. Letterbooks did continue into the 1940's but fell out of use as the telephone became more widespread. Reading some of the letters brought challenges, as Scots vocabulary, farm words and occasional idiosyncratic turns of phrase were included, and, at times the ink had not made sufficient impression on the page, but this selection contains insights for those interested in farming or local history and the Scots language.

Hugh Miller had married Jane Whiteford and moved to West Fortune Farm in 1909 with their four children. Later, their 15 grandchildren spent most of their childhoods locally. Over the decades descendants have farmed in the North Berwick area – Prora, Congalton, Bonnington and Castlemains – and there were also close connections with other Ayrshire farmers who had moved east.

Our grandfather was a man to be respected, and occasionally feared, although his grandchildren probably experienced a milder side than his own children had done. Memories remain of him enjoying porridge in the old-fashioned way with a separate cup of cream into which each spoonful of porridge was dipped, and cream was always supplied to accompany strawberries or rasps from the garden too. Hugh Miller was respected in agricultural circles in East Lothian and beyond, and I have compiled this to record memories of his life.

Hugh Miller came from an Ayrshire farming family and I have appreciated the effort of those recording the genealogy of the Millers of Shaw. Hugh's grandfather, Robert Miller (1787 – 1864) was a tenant farmer in Bellsland (115 acres), near Kilmarnock, and he and Mary had 8 children: Hugh, William, James, John, Thomas, Robert, Euphemia and Marion, at least 5 of whom were farmers. James (1830 – 1890), Hugh's father, married Elizabeth Bowie (1834 – 1899) in 1864 and James continued as tenant farmer of Bellsland until 1871, according to the custom of tenancy being passed from father to son for a limited period. Whether James did not realise that he had to renew the tenancy is unknown, but his brother, William, who was farming elsewhere managed to inveigle his way into being granted the tenancy by the new laird, ousting his brother, James, who had to move to a new tenancy at Shaw (122 acres) near Prestwick, in 1871.

James and Elizabeth had 4 children while at Bellsland: Mary (1865), Bessie (1867), Robert (1868) and George (1870) and then 3 more at Shaw: Hugh (1872), James (1874) and Phemie (1877). George and James trained in banking and accountancy, Robert and Hugh farmed and all the girls married farmers.

Standing: Robert, Mary, Bessie. Middle: Elizabeth, Phemie, James, Hugh. Front: James, George Circa 1883

After the census of 1891, Hugh left Shaw for Grassmillees to help his unmarried uncle – another Hugh – who was always referred to as being 'jilted at the altar'. Following his uncle's death in 1893 Hugh assumed the tenancy and in 1896 married Jane Whiteford (1871 – 1964), the eldest of another Ayrshire family with farming connections living at Ashbank, Stewarton.

They had 4 children: Janie (1898), Jim (1900), Betty (1905) and Hugh (1908), all born at Grassmillees. Hugh's brother, Robert, had moved east in 1901 and encouraged him to follow. In 1909 the family along with the farm animals made the journey in a specially chartered train to Drem Station where the carts and horses were put to use to transport family and chattels to their new life at West Fortune (460 acres), 2 miles from Drem.

The Whiteford family circa 1895. Standing left to right: James, Phemie, George. Seated left to right: Hugh, Bessie, Robert, Mary.

Hugh, Janie, Jim, and Betty Circa 1911.

The farm was factored by two Guild brothers, lawyers in Edinburgh, one of whom had the tenancy of Rhodes Farm, east of North Berwick. Numerous letters were traded over permission for improvements in the farm steading and land before Hugh eventually purchased the farm in 1919 for £20,000 – equivalent to £1,000,000 in the 21st Century. Over the following 20 years he also puchased Prora (224 acres) and Congalton (296 acres, with 60 in permanent grass – the Braes). These were farmed as one unit by Jim with input from his father. Congalton Gardens was sold as a separate entity in 1940 and Hugh and Jane 'retired' from West Fortune to the house at Congalton in the early 1940's. In spite of recording frequent complaints about the weather – too wet, too dry, too hot, too cold – and the poor price of potatoes, turnips or grain, he obviously prospered after his early days of requiring loans and being overdrawn. He fastidiously looked after the pennies and the pounds must have looked after themselves.

The family went to primary school in Athelstaneford (known as Elshinford), a mile from West Fortune. Janie and Jim also went to North Berwick, as ascertained by book prizes recently discovered on a bookshelf, which had been awarded to Janie in 1912-1913. The family moved to George Watson's School for Boys and George Watson's Ladies College, Edinburgh for High School. Jim and Hugh boarded (which Hugh hated) but the girls travelled daily from Drem Station. There are references of occasional trips to Ayrshire to allow Jane to visit her parents at Stewarton, usually accompanied by perhaps 2 of the family. Her mother died in 1912 but her father David Whiteford lived until 1927.

David Whiteford with Betty at West Fortune.

Grandpa travelled more frequently, meeting his brother-in-law, John Hannah, (married to his sister, Phemie), his brother, George, a banker in Ayr who assisted with his financial affairs, and his sister, Bessie (married to George Osborne and then after his early death, to James Henderson – both farmers). Another reason for returning to Ayrshire was to visit the Mauchline Mission and to support the work that was done at the Mission Hall where he had been involved while living at Grassmillees. Hugh's Christian commitment resulted in his establishing a barn service in a loft above the farm steading for anyone around the West Fortune community which continued until the early 1960s.

As all 15 grandchildren lived within a radius of about 4 miles of Congalton we shared many memories of his time in retirement. His garden flourished with roses, sweet peas and soft fruit but much of his time was devoted to tending to the tomatoes and grapes in his large greenhouse . When these were ripe he would carefully cut them and lay them in a small basket atop a vine leaf before sharing them round. The flowering of the Yucca plant on the south side of the lawn around 1950 was a notable event.He gardened with dedication and energy, purchasing a new jacket for the enterprise, but Granny told him it was too good for the garden and he was not allowed to use it. Another family member, on observing him, commented, 'If he continues to mow the lawn at that pace he will explode!' He was reprimanded in his 90's when discovered up a ladder because the greenhouse roof was in need of attention. His workshop was also a place of creativity and many repairs and constructions emerged from there. Replacement knobs for cooking pan lids were crafted out of thread bobbins on several occasions.

There are also memories of his displeasure being expressed in no uncertain terms – when the bullfinches had eaten the blossom on the cherry tree, or the rabbits had found their way into the garden, or the cattle had escaped and were on the front lawn (usually on a Sunday morning).

I have clear memories of Grandpa's Sunday evening meetings which he had started in 1911 purchasing a pedal organ for £4. The grandchildren awaited the arrival of Grandpa's car from Congalton and rushed down the road to jump on the running boards for a ride up the hill with the farm collie adding to the fun. One evening something had been forgotten and one of the grandsons accompanied him home and reported that they had turned into the Congalton

Yucca in flower 1950.

entrance at 60mph. Each week, some of the children had duties to unlock the loft, sweep the floor and open the windows before the meeting and a favourite role was writing the hymn numbers on the blackboard. Granny or Janie had played the organ in the early days, but Betty had that responsibility from 1945 and was often challenged by Grandpa trying to increase the pace as he kept the beat on his desk and sang with vigour. Some of his talks were memorable such as his summing up of the parable of the Sower: 'No sproot, no root, no fruit, and much fruit'. Occasionally he had a friend come to speak at the meeting and their arrival in a Rolls Royce was quite an event!

Jane was a quiet, gracious lady who had a knack of managing people well, including her husband. She was someone who practised the advice of 'Is it true, is it kind, is it necessary?' before speaking. She was also quite strong-minded in her giving: having gifted some strawberries to a friend at church one Sunday and then being given eggs in return the following week she graciously refused to take them – payment for her gift was not wanted! In later years she had suggested to Hugh that due to hearing problems they should move further forward in church, but his response was that they would sit where they had always sat (the second back pew). She later recounted to her daughter-in-law that it so happened that there were a few extra duties to be attended to before they set off for church that morning and when they arrived, the church was fairly full, and they had to sit further forward. Jane once dared to suggest that there was occasional justification for a little white lie, but Hugh being a man of strong principles emphatically disagreed. She apparently confided that "Hugh could be a difficult man but she had learned to manage him in ways that he did not realise he was being managed."

Although Hugh was somewhat severe in demeanour, he had a great way with small children bouncing them on his knee accompanied by some doggerel rhyme or other, a favourite being 'There was a weddin' in Tranent'. His own family reported that they had only ever known the attitude of 'You could have done better' – any form of praise had been lacking. His Christian principles did not allow any work on the farm apart from essentials on a Sunday – a position which was tested on occasion when the grain was ready for harvesting and the weather was fine, but he remained true to his conviction. Granny had to accept that farming took priority in their lives. When members of the family were visiting her and sharing family news, somehow Grandpa knew they were there

A Farmer in East Lothian 19

Jane Miller with daughter, Janie, grandson, James Simpson and great grandson, Bob Simpson.

Jane Miller with daughter, Betty Murray, granddaughter, Margaret Cannon and great granddaughter, Fiona Cumming.

and appeared from garden or workshop and as he passed the lounge window she would say 'Oh no here he comes, it will be all farming talk now'!

Hugh Miller with Grandson Douglas Murray at West Fortune 1934.

He was someone who took on committee responsibilities such as the Athelstaneford School Board and County Education Committee; a Director of the Scottish Chamber of Commerce; Chairman of the Chamber of Agriculture; Council member of the Southern Morocco Mission (SMM). He was also well regarded through his involvement in farm valuation and agricultural arbitrations. He kept an ear to the ground through his weekly visits to markets in both Edinburgh and Haddington.

I hope that this background will have introduced the writer of these letters and enhance the understanding of some of his attitudes and concerns.

History of Agriculture in East Lothian

In the early 18th Century, there had been few trees in the county and the farms and fields were generally unenclosed, but by 1800 enclosure and tree planting had taken place. The infield and outfield system was followed – there was continual cropping and manuring on the former and constant cropping without manuring on the latter. The outfield was often some distance from the farmstead. Fodder was often in scarce supply and animals were emaciated. Villagers had cultivated strips (cotlands) and animals were often grazed on common grazing. Tile-draining of hollows brought marked improvement of heavy loams and fallowing (leaving unploughed or unseeded for a year) also brought improvement, leading to the Agricultural Revolution of 1770-1800.

Yields of grain and root crops in East Lothian were amongst the highest in the world by the mid 19th Century – quite a change from the previous century. In the early 1800s very high wheat prices encouraged the building of new and larger farmhouses and steadings, large quantities of wheat were exported from North Berwick and Dunbar, and Haddington was one of the greatest corn markets in Scotland.

The repeal of the Corn Laws in 1846 caused strains in relationships among those connected with the land. Farms were let to the highest bidder, ousting long standing tenants, and the flitting of workers at the Whitsunday Fair became much more frequent. Game preservation restrictions were also imposed.

In the 1850s and 1860s East Lothian agriculture was famed for its efficiency. Rents and wages had increased and there was plentiful grain, roots, and well nourished livestock. The purchase of concentrated animal foodstuffs increased markedly. Mechanisation increased and most farms had steam threshing mills installed. The reaping machine was introduced in the 1850s, reducing the need for gang workers to be hired. The bondager system which had involved a worker having to be able to supply a woman for so many weeks during harvest in order to enable him to be given employment and a cottage, was gradually fading out, but the provision of the 'Tattie Squad' (often mainly women) continued into the 1950s. The first female worker named on the West Fortune valuation accounts was a Margaret Steele, described as an outworker in 1918 and 1919.

East Lothian was hit by the Agricultural Depression of the 1880s following the import of large quantities of wheat from the American prairies. Permanent grass was increased, and sheep and cattle rearing increased. The Ground Game Act of 1880 allowed farmers to kill rabbits and other game on their farms.

East Lothian looking north from Traprain with North Berwick Law in the right background. West Fortune lies in the central distance.

By the 1890s slow recovery had begun. Few of those families who had known the good years in the 1850s and 1860s were left, having been unwilling to accept a diminished standard of living. Rents were lower and attractive to enterprising grieves or farmers from elsewhere, particularly Ayrshire. Robert Miller (Hugh's older brother) was an early arrival from Ayrshire in 1901 to Ferrygate, Dirleton, and along with his neighbour, James Simpson of Castlemains, pioneered the growing of early potatoes which proved highly successful in their coastal location. Around that time, East Lothian was described as the Garden of Scotland, and the lowland plain was one of the largest areas of high yielding farmland in the country.

The expansion of grain growing and increased prices of 1914 – 1918 were followed by a collapse of prices and economic depression. The area of permanent grass increased again and flocks of breeding ewes and grazing cattle became more common but the import of chilled meat from South America, Australia and New Zealand caused a fall in meat prices making winter indoor feeding uneconomic. The low and fluctuating prices made farming a perpetually uncertain business and many farms changed hands.

From the mid 19th Century until the early 1920s farms were usually run on the Lothian six crop rotation of Oats – Potatoes – Wheat – Turnips & Swedes – Barley – Grass (used as pasture or cut for hay). Elasticity in cropping allowed the introduction of sugar beet, silage, kale or rape. Heavy cropping, especially of potatoes was made possible by the liberal use of animal manure, and of imported cake and maize used to feed the cattle when indoors. After 1939 permanent grass was reduced once again, sheep flocks disappeared and the wheat-growing county of 100 years previous, became a barley-growing county with wheat and potatoes still of great importance.

Threshing was done by a built-in mill driven by oil, engine, electricity or tractor or by a travelling mill driven (pre-1940) by steam engine, then by tractor. Much of the grain was sold at the Haddington Corn Exchange with market day being a Friday but Hugh Miller made regular Wednesday trips to the Gorgie Corn Exchange in Edinburgh. Potatoes were traded mainly through merchants in Glasgow and Edinburgh – ware potatoes going there (or to Newcastle); seed potatoes going further south in England and new seed stock coming from the north of Scotland. Fat stock markets were held on alternate Mondays in Haddington and East Linton and there were also markets in the Borders, especially St Boswells for sheep sales. The auctioneers were John Swan & Son, Ltd. Edinburgh with a branch office in Haddington. Tranent was characterised by the East Lothian Cooperative Society which became one of the most active and successful in the country.

The Farm Servants Union formed in 1912, managed to obtain an increase of one shilling to weekly wages of 17 shillings in 1913 and further to 19 shillings in 1914. A Saturday half day was eventually granted on some farms in 1914 and on most by 1919 – in a working week of six 10 hour days. In the years of falling prices and depression following the First World War, a considerable wage reduction was accepted surprisingly smoothly but a suggestion of adding half an hour to the working day led to a strike. This was resolved following arbitration with an additional twenty hours worked annually. The Union was also involved in the pressure to upgrade farm cottages and accommodation.

Andrew Meikle (1719 – 1811), a local farmer and millwright, was the inventor of the threshing machine and also had an influence through his workshop on another member of Prestonkirk Parish, John Rennie of Phantassie, East Linton. John became a well-known civil engineer and builder of canals and bridges. John's brother, George, gained acclaim in farming and brought many international visitors to learn about farming practices at Phantassie.

Farm workers were employed through Hiring Fairs which were held in East Lothian in Dunbar on the first Tuesday in February and in Haddington on the first Friday. Men and women were hired at the fairs – farm servants, ploughmen, dairymaids and domestic servants. The farmers would be recognised by their top hats or bowlers and the workers would be wearing caps. The hiring terms were Whitsun in May and Martinmas in November. Married men were generally hired for a year and were expected to supply a female worker to help out when needed, such as at harvest. Single men were hired for 6 months. There was much criticism of these fairs as being little more than slave markets where men were judged on their appearance of strength, and the short terms were unsettling. Drunkenness was also said to result from such occasions although this was refuted by the workers enjoying their rare day out in the fun of the fair. Certainly, their token advance payment of 'arles' (about 1 shilling), given to seal their contract was generally spent at the stalls set up on the day of the fair or in local pubs,

Women workers would be in the fields 6.00am – 6.00pm, often coping with dirtier work and very poorly paid (9 or 10 shillings per week). Piece work for singling[1] or shawing[2] turnips was 1½ – 2 pence per 100yds. £1 extra might be given for a hard month's harvest work. Church attendance was expected on Sunday and was frequently a condition of farm workers' employment in Scotland.

Seaweed (or ware) being harvested for use on Castlemains Farm circa 1950, with the island of Fidra in the background. Hugh Miller did not appreciate seaweed being used as fertiliser and complained about a dung delivery having too much ware mixed into it. The collection of photographs from the 1950s were taken by Hugh's grandson, James Simpson and, although not contemporary to the text, add perspective to aspects of farming in East Lothian.

The Manure Man

Money is like manure, of very little use except it be spread.
– Francis Bacon. 1561–1626

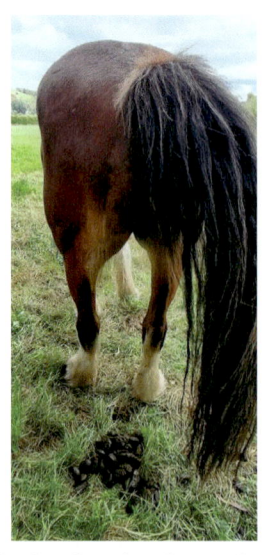

The spreading of dung on the land as fertiliser, along with improvement of the drainage were the main methods of improving the condition of the soil through the 18th and 19th Centuries and there is archaeological evidence from soil samples of the use of livestock manure dating back 8000 years to Neolithic times. Horse dung is rich in nitrogen which is good for potato growing and although current composting guides suggest letting it mature for months to years before applying it, the loads were probably spread on the fields fairly fresh.

Working the land generally requires getting your hands mucky, and this has been reflected in the language of Britain and Ireland over the centuries with phrases such as 'Where there's muck, there's luck' and 'Where there's muck, there's money.' [1]

Most human occupations involve some dirty work, but this series of letters indicate a job with no escape from hard manual labour. Many of the letters are addressed to a Mr McNally who is recorded as being a 'Manure Merchant', and the organisation of delivery of loads of dung to be used as fertiliser caused Hugh Miller frustration. J.& P. McNally (probably brothers) supplied the dung and deliveries came from Bonnington Station in the Newhaven area of Edinburgh. The Edinburgh, Leith & Granton Railway connecting this station opened in 1846 and eventually closed in 1968.

It is challenging for us to picture the city streets almost entirely traversed by horse-drawn vehicles in the early 1900s. Apparently, a large horse will produce approximately 9 tons of manure a year which would require a lot of shovelling. The McNally brothers presumably based their business from stables and Hugh Miller engaged them.

Complaints about the manure being too wet for the horses to walk on as they would be pulling the spreading carts are understandable, but a high proportion of ware (seaweed) was also criticised. These letters show Hugh's diligence in keeping track of deliveries and of the bills paid, ensuring every penny was accounted for.

***

174. Nov 16th 1911
J McNally Esq
Dear Sir,

I have this morning received your P.C. intimating the dispatch of seven waggons of manure. I have lifted some of it today, but cannot accept delivery as there is far too much rubbish in it. About half of what I have lifted is sea ware.

Please say what is to be done with the rest of it.

Yours faithfully,
H. Miller

***

184. Dec 7th 1911
J McNally Esq
Dear Sir,

I have your a/c for 131 tons 7c dung, but you have made no reference to the sea-ware etc that I wrote you about, in the last seven waggons that were sent. I cannot say how much there would be of it but I would consider 15 tons a very moderate estimate. I expected to see you in the market yesterday and arrange about it.

If you can promise to send the right stuff, I would take a quantity more, but it will have to be right. Let me hear from you by return and we will get a/c squared.

Yours faithfully,
H. Miller

***

203. Jan 16th 1912
West Fortune
Drem.
Mr P. McNally,
Dear Sir,

You might try and send me as much dung as possible during the next two weeks, as I have parts of the fields to finish that I wish to get ploughed up. I hope you will see to this.

Yours faithfully,
H. Miller

***

229. Apr 19th 1912
P McNally Esq.
Dear Sir,

I have your a/c for the two waggons of manure and find that they were paid to you in the Jan a/c.

I find also that I am overcharged 2 t 17 c 3 q in the Feb a/c. I had not the Ry. Co. a/c to check this when I paid you the balance. The two waggons you sent the a/c for are charged in the Jan a/c on the 29th.

Yours faithfully,
H. Miller

***

267. July 19th 1912
Mr P. McNally,
Dear Sir,

I have sent you herewith a cheque for £29.11.6 in payment of enclosed a/c. You could send me a few waggons next week, but do not load any before Friday. Some of the first waggons were very wet & mucky. You might see that this does not occur as

the horses cannot go on to the heap when it is so wet.
Please acknowledge receipt of cheque.
Yours faithfully,
H. Miller

***

268. Aug 7th 1912
J. McNally Esq.
Dear Sir,
Do not load any more dung at present as harvest is approaching and I will not be able to cart it.
Yours faithfully,
H. Miller

***

From the 1881 census records it appears that Peter McNally was born in Dunbar in 1878, and was living with his parents and younger brother, George in Leith. His father seemed to vary his occupations including Cooper, Spirit Merchant and Carting Contractor. There is a record of Peter's marriage on 8th December 1897 to Marion Jane Watson who at age 20 was a year his senior. The 1901 census lists Peter living with his father and seven others in the house including his brother John then aged 17 and described as an architect. The house is listed as having ten rooms containing a window and there was also a servant, Maggie, so they appear to have been prospering. Intriguingly his wife is not listed on the recording day. She did outlive him as she is named in attendance on his death certificate on 29th October 1912 from pneumonia. He was aged 33.

***

272. Aug 16th 1912
Mr Peter McNally,
Dear Sir,
I have your a/c and have sent you herewith a cheque for £50 to a/c of manure. I do not want any more just now as we are harvesting. I will see you in Edinburgh market some day regarding the balance.
Yours faithfully,
H. Miller

***

280. Sept 6th 1912
Mr P McNally
Dear Sir,
    I had your note of 5th inst. I was anxious to see you on Wed. as I consider I have been a good bit overcharged on the dung, owing to short weight. You might furnish me the weights of the last four waggons you sent me from Bonnington.
    Yours faithfully,
    H. Miller

***

285. Sept 13th 1912
Mr P McNally
Dear Sir,
    Yours of - received yesterday, with the nos. of the waggons of manure. What I asked for and wish to know is the weights respectively of the last four waggons, viz. 51139 - 36127 - 50486 - 52004.
    Please let me have this at your earliest convenience.
    Yours faithfully,
    H. Miller

***

287. Sept 16th 1912
Mr P McNally
Dear Sir,
    I have received you letter of 13th inst. but you do not give me the information I asked for. You might ascertain from the Ry. Co. the weight of the four waggons I referred to in my letter of Sept 13th. If you have it on Wed you could see me in the market.
    Yours faithfully,
    H. Miller

***

294. 25.9.1012
To P.McNally
West Fortune
Drem

I sent your a/c a week ago requesting you to receipt and return it.

Pleased do so as I require all those odd things for reference, and I want the dung a/c all in one.

Yours
H. Miller

***

297. Sept 27th 1912
Mr P McNally,
Dear Sir,

I have received yours of date Sept 17th tonight, stating disappointment at not receiving a cheque. Unless there is some mistake regarding the addressee of that letter, I am afraid your disappointment will be increased when you receive this one.

It seems to me that you have a very short memory or that you take other people to be a great deal simpler than yourself.

Without any more bluff I will be glad to have the account returned receipted, on which I paid you fifty pounds on Aug 12th and twelve

pounds as balance on Sept 18th.

Yours faithfully,
H. Miller

***

355. July 21st 1913
Messrs McNally Bros.
Dear Sirs,

I could take a few waggons manure this week - not more than 40 tons per day, and please see that the weight is put down for every separate waggon that I may have some cheque on what I am getting. I am going to spread it on the land so please send me stuff suitable for this.

Yours faithfully,
H. Miller

***

365. Sept 27th 1913
Messrs. McNally Bros.
Dear Sirs,
    Do not exceed 150 tons manure to me in the meantime. When you have this quantity on rail, see that you stop loading at once. Rather be under the quantity than over it.
    Yours faithfully,
    H. Miller

***

367. Oct 16th 1913
W.D.7508
Demurrage[2] a/c 18/-
T. Philip Esq.
Dear Sir,
    I have your letter with a/c for 18/- encl.
    The consigner in this case continued loading manure after I had ordered him to cease, and I took delivery of these extra waggons for his convenience, and for that of the Ry. Co. I therefore do not consider that I am in any way responsible for the demurrage.
    Yours faithfully,
    H. Miller

***

367. Oct 22nd 1913
P McNally decd.
J Robertson Esq.
Dear Sir,
    I am in receipt of your letter of 21st inst. re manure transactions with the above P. McNally.
    I squared my account with him on Sept 18th 1912 and had no further transaction with him.
    Yours faithfully,
    H. Miller

***

368. Oct 29th 1913
The N. B. Ry. Co.

There falls to be deducted from the enclosed a/c for manure carriage £5.14.11 representing the carriage on 57 tons 8c 3qrs of which the consignment was short.

I have therefore deducted this amount from my a/c and trust you will find it in order.

Yours faithfully,
H. Miller

***

386. Dec 24th 1913
Mr Edington,
Dear Sir,

I am in receipt of your letter of 23rd inst re the carriage of manure which I did not get delivery of.

I am quite prepared to pay the carriage on the manure referred to, whenever the Ry. Co. delivers the same to me at Drem Stn but not till then.

Yours faithfully,
H. Miller

***

398. Mar 6th 1914
R.T. 775/814
T. Philip Esq.
Dear Sir,

I am in receipt of your letter of 4th inst. enclosing a/c for carriage of manure said to have been received by me at Drem, and which you state I have refused to pay.

I beg to state that I have not refused to pay the carriage of the manure I received, as ascertained by your own weights at Drem. I have only refused to pay for what I did not receive, and regret that I cannot accede to your request to remit £5.14.11.

Yours faithfully,
H. Miller

***

412. Aug 21st 1914
Mr Edington,
Dear Sir,

I find in the statement of the enclosed a/c that there is a difference of 22 tons 3 cwts 3 qrs in the weight of manure received here compared with the weight at North Leith.

I therefore consider that the carriage on this quantity should be deducted, but without prejudice I am willing to pay the half of it. I have therefore deducted £1.2/- - the carriage of 11 tons - from the a/c, which I trust you will find in order.

Yours faithfully,
H. Miller

***

Potatoes

*What I say is that, if a man really likes potatoes, he
must be a pretty decent sort of fellow.
– A.A.Milne 1882–1956*

The significant famine of 1845 was due to potato blight, a fungal disease. Following this a serious effort was made to breed blight resistant varieties. It was identified that the conditions contributing to blight tended to be less on the drier east coast of Scotland.

Archibald Finlay of Auchtermuchty in Fife bred 'Up-to-Date' (1894 – main crop) and 'British Queen' (1894 – second early) which became the leading varieties in the early 20th Century. 'British Queen' is once again a popular variety, having been reintroduced. Mr Finlay also bred 'Majestic' (1911 – early main) which later accounted for 60% of UK production. Donald Mackenzie of Lamlash, Isle of Arran, was another contemporary breeder producing several Arran varieties including 'Arran Comrade' (1918 – second early). Kerr's Pink bred by Henry Kerr in Cornhill, Banffshire remains one of the most popular varieties in the north of Scotland. It has also become widely grown in Ireland and is regarded as an Irish potato.

English merchants were initially keen to have seed[1] potato tubers from Scotland, but, glimpsing a potential income stream, began producing more plants from stem cuttings, marketing these a year later as 'once-grown Scotch seed'. This seed tended to become infected by viral diseases in the milder conditions of the south.

Messrs. R. & S. Paton were the local potato merchants generally used by Hugh Miller. Prices fluctuated with £45 per acre being the price in 1919 and £80 per acre in 1920.

It appears that the usual arrangement was for the seller to lift the crop and put it into a pit (or clamp). This involved the potatoes being covered with straw and then earth allowing some ventilation through the straw chimney of the elongated pit. The buyer was then responsible for lifting the purchased crop from the pit.

***

1. Sept 15th 1910
Messrs. J & A McArthur
Dear Sirs,
    I beg to confirm having sold to you about fifteen acres of British Queen Potatoes at £16 per acre.
    Yours faithfully.
    H. Miller

***

3. Oct 6th 1910
Messrs. J & A McArthur
    I beg to confirm having sold to you about 12 acres Up-to-Date potatoes at £20 (twenty pounds) per acre with endrigs round plot thrown in, I to do the horse work of digging and carting and also take the brock[2] at 17/6 per ton in your option.
    Yours faithfully,
    H. Miller

***

5. Oct 10th 1910
A Pollock Esq.
Dear Sir,
    I daresay you will have heard from Messrs. A & J Main regarding the potato digger that I had on approval. The pinions began to skip teeth when it had wrought little more than half a day. Mr Poole proposed that you should come and see it, but while I am quite willing that you should do so, I feel it would be a waste of time, as the machine needs to go back to the shop before it is further tried. I am sorry I have had this experience with the machine as I thought its action to be an improvement on the old system. I found, however, that it missed a screw and also a bar on the frame forward the shaws where these were strong.
    Yours faithfully,
    H .Miller
    The digger is lying at Drem Station. H.M.

***

43. Jan 28th 1911
Wm Atkinson Esq
Dear Sir,
   I received the Rising Sun potatoes yesterday. There is a great deal of ware[3] amongst them, but their worst fault is a lot of frosted ones through them. This has taken place some time ago, and they have been lifted very wet from the pit. After they are dry, I will dress them over, and I suppose that you will be willing to accept of my word as to the quantity of waste. The bags will be returned forthwith.
   Yours faithfully,
   H. Miller

***

59. Mar 4th 1911
Messrs J. & A. McArthur
Dear Sirs,
   Referring to our conversation yesterday re the Rising Sun seed potatoes I got from you on 18th & 19th Dec last from Cardross. I found on testing two cwt. of them lifted at random from the lot, that there was 26lbs of diseased ones.
   This means a total of 25cwts in 10tons 17cwts which is the quantity I got.
   The dressing of them will cost me 2/6 per ton but I am willing to bear this part of it. The loss apart from this will be

   25cwts@ 2/6 - £3. 2. 6
Ry. Carr. of same @ 11/8 - 13. 7
         Total £3. 16. 1

I have got as many epicures as I need.
Yours faithfully,
H. Miller

***

131 Sept 2nd 1911
Messrs Allan, Souness & Speirs
Dear Sirs,
 Would you please give me a quotation for 500 potato boxes, both made and unmade. My brother at Ferrygate mentioned that he got some from you. The size of those I have at present is 31 ¼" x 21 ¼" over all and the corner pieces are 6 ½" long.
 I would prefer them this size if possible, the price as arranged.
 Yours faithfully,
 H. Miller

***

138. Sept 12th 1911
The S.C.W.S. Ltd
Dear Sirs,
 I beg to confirm having sold to you about 52 (fifty two) acres potatoes at £24 (twenty four) pounds per ac. With £1 (one pound) per ac. up or down in buyer's option.
 Seller to pit them and buyer to lift them from the pits.
 Yours faithfully,
 H. Miller

***

141. Sept 18th 1911
Messrs Souness & Speirs,
Dear Sirs,
 Yours of 8th inst. duly received.
 Please make up 500 potato boxes and rail them to Drem Station. Would you see that the handles are slightly rounded before putting them together.
 Yours faithfully,
 H. Miller

***

142. Sept 21st 1911
Thos Russell Esq
Dear Sir,
 I am wondering if you could supply me with some fruit hampers for potato gathering. Such as plum or greengage hampers - the round pattern - would suit very

well. If you have them you might say what they would cost, and if I could have 100 next week.

I dare say you will recognise the writer. I was formerly at Mauchline.

Yours faithfully,

H. Miller

***

166. Nov 1st 1911

Messrs Souness & Spiers

Dear Sirs,

I herewith enclose cheque in payment of 500 boxes per a/c.

You might please make me other 500, but see that the bottoms are closely fitted on as this gives more strength to the box. A few of the sides too are cut thinner than others.

Please see to this.

Yours faithfully,

H. Miller

***

273. Aug 19th 1912

H Campbell Esq.

Dear Sir,

Yours of 16th inst. to hand re brock potatoes. I am sorry you have not got a waggon sent to me as the last I have were boiled today, and I have nothing to substitute them for the pigs. I trust you will manage to send me some on Monday as it is now desperation.

Yours faithfully,

H. Miller

***

405. May 6th 1914

H. Campbell Esq.

Dear Sir,

Yours of yesterday's date to hand. I used 30 tons of planting your field. The half ton of manure costs £3.6/-. The balance of the seed left for broke is 5 tons 8 cwt.

I have railed the waggon of "ware" today, and the weight is as follows: 3 tons 12 cwts.
Yours faithfully,
H. Miller

***

407. Aug 3rd 1914
The S.C.W.S. Ltd.
Dear Sirs,
Thanks for cheque in payment of potatoes but there is a slight discrepancy in the amount I am charged for the seed.
I had 40 tons @ 75/- £150.3. 9
I am charged £150.11 .2
An overcharge of 7. 5
Yours faithfully,
H. Miller

***

The following letters are addressed to a Miss Quarrier, presumably of 'The Orphan Homes of Scotland', Bridge of Weir, a charity supported by Hugh Miller. William Quarrier was a prosperous shoe merchant in Glasgow but is recorded as meeting a young orphan boy in tears one night in 1864. Following this he worked to establish charitable support for orphans resulting in the building of a collection of houses on farmland outside the city. Gradually the village grew to include almost forty houses, a church, a school, and a training ship where boys could be prepared for entry to the navy. William Quarrier died in 1903 and his family continued this work. Changes in healthcare and sanitation had an enormous impact on the number of children orphaned and the charity has changed its name to 'Quarriers' continuing to support people living with a disability, those with a diagnosis of epilepsy, young homeless and carers.

***

474 & 475. Mar 17th 1917
Dear Miss Quarrier,
My brother spoke to me the other day about a communication he had from you regarding potatoes. I really had sold all I had to spare to a merchant, but I arranged all right with him and have sent you a waggon (four tons) today. They are much smaller than we get in ordinary times, but you will find the quality all right.

In the course of a week or two I could perhaps send you other four or eight tons. I hope this quantity will put you more than an arm's length from famine. I would have sent you a larger quantity, but I must not break faith with the merchant to whom they were already sold.

I will send the a/c for the lot after they are railed.

These are trying times we are passing through and the difficulties of maintaining your large family, will be much increased, but when we 'Consider the ravens' and remember the Hand that feeds them we conclude that our Father has a deeper interest in us.

Jehovah-Jireh.
With kind regards,
Yours faithfully,
H. Miller

***

478. Apr 26th 1917
Dear Miss Quarrier,

I have today sent you another waggon (4 tons) of potatoes which I trust will reach you all right. I am sorry I cannot send you any more than this as my stock is now exhausted. I enclose a/c as requested.

The potatoes were sold at £11 per ton, but I am charging yours at £10 which I hope will be satisfactory to you.

The future months are not bright at the moment, concerning our food supplies, but 'The Lord reigneth', and the assurance the earth and the fullness thereof belong to Him, gives us confidence that we shall not want.

May the Lord bless you & yours.
Yours faithfully,
H. Miller

***

533. Aug 19th 1920
Chas. Weatherall Esq.
Dear Sir,

I am in receipt of your communication regarding the inspection of my potatoes, and I must say I am disappointed with the report. I am sorry I had not the opportunity of explaining to the inspector that there had been a mistake in planting the Tinwalds and I intended the mixed portion to be left out altogether.

As for the Majestics these were rogued[4], and I challenge the inspector to find 0.5 per cent of rogues amongst them.

The Golden Wonders were not rogued but these I am not concerned about.

Then I have 2 ac. of Arran Comrade, and 2 ½ ac. of Kerr's Pink which are as near as possible pure. Why are these not referred to in the report?

I consider I have not been fairly treated by the Board, and will be glad to have your observations.

Yours faithfully,
H. Miller

***

535. Sept 15th 1920
<u>Inspection of Potatoes</u>
J. Handfour Esq.
Dear Sir,

Referring to your letter of 25th Aug., if you will be good enough to send out your Inspector by appointment to meet me on the ground and point out the rogues in the Majestics plot, I will be glad to take them out. I may say that I have gone through them again and removed anything I could find that was wrong. I also took an expert over them, and he was perfectly satisfied with their purity and would have bought them for seed purposes on the spot. In these circumstances I trust you will be able to meet me, and that you will find the potatoes worthy of being certified.

Regarding the Tinwald Perfection - I was prepared all along and never thought of anything else than to scrap the mixed drills and I trust you will see your way to certify the balance of them.

Yours faithfully,
H. Miller

***

541. Jan 26th 1921
Messrs R. & S. Paton ltd.
Dear Sirs,

Referring to my call at your office three weeks ago when you paid me £1000 to account on our transactions. I offered then to make a concession of £200 if you settled the balance forthwith. This you arranged to do the following week, but as it has not been done, you will not expect me to continue my offer indefinitely.

I will be glad to hear from you on the subject.

Would you please send me a note of the various items as the 4 tons 2c. of Majestics you got in April and the Epicure tops in Aug. and also the Epicure seconds (24 c.) & Epicure thirds (27c.) in Dec. were left to you to make the price.

Yours faithfully,
H. Miller

***

545. Feb 25th 1921
Messrs R. & S. Paton Ltd.
Dear Sir,

I have your favour of 25th inst. with cheque enclosed for £218.14. 6 which squares up the transaction of 43 ac. 2rds. 14pls. of Epicures, and for which I thank you.

There still remains outstanding some Majestics and some Epicure seconds which I would be glad if you can get squared up. The price of these was I think left to you, although I think £14 a ton was spoken of for the Majestics.

Yours faithfully,
H. Miller

***

662. July 16th 1932
Messrs Reid, Grahame & McRobbie
Dear Sirs,

I have your letter of 11th inst. regarding the two waggons of potatoes.

There is much I might say but perhaps it will be better left unsaid. I agreed to be responsible for the former waggon, never for a moment thinking that the price was to be quartered, but as promised, I herewith send you cheque for £26.12.8 which you say is the loss.

Regarding the latter waggon, if you say this is fair treatment to me then I have nothing more to say on the matter.

This however I will add, I had several other customers getting the same potatoes at the same time, and I had no other complaint whatever the whole season. I am only sorry now that I did not ask for the potatoes to be returned.

Yours faithfully,
Hugh Miller

***

The following correspondence outlining a proposition to establish trade with the West Indies was a surprise and coming in the last pages of the letterbook there is no indication as to whether this developed into a commercial enterprise before war broke out. The *S.S. Magician*, built in 1925, sailed as a cargo ship between London and Trinidad. She sank off the coast of Peterhead, Scotland in 1944.

***

667. May 17th 1934
Messrs Aitken Lilburn & Co.
Dear Sirs,
 I have been communicating with Messrs B.E.Cooper & Co. Ld., Australia House, London, about the possibility of exporting potatoes to the British West Indies. They state they are known to you, and asked me to get in touch with you, about getting a sample case sent to Trinidad.
 Would you be good enough to tell me when the sailings are for that port - or I should say - Port of Spain, and give me any instructions that you think necessary.
 Of course, this is only an experiment, and it will all depend on the cost of freight and what the potatoes can realise whether there can be further business of not.
 Yours faithfully,
 Hugh Miller

***

668. May 17th 1934
Messrs B.E.Cooper & Co. Ld.
Dear Sirs,
 I thank you for your letter of 14th inst. and I am now endeavouring to arrange to send a sample of potatoes to Port of Spain.
 I have written to Aitken Lilburn & Co. of Glasgow, and have asked their instructions as to getting a sample shipped. I am thinking just to send it to The Trinidad General Sales Co. and ask them to take charge of it.
 When I have anything further of interest, I will communicate with you.
 Yours faithfully,
 Hugh Miller

***

669. & 670. May 24th 1934
The Trinidad General Sales Co.
Dear Sirs,
 Messrs B.E. Cooper & Co. Ld. of London have been communicating with me about sending potatoes to the B. W. Indies, and recommend you as reliable consignees. The season is almost past now for our Main Crop potatoes, and it might be questionable whether our early crop varieties would carry successfully or not, but as an experiment I am sending you a sample case from Glasgow by the S. S Magician on the 30th curt. I have made up a case in two divisions of 29lbs each of "King Edwards" and "Majestics". I hope they may arrive in good condition, and I would like you to give me a full report of how they have stood the journey, and whether they are acceptable or not, also how the sample could be improved upon. If they have not kept well on the journey I would rather you did not offer them on the market at all, but if they reach you in a sound condition, please do the best you can with them on a competitive market.
 If it can be made worthwhile, I have no doubt it will lead to further business.
 Would a bulk shipment carry well in sacks?
 I am,
 Yours faithfully,
 Hugh Miller

***

46 A Farmer in East Lothian

Potato Dresser Or Grader

Grain, Hay and Straw

You'll never plough a field by turning it over in your mind.
– Irish Proverb

This chapter brings together a portion of the letters regarding the seed harvest. Originally the binder was horse-drawn and later by tractor. The grain was cut, tied in sheaves and then stooked by workers in the field. The sheaves were stood on end, leaning against one another to allow them to dry. In due course they were carted off for stacking.

The traditional agriculture in East Lothian and its climate has been well suited to growing barley. It is slightly incongruous that Hugh Miller was a supporter of the Temperance Movement but harvested his barley and traded it with the Malthouses in Athelstaneford and Haddington.

***

8. 18th Oct 1910
D Dale Esq
Dear Sir,

You might let me know if you have any whitechaff squarehead wheat suitable for seed as usual, and the price. I will require nearly 60 bolls. You might please send sample. We have had beautiful weather for potato lifting, but today has broken down. There are large breadths of potatoes still to lift.

Yours faithfully,
H. Miller

***

13. Nov 5th 1910
Messrs Jas Aitken & Son
Dear Sirs,

I have railed today to your address - Duddingston - two waggons second crop hay as arranged.

	Tons	c	qr	
61359 - 28 bales	2	2	1	
59382 - 28 bales	2	2	3	weighed at Drem.

Yours faithfully,
H. Miller

***

34. Dec 17th 1910
Messrs A Hamilton & Sons
Dear Sirs,

 I am in receipt of your favour of 16th inst. Re black oats sample. I have just called to mind that I put the sample into a bag in which I had a sample of barley at the market on Wed. last and omitted to invert it before doing so. There was not a barley pickle in the sample I rubbed. The price is not tempting but I will likely be in the market on Wed. and will see you there.
 Yours faithfully,
 H. Miller

***

41. Jan 21st 1911
Messrs A. Hamilton & Sons
Dear Sirs,

 I have sent you today per Pass. Train a large sample of the black oats (Rival) when I hope they may prove suitable for your purpose. To procure this sample I have to pass them first through a hand riddle and then through the fanners[1]. I cannot take the last of the robin seed out, but there is not much left. The sample is much stronger on account of the hand riddling.
 Yours faithfully,
 H. Miller

***

86. May 3rd 1911
Messrs J Montgomerie & Co Ltd
Dear Sirs,

 I loaded today at Drem on account of G. McLennan Esq. 55qrs wheat, and I regret that a few of the bags got a shower on the way to the station. I don't know to what extent they were wet, but if you get them emptied out as soon as possible, the wheat may not be much the worse, and I will be responsible if it is. Let me know how it turns out.

    Yours faithfully,
    H. Miller

***

107. June 26th 1911
A Campbell Esq
Dear Sir,

    I find that the receipt for two waggons hay loaded today are marked 'Hay damp when received'. This is far too general a statement, and I cannot accept of it. The men who baled it state that it was dry, the man who loaded it states that it was dry, and I was among the bales myself and saw no wet bales. While not admitting that any of the hay was damp, the number of bales must be stated.

    Yours faithfully,
    H. Miller

***

215. Feb 9th 1912
Messrs E Chalmers & Co
Dear Sirs,

    You might please send me 100 sacks similar to what I got on Nov 18th last year. These were plain flour sacks. Please see that they are whole as they are for holding grain. Send to Drem Station at your earliest convenience.

    Yours faithfully,
    H. Miller

***

223. Mar 21st 1912
Messrs Gortons Ltd
Dear Sirs,

    I find that the two quarters of Waverley oats you sent me on Feb 15th have a good many black ones through them. This was not observed till they were being sown. They should have been pure as the sample I bought them from had nothing of the kind in it.

    Please look into the matter.
    Yours faithfully,
    H. Miller

***

248. June 19th 1912.
Messrs Mungo Gray & Co
Dear Sirs,
    I wired you this afternoon that I had loaded two waggons of wheat straw to your order, and asking you to send me an address for it. I expected to see Mr Mungo Gray in the market at Edinburgh but did not see him. When I sold him the straw, he said I was to rail the half of it when threshed but the Ry. Co. had no order, and I did not know this till after it was loaded. I trust you will have no inconvenience, through these two waggons being loaded, and in the meantime, I have stored up the remainder - about ten tons.
    Yours faithfully,
    H. Miller

	T.	c.	q.
No 50654	2	9	2
38989	2	10	1

***

262 July 9th 1912
George McLennan Esq.
Dear Sir,
    Through a misunderstanding I charged you 39/- for the last 300 qrs. of wheat you got, as I understood I had sold an equal quantity to Wm Kay & Son at this figure, and they reckoned the sale was 38/6. I conceded the 6d per qr. to them and will refund you 10/-. I need not say that it was in good faith that I stated 39/- to you as the price.
    Yours faithfully,
    H. Miller

***

301. Oct 23rd 1912
John Howie Esq.
Dear Sir,
    I had your letter of inquiry regarding seed wheat, and as I did not see you in the market today I wired you that I had not any suitable. The fact is, I had red-chaff growing in the same field, and I made up my mind that I would not offer it for seed at all. It was my first experience of red-chaff and I think it is likely to be my last. It

was a good enough crop, but we got a very high wind before it was cut, and I thought it much worse shaken than the white chaff.

I have written Dale of Flint asking if he has any. If he has it to spare, would you care to have his?

We will scarcely finish potatoes this week. We have too much disease in places.
Yours faithfully,
H. Miller

***

322. Dec 6th 1912
Messrs Wm Kay & Sons
Dear Sirs,

With reference to the barley I sold to you on Wednesday, I delivered to the Maltings at Athelstaneford 80 bags Standwell barley yesterday.

I told the carter to get a receipt for this quantity, but the foreman at the maltings refused him this.

I wish now to inform you that under existing circumstances I will sell no more barley for delivery at Athelstaneford, as I prefer to find a market where I will meet with ordinary business civilities.

Yours faithfully,
H. Miller

***

323. Dec 20th 1912
Messrs Wm Kay & Sons
Dear Sirs,

Referring to conversation in Haddington market today regarding the delivery of the barley at Athelstaneford, I am now prepared to prove that a note of the quantity was sent and handed to Webster, and even the number of Miller's bags and the number of the Maltings' bags mentioned in the consignment. The carter also states that he did ask for a receipt as the time and was refused it.

I just mention this in confirmation of what I said in the market today.
Yours faithfully,
H. Miller

***

331. Jan 10th 1913
C Charlton Esq.
> Dear Sir,
> Mr John Middlemass told me today that you were inquiring about hay. I supplied some to Messrs Posgate, Butchers, whom you may know, and would be pleased to supply you with the same class of hay this month at 90/- per ton on rail in bales. You might please say if you can take in a quantity - say ten to twenty tons at a time, as this suits me best.
> Will be pleased to have your order.
> Yours faithfully,
> H. Miller

***

333. Jan 18th 1913
Messrs Boyd & Finlay,
> Dear Sirs,
> I am in receipt of yours of this date, and am surprised at the complaint about the hay. It might be there was an odd bale not as good as the rest, but I have delivered over 30 tons this season and yours is the first complaint I have got. However, if you have lifted it from your customers, I will arrange about the disposal of it on Wednesday at the market.
> Yours faithfully,
> H. Miller

***

334. Jan 21st 1913
C Charlton Esq.
> Dear Sir,
> I have your favour of a recent date and find that the carriage of hay from Drem to Sunderland is 15/- per ton for a minimum of 2 ½ tons. The R. Co. have restricted the size of the load of late, and I can only manage to load about 2 tons on the waggon, so the actual cost will be from 18/- to 19/- per ton. I would make the price 87/6 per ton on rail. Will be glad to hear from you at your earliest.
> Yours faithfully,
> H. Miller

***

335. Jan 30th 1913
Messrs Arch. Hamilton & Sons,
Dear Sirs,

I am in receipt of your favour of 29th inst. Regarding the oats, I do not think I could promise more than 160 bags of 112lbs each in the meantime, as I have another order to fill, and I do not wish to leave myself short.

You would perhaps be better to do as you suggest and get 45 bags from Ferrygate.

Yours faithfully,
H. Miller

***

Feb 1st 1913
Messrs J E Postgate & Sons
Dear Sirs,

I had your note today ordering a waggon of hay, and dispatched the same this afternoon.

No Bales   T   C   Q
49692   25 1   19   3

If you could do with another waggon in the course of a fortnight, I would send it on, as I am removing some I have stacked in the field and may not be baling more for some time.

Suit yourself, however. The price will be 87/6 per ton.

Yours faithfully,
H. Miller

***

337. Feb 11th 1913
C Charlton Esq.
Dear Sir,

I have your P.C. for two waggons - "if I can lower the price". I am sorry I cannot lower the price, viz. 87/6 per ton on rail at Drem. You might let me know by return if you wish me to send it on at these terms, as I am getting through with this lot of hay, and there will be an increase in price shortly.

Yours faithfully,
H. Miller

***

482. July 20th 1917
J. H. White Esq.
Dear Sir,
I have your wire asking "Why sending such small loads straw to Oakham, incurring unnecessary carriages, and unnecessary use of stock". I don't know why you complain now about the weight of the loads of straw. I began loading on June 26th and finished on July 13th and if you had any fault about the loads why did you not complain sooner? In any case I suppose you will be aware that the Rlwy. Co. have a gauge for the height of loaded waggons, and I had to go by that.
Yours faithfully,
H. Miller

***

The following letters in late 1917 and early 1918 reflect some of the impact of the war. Some of the wheat straw was going to the Paper Mills at Inveresk. Whether this had occurred previously or was a necessity precipitated by wartime shortages is not clear. Although none of the West Fortune horses were requisitioned for the war effort, some of the hay went to meet Government requirements.

***

Nov 28th 1917
The Paper Manuftg. Co.
Inveresk
Dear Sirs,
Regarding our conversation on the telephone this evening, I hereby offer you from twenty to thirty tons wheat straw, steam baled free on rail at Drem Station, at £3.10/- per ton. Delivery as soon as I can get a mill to thresh it, which I expect will be about the second week in Dec. weather permitting.
Yours faithfully,
H. Miller

***

487. Dec 5th 1917
Capt. Anderson
Dear Sir,
I have signed & herewith return purchase notes for 46 tons hay.

Regarding clause 6 of the conditions of sale, I beg to state that I am fully insured with the "Guardian Insurance Co". I can exhibit the receipts if you wish.
Yours faithfully,
H. Miller

***

506. Nov 5th 1918
Captn. Anderson, D. P. O. S.
Dear Sir,
I have a quantity of hay to offer you for the Government and will be glad if you can examine it at any time at your convenience.
Yours faithfully,
H. Miller

***

514. Aug 15th 1919
Messrs Gartons Ltd.
Dear Sirs,
I regret to inform you that the eleven qrs. of Abundance oats I received from you under invoice dated Feb 7th last have turned out to be badly mixed with barley. I am exceedingly disappointed at this as I meant the produce for my next year's stock of seed. I thought of roguing the crop but found it was impossible to do so satisfactorily. The crop is now ready for cutting but the barley will still be seen in the sheaves.
I will be glad to hear if you have any suggestion to make on the matter.
Yours faithfully,
H. Miller

***

520. Oct 31st 1919
Messrs Hugh Baird & Co.
Dear Sirs,
I delivered a quantity of barley into the maltings at Athelstaneford this week, and I am sorry that again I have to make a complaint regarding the man Webster. He seems to take a delight in keeping my carts standing over a meal hour, although they are forward in time enough to be emptied. This took place on Tuesday last.

I have only to say that however suitable the delivery may be into the maltings otherwise, I will sell no more barley for delivery there, unless I get a guarantee that matters will be different from what they have been.

Yours faithfully,

H. Miller

Raking the hay.

From coil to hay rick.

Hay being loaded to go to yard for stacking.

Binder working in the 1950s.

Livestock and Keeping Them Fed

Cattle
A cow is a very good animal in the field; but we turn her out of a garden.
– Samuel Johnson

The cattle at West Fortune were probably Aberdeen Angus or Beef Shorthorn and these would have been driven on foot from the farm and herded into a waggon at Drem station bound for the Meat Market at Gorgie in Edinburgh.

***

1. Sept 12th 1910
R. Thompson Esq
Dear Sir,
    I beg to confirm having let to you about 50 acres turnips to be consumed by cattle on the farm, say £8 per acre, swedes at £9 per acre (nine pounds) and the 2acres yellows at £7 (seven pounds) according to results with the right for you to reserve 5/- per acre (five shillings) according to how the crop turns out. One acre allowed off for black spots in Quarry Field.
    Yours faithfully,
    H. Miller

***

14. Nov 8th 1910
R Thomson Esq
Dear Sir,
    Yours of yesterday's date to hand. I have put the big cattle in the boxes on to about 8lbs of cake and the others are getting about 6lbs. I am mixing it at the rate of two cakes of cotton cake to one cake of lintseed.
    Yours faithfully,
    H. Miller
    I think I said to send not more than 35 cattle next week. H.M.

***

45. Feb 7th 1911
R. Thomson Esq
Dear Sir,
   You might send me some more cake, both Bombay and Lintseed. 4 tons Bomy and 2 tons Lintd suits best for the mixture the cattle are getting. I will require it not later than Monday. If you wish me to draw a waggon of cattle for Monday you might let me know by Saturday, as I might not be at home on Monday and I would get them marked.
   Yours faithfully,
   H. Miller

***

63. Mar 14th 1911
R Thomson Esq
Dear Sir,
   One of the bullocks has been off his food for a few days. I gave him salts and treacle and oil as well. His medicine acted but he is not coming to his food as I would like. There does not seem to be anything else wrong, and we will try to coax him on. I wired you this morning for some more cake.
   Yours faithfully,
   H. Miller

***

64. Mar 18th 1911
R Thomson Esq
Dear Sir,
   The bullock I wrote to you about has not come to his food, and I think the best thing to do with him is to get him away. If you were coming on Monday you would see, and I think you could get at least half a waggon if not a whole waggon. If you can't come send me word what to do.
   The bullock referred to is fair flesh.
   Yours faithfully,
   H. Miller

***

86. May 3rd 1911
R. Thomson Esq.
Dear Sir,

Unless you are anxious for cattle on Monday, I think it might be as well to hold off them for a week to get through the turnips while they are good. I would say there are plenty of turnips to keep them all for at least two weeks after this one, but if you are here on Monday you will see. I won't see you beat for some mangolds[1] to finish the last of them.

Yours faithfully,
H. Miller

***

104. June 14th 1911
R Thomson Esq
Dear Sir,

I herewith enclose your account as requested. I have put in the turnips at £8. 15/- and allowed you £10 besides which will help you a little. I have charged nothing for the mangolds that were eaten here. I think you will agree that the turnips were quite a good crop, if only the trade had been better.

I enclose the measurement, but you might return it.

We are having a severe drought and things look serious now.

Yours faithfully,
H. Miller

Carting Turnips

***

105. June 23rd 1911
Profsr. McAlpine,
Dear Sir,
   I would be obliged for an expression of your opinion as to what is the cause of the damage to the enclosed turnip plants. Quite a number are affected in a plot that was singled a fortnight ago. If you consider a reply to be of general interest, you could reply through the S.Farmer if you care to do so.
   Thanking you in anticipation,
   I am yours faithfully,
   H. Miller

***

Newspaper articles reporting on the Haddington Show in the late 1930s indicate that James Miller of Prora impressed the judges with his Mangold Wurzels and Sugar Beet more than Hugh Miller of West Fortune (his father).

Prora Farmhouse

113. July 6th 1911
Wm Vivers Esq
Dear Sir,
   I herewith enclose cheque £9. 8/- in payment of turnip seed. The turnip crop around here may in the end not turn out so badly, but there are a number of fields that are still very red. I have about 6 acres that will be a little patchy but the rest are looking fairly well. Your seed did not braird[2] so vigorously as some other lots I had. The Gale's Champion was perhaps worse than the X.L. All. There are some very poor fields of oats. And straw crop generally will be deficient. We have about 100 acres of hay in hand, but this week will I hope, see it nearly all in the tramp rick.
   I hear that turnip in your quarter are making a poor show. They have grown slowly since the rain here, the weather having been cold but yesterday and today are improved.
   Yours faithfully.
   H. Miller

***

145. Sept 27th 1911
R Thomson Esq.
Dear Sir,
   I will be quite pleased to let you have the turnips by the week, but considering the scarcity, the price would need to be 4/-. I would be augmenting their fodder with treacle which might be a benefit to both parties.
   You can let me know what your mind is.
   Yours faithfully,
   H. Miller

***

150. Oct 2nd 1911
Wm Middlemas Esq
Dear Sir,
   I hereby confirm having let to you my turnips for cattle and sheep as follows-
   Cattle under £12 cost at 3/6 per wk.
   Shearling sheep[3] on break[4] at 5d per wk.
   Hoggets[5] on cutter[6] at 4 ½ d per wk. with 20% back for cake consumed by cattle.
   Rape 5d per week for sheep.
   I trust you find this in order.
   Yours faithfully,
   H. Miller

***

187. Dec 11th 1911
East Lothian
Messrs Sutton & Co
Dear Sirs,
   Could you give me any information regarding "French Kail"?
   Do you supply the seed?
   What is the habit of the plant?
   Compared with turnip or mangold what is the most suitable time to sow?
   Is it a crop that is best eaten on the ground or is suitable for pulling and feeding to stock in the house?
   Will it stand frost in the end of the year?

I will be obliged if you can supply me this and any other information regarding it that would be useful. Might it have a fair chance of succeeding here in East Lothian?
Yours faithfully,
H. Miller

***

230. Apr 22nd 1912
Messrs Kent & Brydon
Dear Sirs,
I am in receipt of your favour of 20th inst. with catalogue enclosed.
You might please send me 40lbs of "Darlington" swede seed, and 60lbs "Monarch".
I hope they may do well as I have some land affected with finger and toe[7].
Yours faithfully,
H. Miller

***

295. Sept 26th 1912
W Middlemass Esq.
Dear Sir,
I beg to confirm having let to you turnips for lambs at 4 ½ d per week, and for young sheep at 5d per week, with ten per cent refunded for cake
consumed by them. Also turnips for cattle at 3/6 per wk, with anything further left to your option if cattle do well, and with twenty per cent refunded for cake consumed by them.
Yours faithfully,
H. Miller

***

406. July 11th 1914
Dear Sir,
On bringing in the cow this morning to send her away, I found she had a thick quarter - the far fore one - so did not think of sending her to you in that condition.
If I get her anything like right in the beginning of the week, I will send her on but if not, I will perhaps see you on Wednesday.

I do not know how she has come by it at all as she has never had a weed[8] all the time she was milking.
Yours faithfully,
H. Miller

***

441. Oct 13th 1915
A. Swanston Esq.
Dear Sir,
Referring to our conversation in the market today, I will put the turnips on offer to Mr. Stevenson @ 4/3 per wk. and will allow ten per cent off for cake.
If he cared, I would sell him the cattle I have in, but he can please himself about this.
Of course, I would like to know at once what he decides. I could take the cattle in by the end of next week.
Yours faithfully,
H. Miller

***

443. Oct 18th 1915
J. Stephenson Esq.
Dear Sir,
I have your letter of Saturday regarding the turnips.
I am sorry I do not see my way to give 20% of the cake but I will give the cattle some refuse potatoes which this year will be very good feeding. The cattle, if we arrange, will be looked after as if they were my own.
Regarding the cattle which I have in the courts, I thought they should be a little more than cost price, but seeing the stores are a little easier, I would take cost price for them. They cost £20 a piece.
Please wire me tomorrow on receipt of this, as I wish to know before Wednesday that I may get some cattle at Edinburgh.
Yours faithfully,
H. Miller

***

445 & 446 Nov 10th 1915
J. Stephenson Esq.
Dear Sir,
    You might please let me know if you are taking over my 24 cattle, as it is time they had some cake, and I wish to get them started.
    Indeed, all the cattle would be much the better of some cake as they are inclined to scour[9] with turnips alone.
    Please let me know by return.
    Yours faithfully,
    H. Miller

***

448. Feb 22nd 1916
J. Stephenson Esq.
Dear Sir,
    I had your note this morning asking about the cattle. The heifers are being fed on both sides of the court, and I do not consider it is necessary to do this in the other courts where the cattle are agreeing.
    If you think they are not doing well enough, I know they are eating more than four baskets of turnips per head per day. I think the cattle are doing exceedingly well, considering all the cake they are getting, and I can see that so much interference will not be conducive to the attendant interesting himself in them.
    I have told him however to put some turnip on the other side.
    Yours faithfully,
    H. Miller

***

505. Oct 28th 1918
Messrs Bond & Sons
Dear Sirs,
    The heifer "Halsall Maiden" no 98 in the catalogue of sale held on the 18th inst. at Ipswich, and described as served on July 14th, 1918, is today in season, and is consequently not conform to warranty. The seller is therefore due me £4 .2/- according to the conditions of sale.
    Please give the matter your attention.
    Yours faithfully,
    H. Miller

***

507. Nov 8th 1918
Major C. L. Blundell
Dear Sir,
    The heifer - Halsall Maiden - which I purchased at the Red Poll sale at Ipswich on 18th ult., number 98 in the catalogue is not in calf. She was in season ten days ago. According to the conditions of sale you will be due me £4. 2/- which is ten per cent of the cost price.
    Yours faithfully,
    H. Miller

***

508. Dec 20th 1918
C. H. Clark Esq.
Dear Sir,
    Please register my prefix with the R. P. C. Socty. as "Fortune", for which find value for 10/6 enclosed.
    I am not quite sure if you transferred the bull Marham Jester 11172 - no. 174 in the catalogue of the Oct. sale to my name. If not, please do so.
    My heifer - Mendham Belle 25788 had a bull calf on Nov 20th. Please register this as "Fortune Aerodrome".
    Yours faithfully,
    H. Miller

***

Sheep

Sheep, like people, are ungovernable when hungry.
– John Muir 1838–1914

***

491. Apr 9th 1918
Chas. Ritchie Esq.
Dear Sir,
    With reference to 78 sheep sent by me to Messrs Dewar & Davidson last week to kill, and which were allocated by you as follows -
    48 to Centl. M. M. Co. &

30 to Edinbr. M. M. Co.

I find that in my returns I am charged in name of Comsn. £4.3/- on the former and £1.16.2 on the latter.

This is surely quite out of order, and I will be glad if you give the matter your early attention with a view to recovering these amounts.

Yours faithfully,
H. Miller

***

492. Apr 20th 1918
Messrs Dewar & Davidson,
Dear Sirs,

I beg to acknowledge receipt of cheque for £277.15.4 in payment of 78 carcases of mutton consigned to The M. W. M. S. Asscn. Birmingham. I note the deduction they have made on the carcases and have written to Mr. Ritchie on the matter.

I hope however they may remit the difference to you. In the meantime, I do not accept of the cheque as payment in full.

Yours faithfully,
H. Miller

***

492. Apr. 20th 1918
Chas Ritchie Esq.
Dear Sir,

I have today received from Messrs Dewar & Davidson cheque for £227.15.4in payment of 78 carcases of mutton allocated by you to The M. W. M. S. Asscn., Birmingham.

They have deducted 141lbs of mutton of 5269lbs. I do not think you will expect me to accept of this and will be glad if you will take steps to recover the difference of 141lbs @ 1/1 £7.12.9.

Messrs Dewar & Davidson's weights were promptly advised & invoiced, and these were never challenged.

Yours faithfully,
H. Miller

***

495. May 11th 1918
Chas. Ritchie Esq.
Dear Sir,
    I have now received the balance of the mutton which was deducted from the lot that went to Birmingham, but I have not heard further regarding the amount deducted in name of commission, by the two Edinburgh firms,
    viz. £1.16.2 by The E. M. M. Co. Ltd
    & £4.3/- by The C. M.M. Co. Ltd
    As it is well enough understood that this must be paid, and this fact was corroborated by you, I cannot understand the delay in settling it.
    I will be glad to hear from you on the matter.
    Yours faithfully,
    H. Miller

***

499. July 3rd 1918
Thomson Esq.
Dear Sir,
    On the 11th of Apr. last I consigned 78 sheep to Messrs Dewar & Davidson - to kill. Those were allocated by the Live Stock Commsnr. - Mr Ritchie - as follows -
    48 carcases to The Central Meat Market Co. Ltd. - Edinburgh
    &30 do. to The Edinburgh Meat Market Co. Ltd - Edinburgh.
    The Govt. was paid the usual charge of 1/6 per head, but my complaint is that these two companies each charged commission again on their consignment, the former £4.3/- and the latter £1.16.2.
    I think this is quite an unjust charge and I will be glad if you will look into the matter and let me know what is right, and who should pay.
    I enclose for your perusal and return the statements of both lots of sheep.
    Yours faithfully,
    H. Miller

***

501. T/A.D.K. July 23rd 1918
Thomson Esq.
Dear Sir,
    I have your favour of 19th inst. and in reply beg to state that the offals referred to were sold by Messrs Dewar & Davidson who accounted to me for them.
    Yours faithfully,
    H. Miller

***

G./A.P.
502. Aug 9th 1918
Weston Thomson Esq.
Dear Sir,
    Yours of 1st Aug duly to hand. With regard to the offals of 78 sheep in question, I stated in my letter of July 23rd that these were sold by Messrs Dewar & Davidson who accounted to me for them. I do not see that the particulars of these offals has anything to do with the matter. Also, what I asked in my first letter of July 3rd was, who should pay that commission.
    Other firms got sheep from me under exactly the same conditions and no commission was charged. I will be glad if you will give me the information that I asked for, and return the enclosures I sent to you on July 3rd.
    Yours faithfully,
    H. Miller

***

506. Nov 5th 1918
The N.B. R. Station Agent
St Boswells
Dear Sir,
    On Sept 5th when a waggon of lambs off Upper Huntly Wood, bought by me at Swan's sale was being loaded, one lamb got its leg broken. The Railway officials took it out of the waggon and retained it. This lamb cost me 53/6 and I will be glad to have this amount refunded.
    I cannot understand why you have refused to settle with Swan's people on my behalf.
    Yours faithfully,
    H.Miller

***

507. Dec 4th 1918
D. Hutchison Esq.
Dear Sir,
    On Nov 5th I wrote to the Station Agent at St Boswells, claiming 53/6, the cost of a lamb which I bought at Swan's sale on Sept 5th & which got a leg broken in the N. B. Ry. Co.'s hands, and was appropriated by them. He has not acknowledged that letter, and I ask you who are on the spot to collect this for me. You are conversant with all the circumstances, and I do not need to detail these.
    Yours faithfully,
    H.Miller

***

512. Mar 20th 1919
G/A.P.
J. Weston Thomson Esq.
Dear Sir,
    Referring to your letter of 1st Aug. last, I wrote you on Aug 9th asking you to return to me the enclosures I sent to you at an earlier date regarding the details of sale of 78 carcases of mutton. You have never acknowledged this request, and as I have now ceased to hope for any assistance from such government departments, I again request you to return to me the papers referred to, and I will fight my own battle without that department's help.
    It is clearly a case of the victimisation of the producer again.
    Yours faithfully,
    H. Miller

***

628. Nov 1st 1926
Tranent Co-Op. Socy. Ld.
Dear Sirs,
    I have today received from Mr. J. Thomson a note of the salvage of five lambs which were disabled by one of your vans on Oct 1st, and herewith I enclose a/c for the damage sustained by the flock through the negligence of your driver. I trust you will find the matter in order and will be glad to have your cheque.
    Yours faithfully,
    Hugh Miller

***

634. Apr 29th 1927
Messrs Lawrie & Symington,
Dear Sirs,
    I have your letter of 27th inst. with Mr Armstrong's enclosed.
    I think it will be as well to let the matter stand over till we see how many of the H.B. hoggs prove in lamb. As far as I can make out just now there are three, and if this is all it will not be a serious matter to settle.
    Yours faithfully,
    Hugh Miller

***

Turkeys
A peacock that rests on his feathers is just another turkey
– Dolly Parton b.1956

***

45. Feb 7th 1911
Dear Madam,
    I have your letter of 4th inst. I thought that mine of Jan 25th had gone astray. I would take either of the young turkeys, but do not want the old one as I fear that he would be too heavy. Send me what you consider the better of the two and I will remit the price as I have no doubt but the bird will be satisfactory.
    I am sorry I have no hens to exchange.
    I am willing to pay the carriage in the event of being dissatisfied.
    Yours faithfully,
    H. Miller

***

48. Feb 13th 1911
Dear Madam,
    I received all right but am surprised to find that he has a crooked breast. I am therefore returning him tomorrow as I would not think of using him for breeding with this defect.
    Yours faithfully,
    H. Miller

***

51. Feb 17th 1911
Mrs Fergusson
Dear Madam,
   I have your letter of 15th inst. Re turkeys. I enclose two P O's for 28/- and you can send me on a cockerel at your convenience. I am depending that he will be a right bird.
   Yours faithfully,
   H. Miller

***

335. Jan 24th 1913
The Secretary
B. of Weir Orphan Homes
Dear Sir,
   I sent yesterday to the Homes a turkey, which I hope you may find a use for although Xmas is past.
   With best wishes for all concerned with the Homes.
   Yours faithfully,
   H. Miller
   The turkey was killed yesterday.
   H.M.

***

Pigs
I am fond of pigs. Dogs look up to us.
Cats look down on us. Pigs treat us as equals.
– Winston Churchill 1874 – 1965

***

212. Jan 31st 1912
George Vivers Esq.
Dear Sir,
   You can send me the pigs as soon as it suits you, but if you don't get them on Friday in time to be here before night on Sat., do not send them till Monday. You might let me know when to expect them.

Will they be fit to walk a mile and a half from the Station here, or should they be carted?

I got home all right last night, and found the frost gone, but it caught on this morning again.

H. Miller

***

213. Feb 6th 1912
To Chief Constable
Haddington.
Dear Sir,

Please send me a licence for the removal of thirty pigs from Annan to the above address.

Yours faithfully,
H. Miller

***

214. Feb 7th 1912
Wm Vivers Esq
Dear Sir,

I have here your various communications regarding the pigs. I have applied to the Chief Constable here for a licence to have them removed, and will be able to send it to you by Friday I expect. The wheels of government officials move slowly.

I hope they will come safely to their destination. Book them to Drem Station, N.B.R. and I hope they may do well while they are with me.

We had two very hard nights frost in the beginning of the week, but it is freshening now. Some potatoes have got a nip.

W Taylor has got a good trade for his horses. Another victim of the stock exchange.

Yours faithfully,
H. Miller
Let me know when to expect the pigs
H.M.

***

215. Feb 8th 1912
Wm Vivers Esq.
Dear Sir,

I wrote you last night, and I have the enclosed from the Chief Constable this morning. You can see what he says.

If you return my letter asking for the licence, and the form you are to fill up, direct to him it will save time.

Yours faithfully,
H. Miller

***

220. Feb 21st 1912
Wm Vivers Esq.
Dear Sir,

The pigs arrived all right on Wednesday afternoon as arranged. They were very hungry, but we have managed to satisfy them, I think. The smallest one was to be thrown in, so I enclose cheque for £43.10/-. Is that right?

We had the biggest flood of rain the night before last that we have had since I came here. Things have dried up today, however.

Do you think the pigs would come on as well on raw potatoes cut and mixed with meals as on boiled potatoes? There is a considerable difference of opinion as to the necessity of boiling potatoes. They are getting some turnips & meals mixed and they know how to put it out of sight.

Yours faithfully,
H. Miller

***

244. May 30th 1912
Wm Vivers Esq.
Dear Sir,

I am in receipt of yours of 24th inst. I will not put in any more pigs at present as these I have will need a good while to make their weight. I hope the price of pork is good when I put them out.

Robert's filly is not in foal. She was served the other day.

Turnips are brairded but X L All are distinctly weak alongside other varieties in the same field. I am afraid I may need to resow them.

We could do with a good soaking of rain again, to keep things going on.

Yours faithfully,
H. Miller

***

Horses

I can make a General in five minutes, but a good horse is hard to replace.
– Abraham Lincoln 1809–1865

The purchase of horses suited to farm work presented many challenges. Hugh was unwilling to accept those not reaching his stipulations and several were returned to the seller, involving some perseverance in obtaining the refund for railway carriage and veterinary bills. He was also involved in breeding and there is reference to the sale of a colt for £140 from his mare at West Fortune, served by the stallion 'Scotland Yet'. The Clydesdale Horse Society hired a stallion for the season and members kept one to three mares registered in the Clydesdale Yearbook.

The Clydesdale breed was founded in the early 1800s. By the beginning of the twentieth century there were 2.6 million heavy horses working but this had dwindled to 10,000 by the middle of the century. The first mention of a tractorman at West Fortune was a James Lorimer in the 1941 valuation. There were 61 tractors registered in the county in 1928 rising to 157 in 1938 and 749 by 1947. Combines were rare in the early 1940s but 19 were registered by 1946.

Horses remained a vital part of farm life until almost the 1950s. Ploughmen faced hard manual labour and long hours. Ploughing in East Lothian was done using the 'swing plough' which had no wheels and depended on the ploughman setting his 'irons' (blades on the plough), his eyesight and his skill. The day began at 5am with feeding and cleaning of the horses and stalls, prepared to begin work by 6am. There was a 10 – 15 minute breakfast break at 8am and a stop for dinner at 11am. The afternoon yoke was from 1pm – 6pm without a break and the ploughman then had to attend to the feeding, cleaning and bedding of his horses. This was the traditional pattern for six days each week. The average weekly wage for farmworkers in the early 1900s was 17/- for men,

9/- for women. This increased to £5 for men and £3.10/- for women by 1950.

This photo was taken in the steading at West Fortune in September 1926. Hugh Miller (Jnr) is second from the left, aged 18 with his own pair of horses. He is the only man not wearing a cap and perhaps this is what makes his face more prominent – or the photographer may have focused on the farmer's son.

The first collection of letters are addressed to a Mrs. Norris who was a horse dealer. She appears to meet her match with Hugh Miller as he was awarded £25-6-6 by the court in Berwick when she had sent a horse back to Drem Station after agreeing to purchase him.

***

13. Nov 4th 1910
Mrs Norris
    Dear Madam,
    I have one or two horses to sell, and my brother at Ferrygate gave me your address as a probable buyer. I would like to know at your earliest convenience if you would like to take a look at them, as the Hallow Fair comes on the week after next.
    Yours faithfully,
    H. Miller

***

21. Nov 25th 1910
Mrs Norris
Dear Madam,
   I have still the black horse for sale and if you could bid me about £40 we might have a deal. I have two two-year olds coming in and so must part with something. I have sold the little mare that you saw along with the black horse.
   Let me know by return.
   Yours faithfully,
   H. Miller

***

98. June 1st 1911
Mrs Norris
Dear Madam,
   I could now part with the shivering[1] horse which you spoke to me about. Let me know if you want him at £10.
   Yours faithfully,
   H. Miller

***

201. Jan 12th 1912
Dear Grandfather,
   I saw a useful pony this week that the owner is anxious to sell, and had it not been for what was said about your yellow one, I would have bought it. You might let me know however, what you want for your one, as I don't want it on any other condition than buying it. What age is it?
   Please let me know immediately as I want to be off or on with the other one.
   You might send us an Ayrshire ham, spiced the same as the last one, and a little bit larger.
   I got home yesterday and found all well. I trust you are all well too.
   Yours faithfully,
   H. Miller

***

202. Jan 16th 1912
Dear Grandfather,
   I received your letter yesterday, and was much surprised to learn the conditions on which you propose to send the pony. I never thought of such a thing, but in the

circumstances, I can do nothing but accept of your kindness on behalf of your beloved daughter, and I trust that as often as we sit behind it, it may lead us in the paths of rectitude and righteousness. I trust also that you may often have a share in the same pleasure here. I do not think you need have any concern regarding the treatment that it will get, and I hope it may have many days of usefulness in store.

I never was given to "gush", so please accept of our united thanks for your kindness.

Yours affectly,
H. Miller

***

Jane's father sent the pony (for their trap) as a gift in memory of his late wife.

***

205 Jan 19th 1912
Dear Grandfather,

I got your letter this morning, your wire this afternoon, and the pony came all right tonight. I have only seen it in the stable but will have a better look at it in daylight. I hope it may do well and serve us a long time.

We have had some blustery weather this week, but we seem to be escaping the snow that they are having in places. The land is drying again, and we are busy pulling turnips amongst other things.

The ham came to hand all right and we "freed" it tonight and pronounced it very good.

The weather will be suiting you fine for handling heavy consignments of pigs as you seem to be getting.

I trust you are all well.

Yours affectly,
H. Miller
The children are all very much interested in mother's pony.

***

245 - 247. June 15th 1912
T C Smith Esq.
Dear Sir,
<u>Miller v Norris</u>

Mr Guild has sent me your letter to him of 11th inst. and has asked me to reply to you direct.

I have only had one transaction with Mrs Norris previous to this, and she paid me with cash. I ascertained from the banker in Haddington yesterday however that any cheques issued by her that they have cashed have had two signatures although there is a striking similarity between the two.

There was no letter intimating the return of the horse, but there was a telegram, which I regret was inadvertently destroyed. It merely stated that the horse was sent from Berwick with the five o'clock train. I saw Mrs Norris in Haddington that day – May 24th – and she said that the horse was not satisfactory for he stocked² in his hind legs when he stood in the stable overnight, and "oor" man says he is too dear, and that she was quite willing to give me a fair price for the horse but if he was to be the price he was sold at she would send him back.

I said to her then that I would not take delivery if she did send him back. I received the said telegram in the evening, and the horse duly arrived. Mrs Norris paid the carriage both ways.

When I sold her the horse, or rather before we concluded the bargain she was offering me £25, and urging me to take it, she struck her pocket and said and here's your money now. When latterly I sold the horse to her she was hurrying to Drem for a train and had not time to give me the money but would send me a cheque the next day. Just as we parted I said "Now the horse goes from me as he stands", she said "Yes that's all right".

Regarding the stocking of the horse's legs, that was the only fault she had to find with him before ever she bade me a price of £25.

I enclose Mr Guild's letter, and you will see what he says about pursuing John Norris and his wife jointly. This might be the better procedure.

I suppose you will understand that the horse is standing at livery at Drem placed there by the Ry. Co. at Mrs Norris's instructions.

Yours faithfully,
H. Miller

✱✱✱

256. June 28th 1912
T C Smith Esq.
Self v. Norris
Dear Sir,

Yours of 7th inst. to hand. I called today at Drem Station and was shown a telegram which the agent received from Berwick Station on May 24th when he asked for instructions regarding the horse on my refusing to accept delivery. It was as follows - "Only instructions sender will give is put horse in livery for night", and the Ry Co therefore did so.

Yours faithfully,
H. Miller

***

263. July 11th 1912
T C Smith Esq.
Dear Sir,

Yours of 9th inst to hand with enclosure.

I have made a few corrections in the draft proof, and answered the queries, which I trust you will find in order.

Would it be any use on my part to produce witnesses to state upon what terms Mrs Norris purchased horses from them?

She has bought a good many horses around this district, but I can learn of no one having sold horses to her on approval. I have a brother near who has had several transactions with her, would he be any use? or would outsiders be better? If you let me know what you think of this, I will arrange accordingly. Is the court day the 23rd inst.?

Yours faithfully,
H. Miller

***

264 & 265. July 15th 1912
T C Smith Esq.
Dear Sir,

In further reply to your letter of 12th inst. my grieve had no conversation with Mrs Norris regarding the horse, except that he pointed out to her the particular horse that I was going to sell. The horse was working one of a pair, and was unyoked and taken by the horseman, James Towsie, to the road about sixty or eighty yards away to be examined by Mrs Norris, the grieve meanwhile waiting the other horse which was still in the yoke. I have learned however that Mrs Norris asked James Towsie if the horse stocked or ? in his legs when he was idle. He said however ……
……….. as she was moving round the horse at the time, making her examination.

This man is not now in my employment, but I think I could get him as a witness if you wish. If I got him, would it be necessary to have my grieve in attendance as well?

Yours faithfully,
H. Miller

***

268. July 19th 1912
T C Smith Esq.
Dear Sir,
Miller v. Norris

I duly received yours of 16th July, and I have arranged for the man James Towsie to attend the court on Tuesday.

I will be due at Berwick about 9.00am and will call on you before the court hour if this is convenient for you.

Yours faithfully,
H. Miller

***

273. Aug 17th 1912
T C Smith Esq.
<u>Miller v. Norris</u>
Dear Sir,

I am in receipt of your letter of yesterday's date, regarding the above case. I will settle with Brown & Towsie.

I am pleased that you have got everything satisfactorily arranged.

I spoke with Mrs. Norris in Haddington yesterday and she said we would perhaps have a better deal the next time. I hope so!

Yours faithfully,
H. Miller

***

276. Aug 27th 1912
T C Smith Esq.
Dear Sir,

Yours of 24th inst. to hand with cheque enclosed for £25.6.6 as balance of amount awarded me by the court in my recent case v. Norris.

I am much obliged to you for the interest you took in the case on my behalf.
Yours faithfully,
H. Miller

***

31. Dec 14th 1910
A. Main Esq
Dear Sir,
There is a new horse trough erected near the new stable and I would now like the water led into it. It would perhaps be better if you could find it convenient on an early day to look in and arrange what would be the best course to take. I have had a good many complaints about the spring tap on the cistern at the cottages. It takes several minutes to fill a pail. Perhaps you would have this altered.
I got Mr Guild's sanction to have the rhones etc of the courts and other places repaired, so that matter is all right.
You will likely have the plumber work of the new shed which is now getting on. The brickwork will be practically through this week.
Yours faithfully,
H. Miller
I might say that I want to take possession of the new stable shortly, and I can't conveniently do so till the water is in the trough. H.M.

***

63. Mar 15th 1911
J Crawford Esq
Dear Sir,
The horse's heel is now all right, and I will put him on rail on Friday morning. It has taken longer to heal than I expected.
Yours faithfully,
H. Miller

***

65. Mar 20th 1911
J Crawford Esq
Dear Sir,
I am in receipt of your letter of 18th inst. I am sorry to hear that the horse I sent you on Friday is out of sorts. He was all right when he left here in the morning. You

can let me know in a few days how he gets on.
>Yours faithfully,
>H. Miller

***

72. Apr 1st 1911
John Crawford Esq
Dear Sir,
>I am in receipt of your letter of 1st inst. The horse never had an accident with me within my knowledge. He went lame for a time about the month of October, and the vet said then that he thought that it was his stifle[3]. I am sorry there is any trouble with him but I will depend on you doing the best you can with him. My own secret opinion is that he was never quite right since I got him.
>Yours faithfully,
>H. Miller

***

74. Apr 11th 1911
J Crawford Esq
Dear Sir,
>Yours of 8th inst. to hand. You can put the blister[4] on the horse and send him after it is dead, unless you could put him in a grass field. If he has to be kept inside however you may as well send him back, but it is a pity to spend Ry Carr on him if it can be avoided. I don't know how he has come by this at all. If I had had any suspicion of a hurt, I would have had him blistered long ago.
>Yours faithfully,
>H. Miller

***

110. July 4th 1911
J Crawford Esq
Dear Sir,
>The horse that was lame has now been going sound for a month. There is a mark left however, where he was blistered. He is otherwise looking very well, but if this is to cut his price, I would rather put him into work again. Let me know what you think.
>Yours faithfully,
>H. Miller

***

These next letters, although formal in tone, appear to be addressed to James Whiteford, presumably a relation of Jane.

***

303. Oct 26th 1912
Dear James,
    I expect to go to the Clydesdale sale at Ayr next Thursday, but if I do not get suited, do you want to sell your horse? I suppose the price would be about £60. If you do want to sell him, it would be more satisfactory if you got Douglas to examine him. Is he quiet & true in his work?
    I will be glad to hear from you.
    We are having very broken weather and still a lot of potatoes to lift.
    Yours faithfully,
    H. Miller

***

304. Oct 29th 1912
Dear James,
    I have your letter about the horse. I will see what there is at Ayr, and phone you on Thursday afternoon.
    A horse at less money would do the work all right, and there is considerable risk in putting valuable horses into the hands of men who have neither care nor concern for their welfare.
    We are having broken weather and still a few days' potato lifting. I wish they were all up.
    I trust your mother is keeping better, and the others all well.
    Yours faithfully,
    H. Miller

***

309. Nov 9th 1912
T. Douglas Esq. V.S.
Dear Sir,
    With reference to the horse you examined for Jas. Whiteford at Stewarton the other day, is he much the worse of the spavin[5], and would you advise me to have nothing to do with him?

I am partly in a fix, having sold one to be replaced by this horse on the assumption that he was sound.

You might write me by return, and any information you give me, will be for myself only. Hallow Fair takes place on Tuesday & Wednesday and I might pick up something there if the Stewarton one is to be of no use.

Yours faithfully,
H. Miller

***

313. Nov 16th 1912
Dear James,

I have your letter of 14th inst. with reference to the horse. Jane told me you were sending him back to the man you got him from, and I supposed this would be right. I bought one at Hallow Fair last Tuesday.

Seeing there is this 'if' about him I would not care to buy him just now, but if it would be any use to you, I would take him for a while and send you an older horse to do your work, and if there should prove to be nothing the matter, we could arrange accordingly.

However, please yourself in the matter. I just thought it would be a means of getting the horse away from the district where you now have a poor chance of selling him at his value if he is sound.

I trust you all keep well.

Yours faithfully,
H. Miller

***

393. Feb 14th 1914
T.P. Sommerville Esq.
Dear Sir,

I beg to confirm having sold to you today a yearling colt by "Scotland Yet" out of a mare whose pedigree I enclose, for the sum of one hundred & forty pounds Stg. (£140), said colt to remain with me till the spring at your risk.

It is understood that I get a free service of "Scotland Yet" for my mare, if he has not gone to his season when required.

Yours faithfully,
H. Miller

***

413. Sept 19th 1914
Messrs McFarlane & Cockburn,
Dear Sirs,
   The five year old horse has a quite decided stringhalt[6]. Bannatyne saw him today and confirmed this.
   Let me know if you want him in on Tuesday morning.
   Yours faithfully,
   H. Miller

***

432. July 9th 1915
Wm Sim Esq.
Dear Sir,
   I have had the horses I got from you this week examined by a Vet. Surgeon here and he is of the opinion that the bay horse has stringhalt. I will send you his certificate if you wish it.
   As there was one price named for the two horses the simplest way will be for me to return them both.
   Yours faithfully,
   H. Miller

***

433 July 10th 1915
Wm Sim Esq.
Dear Sir,
   I have just had your phone message and am surprised at your attitude regarding the horses. The horses were sold to me as one valuation to be correct, and it does not matter who gave a certificate of soundness, if one of them is not sound.
   I enclose V. S. certificate of unsoundness of the bay horse and will be glad if you give instruction as to his return. Otherwise, both horses will be sent back to you. I do not wish to put you in the public or do your horses any harm, but you ought to have told me at the time I saw them that the bay horse had been examined and was rejected for stringhalt.
   I will expect to hear from you by return.
   Yours faithfully,
   H. Miller

***

446. Feb 11th 1916
Jas. Fleming Esq.
Dear Sir,
   I herewith enclose cheque for £92 in payment of horse. I had him in the plough for the first time yesterday. He had cold after he came home but was not very bad. He seems all right in his work, but I have not yet had a test of his wind in his work as I did not wish to put him to it when he had cold. We had some snow in the beginning of the week, and the land has been very dirty on the surface since.
   Yours faithfully,
   H. Miller

***

529. Apr 23rd 1920
James Fleming Esq.
Dear Sir,
   I only observed today that the horse you sent me on the 13th inst is a windsucker[7]. Please give me your instructions regarding his return.
   Yours faithfully,
   H. Miller

***

635. Oct 6th 1927
Messrs Lawrie & Symington Ld.
Dear Sirs,
   On Tuesday 4th inst. I bought Gelding No 262, and now reject him as not being conform to warranty in his work. He will not pull in the cart.
   I phoned you to this effect today and now confirm the telephone message.
   Yours faithfully,
   Hugh Miller

***

636. Oct 15th 1927
Messrs Lawrie & Symington,
Dear Sirs,
   Gelding No 262 at your sale on 4th inst. was returned to Jas. Anderson, Campbelton, Twynholm on 13th inst, not being conform to warranty in his work.

A Farmer in East Lothian   89

Grandsons Douglas & Hugh Murray in the paddock at West Fortune 1939.

The joy of horses at West Fortune for the Murray family, circa 1945. Hugh Miller (Jnr) and Hugh Murray on horseback with Douglas and Margaret standing.

I returned him carriage forward, but I paid 17/6 carr. from Lanark to Drem, and the V. Surgeon's fee for examination which is £1.1/-. I will be glad to have the remittance of his price which is £55, along with these two items.
Yours faithfully,
H. Miller

***

637. Oct 19th 1927
Jas. Anderson Esq.
Dear Sir,
I have received from Messrs Lawrie & Symington the price of the Gelding No 262 returned to you, and they refer me to you for payment of my outlays in connection therewith.
These are as follows - Vet's fee £1. 1/-
and Ry.Carr. Lanark to Drem - 17/6
Total - - - - £1.18.6
for which I shall be glad to have your remittance.
Yours faithfully,
Hugh Miller

***

639. Dec 24th 1927
Jas. Anderson Esq.
Dear Sir,
I wrote to you on Oct 19th asking for the refund of the expense I was put to in connection with the purchase of your gelding at Lanark
sale. The amount is £1.18. 6 and I will be glad to have your cheque. There is no good reason why I should require to ask this twice, and you know I am entitled to it. I trust therefore you will have it settled immediately.
Yours faithfully,
Hugh Miller

***

642. Oct 11th 1928
Messrs Lawrie & Symington Ld.
Dear Sir,
I wired you today, "Horse 114 of Tuesday's sale rejected for work - writing."
He refused in both cart & chains, and he also has the vice of striking out when

he is being fed in the box or being approached in the stall. Mr Brown told me the latter fault after the horse was sold, and I said to him this ought to have been disclosed before the sale, and then I never would have bid for him.

I will be glad to have your instructions.

Yours faithfully,

Hugh Miller

***

643. Oct 20th 1928

Samuel Brown Esq.

Dear Sir,

I have your letter of 19th inst. and in addition to the faults already complained of, I have discovered that the horse is a windsucker. If you are not aware of this, you will see it if you watch him quietly in the box. I have communicated with the Auctioneers and have been instructed by them to return the horse to you. I am therefore sending him on to you on Monday morning.

Yours faithfully,

Hugh Miller

***

Miller's Mill

Let the sofa be mountains, the carpet be sea,
There I'll establish a city for me:
A kirk and a mill and a palace beside,
And a harbor as well where my vessels may ride.

Block City R L Stevenson 1850 - 1894

Robert Louis Stevenson's poem describes his essentials for a community – a harbour, a palace, a kirk and a mill. West Fortune had its own mill and there is a variety of correspondence surrounding this.

Threshing (or 'thrashing') was originally done using a flail, a small stick with a longer stick forming the handle. Significant effort was required to separate grain from stalk. The first successful model threshing machine was invented by Andrew Meikle of East Linton in 1786 and it was in general use by 1800. It has been said that few Scottish inventions had such a transforming and lasting impact on rural life.

A mill had three parts: the mill itself, the engine and the buncher. The mill was a self-contained unit with a set of teeth inside which removed the grain from the stalk. The axle with the teeth had a pulley on the outside linked, by a circular belt, to a wheel on an engine. Mills were moveable and came with external wheels which Hugh Miller returned as he planned to fix his mill in position.

The engines driving mills developed with time. The first were steam-powered, similar to the big traction engines seen at shows. These had a pulley which could be attached to the belt on the mill. They were often hired out at harvest but from around 1900 these lumbering steam engines were replaced by internal combustion engines, usually running on paraffin oil. These were less bulky, hence could be accommodated more easily. One of these was installed at West Fortune but this required a 'gas' or fuel tank for the paraffin. The endeavour caused frustrations at West Fortune and elsewhere - the functioning of the mill; the tank; the quality of the paraffin oil; the cost of electricity. Hugh perhaps had some satisfaction between 1913 and 1933 as there is no correspondence in relation to it until he changes to an electrically powered engine in 1933. He then had to embrace the high levels of electricity consumption.

The buncher, purchased for £12 bunched the straw after threshing producing large sheaves as an early form of baler. By the 1940s straw bales were rectangular before today's massive round ones.

Before making his purchase, Hugh Miller sent several enquiries to allow him to compare a Clayton English Mill with the Allan Bros Threshing Mill. A Clayton & Shuttleworth Mill from Lincoln was bought for £135 – with chaff and cavings blast. This involved a means of blowing the chaff and cavings (small pieces of broken straw) away from the separated grain.

A threshing machine at Castlemains in the 1950s.

***

37. Jan 12th 1911
Messrs Allan Brothers
Dear Sir,
   I herewith enclose cheque for £130.2.6 in payment of engine etc. as per a/c.
   In your letter of quotation for shafting etc. of Aug 29th I understand the belt to drive said shaft was included, but this is comparatively a small affair. I will be glad, however, if you can allow me a luck's-penny[1].
   I am well satisfied with the engine as far as I have tested it.
   Yours faithfully,
   H. Miller

***

The following letter was rewritten and copies addressed to T.Miller Esq, J.Dodds Esq, Jas Haggert Esq and D.Walker Esq seeking opinions prior to committing to the purchase of his mill.

***

120 Aug 1st 1911
Messrs A & J McWhirter
Dear Sirs,
   Would you be good enough to give me your candid opinion of the mill supplied to you by Messrs Allan Bros, Aberdeen?
   When was it supplied?
   Is it their own make?
   What do you consider the quality of the workmanship?
   Do you consider it quite equal to an English (Clayton) mill?
   You can depend on any information you give me being treated with the strictest confidence.
   Please reply by return, and thanking you in anticipation,
   I am, Yours faithfully,
   H. Miller

***

130. Aug 30th 1911
Jas Dodds Esq
Dear Sir,
   I said to Clayton & Shuttleworth's men today that I would take the mill, to be

delivered within a fortnight. You will please see to this, but I expect he would tell you today, and I was hurrying for the train and had not the time to see you. The price as arranged is £135, with chaff & cavings blast and all necessary piping and drum belt. Of course, apart from what is here mentioned I rely on your word for putting the thing right.

You might try to arrange for a suitable buncher for me as it is the first thing I will need. Send down your man tomorrow if convenient to arrange about the barn wall.

Yours faithfully,
H. Miller

***

Oct 6th 1911
Allan Bros
Dear Sirs.

I am in receipt of your favour of 5th inst and will be glad if you forward to me at Drem Station at your earliest possible convenience a 36" pulley for the engine shaft, 12" broad. The shaft is 2½" thick.

Yours faithfully,
H. Miller

***

153. Oct 16th 1911
J Dodds Esq
Dear Sir,

The pulley for the engine has come to hand, so I will be glad if you can have it fixed up. I would be threshing the very first opportunity I have now. I am not satisfied with the position of the blow pipe, and I think it should be altered. I wanted it carried along the straw barn on the top of the joists, but "Harry" put it on the underside. You would not be pleased with the job yourself if you saw it.

Otherwise, things are well done.

Yours faithfully,
H. Miller

***

162. Oct 26th 1911
Mr Wm Bickett,
Dear Sir,
 If you happen to know of a good buncher for sale, would you be good enough to let me know? I have put in a new Clayton mill, and am going to put a buncher on but have not fixed on a new one yet to see if I came across a good second hand article. Of course, I would not fix up a machine that would not be satisfactory. You might let me know from you as soon as possible.
 You have had good weather for the backend threshing, at least it has been so here, and I hope you have had your usual good turn.
 Yours faithfully,
 H. Miller

***

166. Nov 3rd 1911
Mr Wm Bickett
Dear Sir,
 I would take the buncher if you would part with it for £10. I find I will be in considerable expense in having it fixed up. Of course, I will expect that the broken parts will be replaced.
 Let me know if you accept of this, and if so, you can send it on to Drem Station.
 Yours faithfully,
 H. Miller

***

168. Nov 8th 1911
Mr Wm Bickett
Dear Sir,
 I have your letter of 7th inst. You can send on the buncher to Drem Station. I will give you £12 but the bargain is to be that the broken parts will be replaced, and that it will work satisfactorily after it is erected.
 See that it is put safely on the waggon, and it might be as well to send it at company's risk, but you will know whether this is usually done with such articles or not.
 Let me know when it is put on.
 Yours faithfully,
 H. Miller

***

191 & 192. Dec 18th 1911
Messrs Allan Bros
Dear Sirs,

 I duly received your favour of 14th inst with your quotation for the gas tank. As you say it is rather expensive but the circular one you mentioned would take up too much room in the engine house. However, on reconsidering the size, I think it would be as well to reduce it to hold two barrels of oil only as this may be plenty to store at a time.

 You might therefore get a tank forwarded of the following dimensions:

 3ft long x 4ft deep x 16" wide. The price will be less than the one you quote, and I will depend on you making it right with the makers.

 I have now had a fair trial of the engine with something approaching a full load, and while it drives the mill all right, I think it has not a very great margin of power.

 I do not suggest that the engine has less capacity than you stated it to have, but I find it would be convenient for me to have one a little larger. I could then have the option of bruising etc while threshing. If you could therefore without disadvantage to yourselves exchange it for the larger size, it would be an advantage for my work.

 I would be glad to hear from you regarding your terms.

 Yours faithfully,

 H. Miller

***

208 & 209. Jan 24th 1912
Messrs Allan Brothers
Dear Sirs,

 I duly received your letter of 20th Dec. last, regarding the engine, and your proposal to sell it for me. I would be prepared to sell it if you can get me nearly cost price for it as it is practically nothing the worse of being with me. If you have an opportunity of disposing if it on these terms, then the sooner the better for sake of the purchaser.

 However, if your engineer is in the district, I would like him to call as soon as possible, as the valves require a little bit of adjusting. I was reading the book of instructions the other day and thought from the description there given that the adjusting screws required a little alteration. I did and made a bad job of it, and have not been able to get the full power out of it since. As I have a lot of threshing to do at present, I am a bit handcuffed on this account.

I have your note tonight announcing that the oil tank has been sent on.

Yours faithfully,

H. Miller

***

219 Feb 17th 1912

C Mann Esq.

Dear Sir,

I got a tank for the oil in the engine house fitted for a tap to screw in, but the hole is too large - 1 ¼". I was thinking there might be a short length of pipe screwed into the hole and a tap fixed into it. A ¾" tap would be quite sufficient.

You evidently misunderstood me when you were here last regarding the overflow pipe from the water tank. I would like if you could fix it in sometime soon. It would do if you could screw it into the return hot water pipe, as we would then be drawing off the hottest of the water.

I hope I have made myself plain. A half inch pipe with a stop cock is what we spoke of for the overflow of the hot water.

Yours faithfully,

H. Miller

***

223. Mar 21st 1912

Messrs Allan Bros.

Dear Sirs,

I have had the oil tank that you sent me set up, and find that it leaks badly, so much so that I cannot use it. Please look into the matter at your earliest convenience.

Yours faithfully,

H. Miller

***

227. April 17th 1912
Messrs. Allan Brothers
Dear Sir,
 I have had the oil tank returned and regret to say that it is still leaking. Indeed, I can see no trace of anything having been done to it at all, and it is the worse of knocking about on the railway.
 Please advise me what to do.
 Yours faithfully
 H. Miller

***

231. Apr 24th 1912
Messrs Allan Brothers
Dear Sirs,
 I am in receipt of your letter of 23rd inst. with the Shipley Tank Co's of 22nd enclosed.
 The tank was not signed for as damaged in transit, as it bore no evidence of damage that would cause it to leak. I said in my last letter that it was the worse of knocking about on the railway, but this meant that it was getting defaced. The cause of the leakage is defective construction, and it would be difficult to know where to have it soldered. I thought the surest way to have it put right would be to regalvanise it, and I was surprised that the makers returned it without having done this. To say the tank was inspected means nothing if it was not tested with paraffin.
 Yours faithfully,
 H. Miller

***

234. May 2nd 1912
The Pumpherston Oil Co Ltd
Dear Sirs,
 Referring to your letter of 15th Apr I have now had the oil tried with the engine, and regret to say that it is quite unsuitable. My engine simply would not drive the mill with it. I am wondering if your man left the right stuff, as others who get your oil for their engines say it does quite well.
 Yours faithfully,
 H. Miller

***

237. May 16th 1912
The Pumpherston Oil Co Ltd
Dear Sirs,
   I duly received yours of the 4th cart., also that of 13th do. regarding the oil for the engine. I am very reluctant to try the oil further as it made such mess of the valves of the engine that I have not got all the deposit quite cleaned off yet. I used all the sample I got from you.
   Yours faithfully,
   H. Miller

***

254. June 25th 1912
The Pumpherston Oil Co Ltd.
Dear Sirs,
   I duly received yours of 15th inst. but I will not now be using much oil till after harvest as my threshing is finished for the season.
   Yours faithfully,
   H. Miller

***

291 & 292. Sept 24th 1912
Messrs Allan Brothers
Dear Sirs,
   I duly received yours of 18th inst. regarding the engine. You suggest a price of £80 if I were to sell it to Mr Riddell, but as this works out as a depreciation of £11.10/- a year, on the prime cost, you surely do not expect the engine to have a very long life. While I would have liked well enough to have exchanged it into the larger size, I am sorry I could not see my way to part with it at the price, and in any case, Mr Riddell would I think prefer to take a new one. My engine is as good today as when I got it, and it has only done threshing for one season though I have had it for two years.
   If any other opportunity turns up of exchanging, we might perhaps consider it.
   Some time ago you spoke of an improvement you had introduced in the valve settings, which increased the power of the engine, and if this could be carried out it might serve my purpose.
   I will be glad to hear from you regarding this.
   Yours faithfully,
   H. Miller

***

329. Jan 9th 1913
The Pumpherston Oil Co Ltd.
Dear Sirs,

I have your letter of inquiry re the oil you supplied to me for the engine. I regret to say that I could not get the engine up to its power to drive the mill, and had to empty the tank and put in what we had been formerly using. Your oil does not seem to suit this engine at all.
Yours faithfully,
H. Miller

***

645. July 4th 1930
H.C.Babb Esq.
Dear Sir,

I have received your letter of 2nd inst. re Electric Current for which I thank you. I am sorry however the terms are prohibitive from an economic stand-point. I can put in a private installation for a very much less initial outlay, which would give me sufficient light for the farm.

I would have been glad to discuss the matter further if there was any chance of a compromise, but if £350 is your final offer I am afraid it would be fruitless.
Yours faithfully,
Hugh Miller

***

663. Jan 24th 1933
The L.E.P.Co.
Dear Sirs,

Herewith I enclose cheque for £10.16.11. I have deducted from the account £8.8.9 part of which I admit I owe, but as you are aware I am not satisfied with the consumption of current for the power. This installation is consuming more than double of any similar installation in the district, and I consider therefore that I should not be called upon to pay this inflated charge. I had hoped that the matter would have been corrected before this.
Yours faithfully,
Hugh Miller

***

664. Feb 2nd 1933
Messrs Compton Parkinson Ld.
Dear Sirs,
 The Lothian Electric Power Co installed an Electric Motor to me on the farm in Oct. last, details of which are as follows:
 No 12311092, H.P. 25, Rev. 930, Volts 400, Phase 3.
 I am not satisfied with the motor as it is taking the double of the current to run my threshing mill, of any other motor driving a similar outfit in the district.
 Could you suggest any reason for this? It takes 18 to 19 units per hour, in spite of the fact that the drum of the mill is mounted on ball bearings.
 I will be glad if you can solve the difficulty.
 Yours faithfully,
 Hugh Miller

***

665. Feb 3rd 1933
H.C.Babb Esq.
Dear Sir,
 Referring to your letter of 26th inst. and also that of 31st inst. with enclosures, I have only to say I am still not satisfied with the results of running the motor. It may be that the speed of the mill is a little more than the speed the makers state it should be run, but the reduction of the speed would obviously not put matters right.
 I beg to refer you to the terms of contract of 11th July last, where you agree that the motor is to be to my satisfaction. I again state that I am not satisfied, and if you have now said your last word on the matter, then I am afraid the only course is for you to remove the motor. I think it is quite unreasonable on the part of the Power Co. to ask me to accept of this installation that is costing double for current of any similar installation in the district.
 I may say that in the mean time I have written the makers asking if they have any observations to make on the situation.
 Yours faithfully,
 Hugh Miller

***

666. Feb 9th 1933
H.C.Babb Esq.
Dear Sir,

I duly received your favour of 6th inst. and am accordingly having the mill tested at a reduced speed, although I have no expectation that this will put matters right.

Regarding my cheque for the way leave and current, please do not imagine that I wish to shirk my obligation, but I now consider that we would be better to have the question of the motor settled and then we can settle accounts.

Yours faithfully,
Hugh Miller

***

Farm Management

'The land: this is where our roots are. There is the basis of our physical life. From the land comes everything that supports life. It is there waiting to honor all the labour we are willing to invest in it. No insurance policy can be compared to an alliance between man and a plot of land.'
– Henry Ford

These letters cover assorted matters ranging from boundary fences, the appointment of farm workers, the buying and mending of machinery and the acquisition of 'metal' for road-making. Road 'metal' refers to broken stones, but a 'metalled' road can be interpreted as being sealed or unsealed.

***

22. Nov 26th 1910
Joseph Lee Esq
Dear Sir,
 I was very much annoyed yesterday to find that one of my men carried the key of the gate into the sand pit from the day before. It was entirely without my knowledge, and I exceedingly regret the mistake and will take care that the like does not happen again.
 Yours faithfully,
 H. Miller

***

38. Jan 18th 1911
Mr Alex Ramage
Dear Sir,
 I have your letter of application for situation as grieve. I have not yet seen Mr Middlemas, but in the meantime you might let me know your age and how long you were in East Lothian. I understand from your letter that you have not been grieve

before, but that would not be an objection if you have thorough practical knowledge of all farm work.

Yours truly,
H. Miller

***

39. Private 18th Jan 1911
Alex Mitchell, G.P.
Dear Sir,

I have an application from Alex. Ramage for situation as grieve. Would you consider him a man with sufficient push and capability for such a position?

Does he keep sober?

You can depend that no bad use will be made of any private information with which you may trust me.

I will be glad to have a reply by return, and thanking you in anticipation,

I am yours truly,
H. Miller

***

19th Jan. 1911
Mr Eaglesham,
Dear Sir,

I have an application for situation as grieve by John Thomson who was with you two years ago. Would you be good enough to give me any information regarding his capabilities and general character? Is he sober? Has he push? Can he control himself and those under him?

I need not say that any information you give me will be treated with the strictest confidence.

An early reply would oblige.

Thanking you in anticipation,

I am yours truly,
H. Miller

***

41. Jan 25th 1911
W.B.D.Gibson Esq
Dear Sir,

I have your letter making enquiry re Richd. Ormerod. He is groom - gardener with me, and does anything else he is required for. I believe he is a total abstainer, and is honest and obliging and willing to do what he is told.

His experience as a gardener is not perhaps very large but he can keep things fairly tidy.

He is leaving me of his own accord.

Yours faithfully,

H. Miller

***

61. Mar 9th 1911

A. Riddle Esq

Dear Sir,

Please send me the following garden seeds by return.

3lbs peas - 1st & 2nd early & late.

½ lb beans.

1 oz turnip rooted beet.

1 oz of a long variety.

Small supplies (1d or 2d worth) of the following -

Dutch & Golden ball turnip.

leek - onion - carrot - lettuce

parsnip - celery - cauliflower

B.sprouts - brocoli

Yours faithfully,

H. Miller

***

Mar 10th 1911

H Campbell Esq

Dear Sir,

I forgot today to ask you could supply me with some plain sacks. I would be obliged if you could send me anything up to 100 tomorrow. I hope you will have these and rail them at once so that I may have them on Monday morning. If you have not got them would you phone Sawers & Co, Robertson St, Glasgow and ask them to send 100 to me at once, and oblige.

Yours faithfully,

H. Miller

***

62. Mar 11th 1911
H. Campbell Esq
Dear Sir,
  I am in receipt of your letter re bags. I thought that <u>Plain sacks</u> would be a sufficient description of what I wanted but apparently <u>East</u> does not understand <u>West</u>. What I want is 20 stone flour sacks for holding grain - with only one hole - and that at the top. They used to cost 4 ½d to 5 ½d but of course they will be cheaper here. If you can send me 100 by return, I will be much obliged.
  Yours faithfully,
  H. Miller

***

164. Oct 28th 1911
Messrs T Sherriff & Co
Dear Sirs,
  I duly received your letter of 21st inst, and thought of seeing you on Friday at Haddn. but I was not over. The price you ask for the Corn Drill is very well on the road to that of a new one, and I do not care to make the exchange at the terms you propose. I thought about £5 and the old machine would have taken it away.
  Yours faithfully,
  H. Miller

***

206. Jan 19th 1912
T Callen Esq
Dear Sir,
  Could you give me an idea when the Roller will be our length? - as I want to cart some more metal immediately before it comes, and have at present quite sufficient of a rough road to traffic over.
  Yours faithfully,
  H. Miller

***

233. Apr 27th 1912
Mr Johnston,
Dear Sir,
  I have hired the man - Little, who is with you, to come here at the term, and as I have several changes I would be obliged if you could let him clear on the Monday

and I would flit him that day, while the term falls on the Tuesday.
 I will esteem it a favour if you can do this, and thanking you in anticipation,
 I am, Yours faithfully,
 H. Miller

✳✳✳

255. June 26th 1912
Messrs J Wallace & Sons
Dear Sirs,
 You might please send at once four knife heads for a Thistle mower, No 63-98, also a dozen fingers & bolts. If the steel fingers are the same pattern as the old ones, send them.
 Yours faithfully,
 H. Miller

✳✳✳

262. July 8th 1912
Messrs J Wallace & Sons
Dear Sirs,
 I have sent you an old reaper as scrap but you will perhaps find that it is better than scrap. If it is worth doing up, do so and send it back, but I will see Mr Wallace in Edinburgh market about it perhaps, before you do anything.
 Yours faithfully,
 H. Miller

✳✳✳

298. Oct 11th 1912
J H Steele Esq.
Dear Sir,
 Would you please give me your price for fencing as follows:
 Best Larch stobs[1] 5ft x 3 ½"
 Five gal. wires No 6
 One barbed wire 4 barbs
 and oblige..
 Yours faithfully,
 H. Miller

✳✳✳

298. Oct 14th 1912
Mr T Trotter
Dear Sir,
   I have your estimate for fence on the Drem road, but I think your estimate too high. The stobs would require to be reckoned at 9ft apart, although some places could do with more, some would require to be less. If you can take the latter price - £23.10/- for this, you can arrange to go with it at once. From Needless[2] down to the metal heap will require five wires but no paling[3].
   Let me hear from you by return.
   Yours faithfully,
   H. Miller

***

332. Jan 18th 1913
Messrs J Wallace & Sons
Dear Sirs,
   The plow metals have come to hand, but the jointer points sent are for the 10A plow, not the 110A as ordered. If you have a customer in the district that could do with these, it will be a pity to return them, but you will know best yourselves what to do with them. In the meantime, please send at once the correct ones as these were urgently wanted in the order.
   Yours faithfully,
   H. Miller

***

353. July 17th 1913
East Lothian
Messrs G E Lewis & Sons,
Dear Sirs,
   I herewith enclose cheque for £6.7.6 in payment of a £6.6/- gun and packing case, No 8 block as described on page 25 of your catalogue. You might send it so that I will have it on Tuesday morning as I wish to have it tried that day. Please add a cleaning brush if you can.
   Yours faithfully,
   H. Miller

***

355. July 28th 1913
Dear Mrs Lee,
   I have your note regarding the sand that I lifted from the sand-pit. I am sorry that the note of the quantity has been mislaid, but it is pretty well on my memory that it was 35 cart loads. This is the information I gave to Mr. Watson.
   Yours faithfully,
   H. Miller

***

This letter is addressed to Mrs Lee as Joseph Lee had died in June 1913 aged 59.

The carts would have been named and these name plates have recently come to light.

***

Jan 31st 1914
Wm Wallace Esq.
Dear Sir,

If you could find a customer for my old D.D. manure sower, I would give you an order for a new one. I could do with one with a larger hopper than what I have. The old one is in good working order and laid past thoroughly clean. I would take £6 or £7 for it.

You might let me know if you have an opening for it.

Yours faithfully,

H. Miller

***

394. Feb 16th 1914
Wm. Wallace Esq.
Dear Sir,

I wired you today as follows, "Can't wait longer on Sower. Send plows and markers complete as arranged at once or must cancel order". I expected to hear from you before this regarding the sale of the old machine, but as I do not suppose you will have sold it, I have wired you as above. If you should have sold it and can let me have a new one by return, of course that arrangement will stand, but in any case, I must have either the parts for the old one or a new machine at once. Let me know how matters stand.

Yours faithfully,

H. Miller

If you should be sending a new machine, I would take the larger hopper.

H.M.

***

399. Mar 10th 1914
Mr T. Brown,
Dear Sir,

I received your letter of application last night and went to Spott this forenoon and saw Mr. Stenhouse. He informed me that he was not going to let you free, so I thought there was no use seeing you today. If your mind is made up to leave and if you can satisfactorily arrange with Mr Stenhouse, then I would try and make an agreement with you.

You might let me know by return how you stand.

Yours faithfully,

H. Miller

***

419 & 420. Oct 29th 1914
Messrs Barlas & Barlas
Dear Sirs,

I have your letter of 27th inst regarding the man Thomas Brown. It seems strange that I never had a complaint from him regarding the house he occupied - and further - he examined the house and its surroundings himself, before I engaged him. On Monday morning last he told me that he was not going to start his work and would give me no satisfactory reason why. He has therefore deliberately and unjustifiably deserted his service, and I mean to hold him responsible for any expense I am put to in filling his place, and the places of those others hired along with him, and I will also object to any other person hiring him.

As to his wages, I find that his woman worker has been overpaid one shilling per day for twenty four days at the potato lifting, according to his contract.

The actual balance of his wages is therefore £2. 6. 6

            less overpaid £1. 4
            less insurance -   .11
                          £1. 4. 11
                          £1. 1. 7

This however I hold at present against any expense I am put to by his desertion of service.

Yours faithfully,

H. Miller

***

421. Oct 31st 1914
Mr Thomas Brown,
Dear Sir,

I am giving you this opportunity of returning to your service and fulfilling your contract with me. However awkward you may think this to be, you will find it will be

the simplest way out of the difficulty you have voluntarily got into. I have written Mr Hope regarding the matter.
    Yours faithfully,
    H. Miller

***

421. Oct 31st 1914
W.W. Hope Esq.
Dear Sir,
    If I am rightly informed, you have taken into your employment a man named Thomas Brown, who deserted his service with me on Monday last.
    I am not clear with him - having not paid him his wages in full, and am giving him the opportunity of returning to his place.
    If he misrepresented his position to you, I trust you will now understand how matters stand.
    Yours faithfully,
    H. Miller

***

422. Oct 31st 1914
Messrs Barlas & Barlas,
Dear Sirs,
    I have your letter of 30th inst. regarding Thomas Brown. The only satisfactory arrangement he can make with me is to return to his work and fulfil his contract. I have written him, giving him the opportunity to do so. I have also written Mr Hope of the Knowes, to whom I understand Brown has gone, telling him the position of matters.
    Yours faithfully,
    H. Miller

***

422. Nov 6th 1914
Mr Thomas Brown,
Dear Sir,
    I have your letter with the charges against me of telling lies.
    Unless you withdraw these charges and give me an apology, I will demand your immediate dismissal by Mr Hope, whether you return to my service or not.

Unless I have this on Monday first, you will be dismissed on Tuesday.
Yours truly,
H. Miller

***

434. Aug 5th 1915
Messrs J. Wallace & Sons,
Dear Sirs,
I have sent today to your address a potato digger to be mounted with a front wheel, and also a set of new pattern forks. I have returned a set of ordinary forks which you can retain and credit me with, but please return the set of forks that is on the digger at present.
Yours faithfully,
H. Miller

***

456. June 14th 1916
J.D. Hope Esq.
Dear Sir,
I am in receipt of your letter of 13th inst. re cutting the hedge sides.
I will not willingly destroy any partridges' nests, but I consider the prevention of weeds seeding on cultivated land is of more importance than the preservation of a few partridges. I think too that it is rather hard that our ploughmen should be called up for military service and gamekeepers allowed to knock around watching a few nests of partridges hatching out.
Yours faithfully,
H. Miller

***

489. Feb 13th 1918
Messrs J. Wallace & Sons
Dear Sirs,
I am in receipt of your letter of 12th inst. and you are certainly quite frank regarding the price of the D. D. & Manure Distributor, but I think your frankness is quite unbecoming in a firm like yours. I ordered the machine from Mr. Robert Wallace early last year, and the price was left to him, as he could not at the time say what it would be. Latterly he did put down the price, and now you are not satisfied with his figures. I think no fair-minded person could do anything but condemn the

action you have taken, and all over a trifle.

However, I am glad to say I can either work away with my old machine or purchase one of another make somewhere else, and thus obviate the risk of you sustaining any loss on the transaction.

Yours faithfully,
H. Miller

***

493 & 494. May 9th 1918
Messrs J. Wallace & Sons
Dear Sirs,

I have sent you three mowers for repair. There are two bags attached with finger & knife Sections, which I got from you last year but did not put on, as I thought it better to send the machines to you. I think the fingers want renewing but there are some good enough ones through them which you might return as they could be useful for later on. If, however you think that some of the fingers would be quite satisfactory with a grease I will leave that to you. I also want the knives filled with new settings.

Look specially to the brackets for holding the ends of the connecting rods into the knives. Some of these are loose. The standard (?) to which the front sections are attached come down on the top of the tractor (?) wheel. Please see that these are set up. The end of the poles has got split at the back end with the bolts getting loose on one occasion. This would be better of an iron plate or perhaps one on each side rivetted on. Though I mention these things I want the machine put absolutely right.

Yours faithfully,
H. Miller

***

526. Feb 16th 1920
Mr. E. E. McClinton,
Dear Sir,

I duly received your letter of 7th inst. and would have replied sooner but I had not the necessary information regarding board & lodging. This can be had in the village of Athelstaneford - about a mile away - for 35/- per week.

My farm is about 500 ac., all arable, sheep & cattle feeding for eight months of the year, but practically no grazing.

I do not propose either to pay wages or to charge a fee, but if you apply yourself to work, the benefit in this direction will be more yours than mine.

If you think of accepting on these terms, you might please let me know, and you could make a start at any time.

Yours faithfully,
H, Miller

***

540. Jan 26th 1921
Mr R. Small
Dear Sir,

I herewith enclose cheque for £14. 4. 10 for waggon of coals on Jan 7th, but I am so disappointed with the stobs that I have not put in the price of them. I have looked for you, both at Edinburgh and Haddington for the last two weeks to speak to you about them. There are very few in them that I would care to put into a fence, and you should surely know by this time, that I would have refused them if I had seen them before they were sent on.

I will send them anywhere near at hand or else pay the carriage on them back to Longniddry.

Yours faithfully,
H. Miller

***

548. Mar 19th 1921
Minimax Ltd.
Dear Sirs,

Referring to your letter of Feb 2nd I have pleasure in stating my satisfaction with the extinguishers you supplied to me last year. I used three - which were all I had - in extinguishing a fire in a cattle court in June last, and since then I added another two to my number.

My opinion is that as a first aid in extinguishing outbreaks of fire they are a great success.

Yours faithfully,
H. Miller

***

562. July 2nd 1921
Dear Mr Dunlop,

Like Pharaoh's butler - I remember my fault this day. At Ayr Show you asked me to look over my list of fixtures which I left to J. Brown when I left Grassmillees.

I find that the water trough in the court is not included, as that was the landlord's property, and should not have been removed by the tenant.

Yours faithfully,
H. Miller

***

572. Aug 25th 1921
T. W. Todrick Esq.
<u>Cotlands March Dyke</u>[4]
Dear Sir,

This dyke has now been repaired and I have settled with Baillie according to his offer, viz. £39. 17/- the half of which is payable by you (£19. 18. 6).

Yours faithfully,
H. Miller

***

573. Sept 6th 1921
Messrs F. D. Cowieson & Co.
Dear Sirs,

I am in receipt of your price list of imported timber, and would be glad if you would send me 20 battens 16' x 6" x 2" at the price mentioned viz. 2 ½d per lineal foot. I suppose 16' will go into a waggon - if not just send 15' lengths.

Consign to Drem Station urgent.

Yours faithfully,
H. Miller

***

576. Oct 10th 1921
Wm Henderson Esq.
Dear Sir,

Some of the march fence between Congalton and this farm have become rather dilapidated, and the time has now come when something would require to be done, as it is impossible to keep stock on their own side of the fence. From what Mr Scott told me the other day I have no doubt but you are aware of what is necessary, consequently need not go into details.

If you agree to half the expense, I will see that the work is carried out satisfactorily and as economically as possible, consistent with a substantive job.

As the matter has become urgent, I will be glad when I hear from you at your earliest convenience.
Yours faithfully,
H. Miller

**

577. Oct 12th 1921
Messrs Stirling & Burnet
Dear Sirs,
<u>Cotlands</u>
I have yours of 11th inst. and hereby confirm the arrangement entered into between Bolton & Herkes, viz. - The former to pay the latter (£25) twenty five pounds in settlement of disturbance and unexhausted improvements claims, and the grass seeds sown to be paid for over and above this.
I think both parties are quite satisfied with this arrangement.
Yours faithfully,
H. Miller

**

579. Oct 18th 1921
Messrs Stirling & Burnet,
Bolton & Harkes.
Dear Sirs,
I have yours of 17th inst. with reference to the sowing of the grass seeds on the Cotlands. You are right in thinking that the Grass Seeds account only is to be paid for. This is the agreement I made with Harkes. There was no mention made of sowing and harrowing.
Yours faithfully,
H. Miller

**

602. May 22nd 1922
Wm Henderson Esq.
<u>Congalton March Fences</u>
Dear Sir,
I have now had these fences repaired and enclose statement of expenses, which I trust you will find in order.
What was serviceable of the old fences I retained - as there were some stobs that

had a grip of the ground and the top wires have, I think a few years wear still. From three to four wires in the bottom are new throughout.

I would point out that if the ditch in Congalton field that marches with me - North of the Rlwy. were cleared and backed up against the fence it would go far to prevent sheep creeping through.

Yours faithfully,
H. Miller

***

618. Sept 12th 1925
Messrs Mackay Ross & Co.
Dear Sirs,

The barrel I ordered from you about Aug 27th has come to hand, and I regret to say is not satisfactory.

First of all, it is not the length you offered me and that I agreed to take - being only 4'9", and then it has two fractured staves.

Had it been sound I would not have complained about the length, but these two weak staves would be on the underside when mounted on the cart as they are opposite the bung.

Please let me know what you think is best to be done in the matter.

Yours faithfully,
Hugh Miller

***

620. Sept 16th 1925
Messrs Mackay Ross & Co.
Dear Sirs,

I have your letter of 15th inst. but I do not see that the barrel you offer me can have the capacity of 160 gallons. Anything less than this will not suit my purpose.

I would rather take one a little larger than one smaller.

I trust you will be able to give me one that will be suitable.

Yours faithfully,
Hugh Miller

***

627. Apr 19th 1926
Messrs H. Alexander & Co.
Dear Sirs,
I am in receipt of your letter of 17th inst. regarding a Fordson Tractor, and have only to state that I made no such arrangement with your Mr. Malcolm.
Yours faithfully,
Hugh Miller

***

David Miller on his rebuilt 'Fergie' in more recent years.

Lawyers' Letters

Law is order, and good law is good order.
– Aristotle 384BC–322BC

Guild & Guild were a firm of lawyers but also factors, including responsibility as factors for West Fortune. They were based in their Edinburgh office but also had farming connections with Luffness, Aberlady, and Rhodes Farm, North Berwick.

Hugh appears frustrated over the slow response from the lawyers when action was needed, eg. having acquired 500 sheep which would readily escape through broken fences and consume turnips meant for other purposes.

Baillie was a builder based in Pencaitland and Trotter a wood merchant.

***

7. 15th Oct 1910
Messrs Guild & Guild
Dear Sirs,

I am in receipt of your favour of 13th inst with fire policy enclosed and I herewith send cheque for £14.0.0 in payment of the premium.

I thought that Mr Guild would probably have been here today to take a look at the fences I spoke of. As I am putting stock in both of the fields next week, I will be glad if you let the matter have your early attention.

Yours faithfully,
H. Miller

***

11. Oct 29th 1910
George Reid Esq
Dear Sir,

I am in receipt of your letter of 26th inst re cottages. I am sorry I was not here when you called. The state of affairs at the two cottages used as bothies no-one can deny. I have urged on the alterations that were agreed upon, ever since these were fixed, but there is practically nothing done yet, except the water turned on.

We have now finished potato lifting and both bothies are cleared out. I thought that Mr Guild might have been here today, but he did not turn up.

Yours faithfully,
H. Miller

***

12. Oct 31st 1910
Messrs Guild & Guild
Dear Sirs,

I am sorry you have not yet been here to arrange about the repair of the fences I spoke of some time ago. I have had sheep on the fields for the last ten days and they are running all over the place. I will be glad if you can let the matter have your early attention.

There are also certain things in connection with the stable that you would have been as well to see for yourself before the work is finished.

I trust that you are arranging to get a start to the shed now as wintry weather may set in at any time.

Yours faithfully,
H. Miller

***

15. Nov 11th 1910
Messrs Guild & Guild W.S.
Dear Sirs,

I am in receipt of your favour of the 9th inst and note what you say regarding the stable. I think that the floor should be completed next week.

I saw Whitehead in Haddington today and was asking him about asbestos slates. He says the merchant will not give a guarantee with them and personally he has a poor opinion of them. I only mention this so that if there is a doubt about them perhaps you could get fuller information.

There was nothing arranged about lighting the loose boxes as far as I remember, but I suppose roof lights will be the most economical.

Yours faithfully,
H. Miller

***

Questions were raised in 1910 over asbestos which had been used in many ways for thousands of years. The negative health effects were noted in 1899 and the first diagnosis of asbestosis made in 1924. The first paper to the UK parliament on diseases of asbestos workers was not until 1930.

***

57 & 58. Feb 23rd 1911
Messrs Guild & Guild W.S.
Dear Sirs,
 I am trying now to get the roadway in front of the shed made up, but it will need a big lot of metal to do it. I was thinking of employing two men to quarry some stones — and break them - from the quarry in the field above the house, as this might be the cheapest way to get stones. If you could see your way to be two thirds of their wages, I would be the other third, and do all the other work. I will be glad to hear what you think of this suggestion. Of course, if the stone could not be got cheaper in this way than at Skade Hill, I would just as soon cart it from there.
 Yours faithfully,
 H. Miller

***

85. May 2nd 1911
Messrs Guild & Guild W.S.
Dear Sirs,
 There are two of the cottages at Dingleton that have been used as bothies, in a rather tumbledown condition, and as I am requiring these after the term, I would be glad if you could see your way to give them a touch up.
 Some of the doors are wrenched off, some of the windows broken and fireplaces need to be looked to, but there won't be much expense incurred in the whole job. I believe the man Stewart in Athelstaneford could do the whole thing if you have no objection to him, but of course I have not mentioned the matter to him.
 Yours faithfully,
 H. Miller

***

117. July 17th 1911
Messrs Guild & Guild W.S.
Dear Sirs,
 I saw Mr Baillie last week and told him he might take a look at the old stable. He

came down and I pointed out to him what we suggested should be done, and showed him the stair of the bothy, and the proposed enclosure for the hot plate.

I saw Trotter on Friday and asked him to come down and see the fence, as he had not then heard from you. The foggage[1] is growing and I would like the fence done as soon as possible. I asked him to include in his estimate two gates for the field that the horses are in, as these are useless.

May I take it that you agree to make the alterations in the barn that we spoke of, as that subject was departed from rather abruptly.

I was asking Mr Callan on Friday if there was any small stuff on hand at the quarry. He said there was plenty. Did you mean me to start and cart some? I could get this done just now rather than later on.

Yours faithfully,
H. Miller

***

119. July 24th 1911
Messrs Guild & Guild W.S.
Dear Sirs,

I duly received your favour of 18th inst. for which I am obliged.

Trotter has started his work and should get through without much delay. I will look as to how it is done. Mr Lothian thought he should have been consulted about the march fence[2]. He is willing to be the half of a moderate expenditure in putting it right, but may I suggest that you send him a note, which would go far to preserve good feeling as neighbours.

Baillie was here on Saturday, and I pointed out the alterations in the barn to him. He said he would send you his estimate for this along with the one for the old stable. As it will not be a serious matter, I hope you may be able to sanction it right away so that I may make arrangements about the mill. This should have been in hand some time ago as the work will take some little time and harvest is approaching.

Yours faithfully,
H. Miller

***

238. May 18th 1912
Messrs Guild & Guild W.S.
Dear Sirs,

Referring to the fence that we spoke of on Wednesday, the length is 232 yards, with a gate at each end, and one in the centre.

Might I say that I would prefer larch stobs, unless the iron standards are of such dimensions as make a stiff job.

I enclose the a/c for repairs done at the cottages in May last year, also for two tons of cement for the binder house floor, which you will remember agreeing to.

I was sorry not to get along today to see your potatoes, but hope to do so sometime soon, as I hear they are good.

Yours faithfully,
H. Miller

***

278. Aug 28th 1912
Messrs Guild & Guild W.S.
Dear Sirs,

I took the liberty of asking Mr Baillie to look over the two stone walls referred to in his two notes which I herewith enclose.

Both walls are in a very discreditable condition and are useless as fences as they are.

There are turnips on both sides of the march walls at the cotlands, and as we will have sheep on our side it would be a great benefit if it were repaired before they were put on.

I think Baillie's estimate quite moderate in both cases.

I have now received my money from Berwick, and enclose Mr Smith's note which you can please return. I have come out very satisfactorily, but the horse will have cost Mrs Norris £45 at least.

Yours faithfully,
H. Miller

***

286. Sept 14th 1912
R Baillie Esq.
Dear Sir,

I have now heard from Mr Guild, and I enclose his letter for your perusal and return.

I will expect you to make a first-class job, seeing you are hedged about by the two proprietors and myself. If the weather is dry, I cannot touch it this incoming week, but you can order the lime or in any case by that time we will see you around.
Yours faithfully,
H. Miller

***

296. Sept 26th 1912
Messrs Guild & Guild W.S.
Alex Guild Esq.
Dear Sir,
I had hoped for some time to see you along, and to talk over some fencing matters, and now with 500 sheep on the farm you will understand something of my anxiety for my own and my neighbour's turnips. If you could spare the time, I would like very much to see you, or otherwise to arrange for something to be done. I simply cannot keep them within bounds.
Yours faithfully,
H. Miller

***

337. Feb 12th 1913
A Guild Esq.
Dear Sir,
I want two waggons of good hard ashes, and as I remember you speaking to me of getting some for Mr Clark, would you let me know where they can be got, or just order them on and send the charges to me.
I am sorry to trouble you in this, but I do not know where I can best get them.
Yours faithfully,
H. Miller

***

340. Feb 27th 1913
A Guild Esq.
Dear Sir,
I duly received yours of 19th inst. which I should have acknowledged sooner but delayed doing so until I would receive the ashes. These have not yet come to hand,

but they will be in a day or two I expect. I had not thought of you paying for the ashes, but as you have so kindly offered to do so, please accept of my thanks.
    Yours faithfully,
    H. Miller

***

402. Mar 19th 1914
Dear Mr Guild,
    I would have liked to see you and explain in detail the matter concerning the cutting of the trees. I am renewing this portion of the roadside fence of the little grass paddock which lies between the road and the railway at my own expense, as you have done a good deal of fencing for me lately, and the cutting of the sticks was, I considered a necessity to get the wires put in their place.
    The trees are not yet removed, and I will not remove them till I hear that my explanation is satisfactory to Mr Hope.
    Yours faithfully,
    H. Miller

***

403. Mar 19th 1914
Messrs Guild & Guild W. S.
Dear Sirs,
    I am in receipt of your letter of 18th inst. referring to the communication you have had from Messrs Blair & Cadell.
    The trees referred to by Mr Hope are situated on the roadside north of the railway and east of my own avenue. I am renewing a portion of the fence there which has been in a very dilapidated condition since I came to West Fortune, and in order to get a run for the wire I cut down two or three ash seedlings that were straggled about. These I may say are of absolutely no value, and in removing them I had no intention of doing anything that would incur the disapproval of either you or Mr. Hope to whom I trust this explanation will be satisfactory.
    Yours faithfully,
    H. Miller

***

414. Sept 24th 1914
Messrs Guild & Guild. W.S.
Dear Sirs,
I am in receipt of your favour of 23rd inst. with regard to the fencing on West Fortune.
While I quite appreciate the desire on the part of Mr George Hope, that everything possible should be allowed to stand over for the present, it will occasion me very considerable trouble and expense if this fencing is included in that category. By mutual agreement it has already been deferred, and I find that the lack of these roadside fences is an unending source of annoyance and expense, and I trust that this side of the question will appeal to Mr Hope's trustees.
As I am most anxious however to have the work done, I would be willing to pay for the fencing according to the estimate and deduct the amount from my next Whitsunday rent, if this would be any advantage.
I will be glad to hear from you at your earliest possible convenience.
Yours faithfully,
H. Miller

**

416
Telephone
Athelstaneford 8
Oct 17th 1914
Messrs Guild & Guild,
Dear Sirs,
I will be glad to hear from you regarding the proposed fencing. The time is wearing on, and I am having the usual difficulty of keeping stock in the fields.
Yours faithfully,
H. Miller

**

436. Sept 10th 1915
Messrs. Guild & Guild W.S.
Dear Sirs,
I am in receipt of your letter of 8th inst. confirming the arrangement come to at our meeting on Wednesday, regarding the taking over of the sheep dipper at my waygoing[3], which is quite satisfactory, and for which accept thanks.

I will be pleased to see you on Saturday to arrange about the fences.
Yours faithfully,
H. Miller

***

460. Aug 16th 1916
Dear Mr Mercer,
I happened to be calling on Mr Guild today, and before parting he told me that there is a claim lodged or to be lodged of £350 against Mr Ogilvy for miscropping etc. at the Brunt. He asked me on the spot to say whether or not I thought any claim was valid. He also said that he had already offered £15 for the cutting of the hedges. I suggested to him that if I were in Mr Ogilvy's place I would be inclined to offer a slump sum[4] of £50 and no more. I do not know whether you would be of this opinion or not, but considering everything and the men you are up against, perhaps 'discretion is the better part of valour'.
I wanted to let you have this information at first hand, so that you would not misunderstand me if you heard it from any other source.
Yours faithfully,
H. Miller

***

511. Jan 29th 1919
Messrs Guild & Guild W. S.
Dear Sirs,
As you are aware of what the state of the cottages on this farm has been for a considerable time, I desire to lay before you the necessity of something being done.
For the last four years it has of course been impossible to have anything done in the way of building, but now my men who inhabit these houses inform me that they are not going to stay in them. This as you can understand will make it impossible for me to carry on. It is also no secret that the sanitary authority has blacklisted these houses, and no doubt compulsion will be exercised by them to have something done at an early date. I however would deprecate any interference from that direction.
The annual hiring is approaching, and I am at my wit's end to know what to do either to get new servants or to retain those I have.

I lay these facts before you in the hope that you will give them the consideration that is due to them, and that you will see your way to do something to help me out of a difficulty which threatens disaster to the welfare of the farm.

Yours faithfully,

H. Miller

***

Hugh faced a dilemma over the poor state of the cottages. Following WW1 there was a nationwide push for improved accommodation and Hugh knew that it was critical for good relations with his workers as the hiring approached, and he contemplated the farm purchase later that year.

Aerial View of West Fortune.

***

519. Oct 14th 1919
Messrs Guild & Guild W.S.
Dear Sirs,
   I hereby offer to purchase the farm of West Fortune for twenty thousand pounds stg. (£20,000), according to the conditions set forth in your communication of 6th inst.
   Yours faithfully,
   H. Miller

***

546. Mar 7th 1921
Dear Mr Guild,
   I duly received your letter of 3rd inst and I have today examined the straw at Nairn's Mains. The stacks generally are in an unsatisfactory condition, and the value of the straw as fodder is very much deteriorated - a considerable quantity of it being quite unfit for this purpose.
   Two of the stacks have evidently been built on the top of the broke (chaff leavings).
   If the stacks as they stand had been all straw, built in the usual manner, I would estimate the quantity at 16 tons, but I consider that a fair estimate of the straw in bunches is 10 tons, and the broke 5 tons, while part of one stack looks like rakings and is in very bad condition which I put at one ton. The tops of the stacks have suffered from the wind and consequently have taken in rain in places.
   I am,
   Yours faithfully,
   H. Miller

***

547. Mar 19th 1921
Dear Mr Guild,
   I have been to Brownhills and herewith I enclose my report of the farm, which I hope will suit your purpose. I have set down what I consider would be a fair adjustment of the claim in so far as I have knowledge of the facts. If you want to ask me anything that I may have omitted, I will be pleased to give you any further information I can.
   My brother & I quite fell in love with the farm when we went over it, and

I am convinced that for an early cropping place it will rank amongst the best. The best crop of turnips I have seen this year was in a field next the shore. The one drawback is that there is not a house for the tenant.

    I am,
    Yours faithfully,
    H. Miller

***

609. Mar 13th 1924
Dear Mr Guild

    I regret to inform you that I have had a small fire on the premises, the piggeries at the cottages having been burned yesterday. They were four in number, built of wood and roofed with lath & tiles. A small boy has got access to matches, and everything being like tinder the place went like a straw stack.

    I put these houses up about three years ago, and estimate their value at the time of the fire at £20. I will be glad if you forward this information to the 'Guardian'.

    Yours faithfully,
    H. Miller

***

Employer's Insurance

Personally I am an immense believer in bed, in constantly keeping horizontal: the heart and everything else goes slower, and the whole system is refreshed.
– Henry Campbell-Bannerman (1836 – 1908)

In the last decade of the 19th Century a compensation scheme was introduced to ensure support for industrial workers who were injured in the course of their employment and left unable to perform their duties for more than two weeks. This has evolved over the decades to the centrally funded and administered scheme today. In 1905 a Liberal Government came to power with the Glaswegian, Henry Campbell-Bannerman, as Prime Minister. Adding the Bannerman to his name was a requirement of his inheritance from his uncle but apparently he did not like the length and insisted his friends referred to him as C.B.

The Liberals, under Campbell-Bannerman, introduced legislation with the title 'Workmen's Compensation Act of 1906'. This ensured all employees received compensation for an injury occurring at work and causing them to be unable to earn their wages for a period longer than one week. Obviously, this impacted employers and insurance companies expanded to offer policies when this came into force on 1st July 1907[1].

Hugh Miller's policy was with The London & Lancashire Insurance Company. When this was established in 1861 it was predominantly a Fire Insurance Company and over the years increased its portfolio as legislation changed. The correspondence with the London & Lancashire Insurance Company highlights the risks of injury inherent in labouring jobs and they give a glimpse of an employer's relationship with his employees. The letters appear to record Hugh Miller wholeheartedly supporting some claims and adopting a startled tone in others. What he might have been inferring by James Coyle's 'Irish reticence' must be left to the imagination.

***

Marion (Mary) Fairgrieve and William Inglis
It appears that the Fairgrieve family had been engaged at the Whitsun hiring. The traditional hiring fairs for farm workers continued in East Lothian until the 1920s as outlined in the chapter on the History of Agriculture. Photographs are available in the John Gray Centre Archive[2]. Traditionally workers carried a tool of their trade as an indicator of their skills. Gradually, as accommodation and conditions improved, in addition to other social changes in the early 20th Century, employees became reluctant to move on and the fairs petered out. One disadvantage of seasonal hiring was the impact on the education of the children who were frequently moving.

***

133. Sept 4th 1911
The L & L Insurance Co
Dear Sirs,
   I beg to intimate that one of my woman workers - Mary Fairgrieve, met with an accident today by falling off a cart. I do not know the extent of her injury, but you will hear in due course.
   Yours faithfully,
   H. Miller

***

137. Sept 11th 1911
The L & L Insurce Co
Dear Sir,
   I herewith return the enclosed form which I trust you will find in order.
   One of my horsemen is also off work with a poisoned arm and hand. He got his hand pricked with something about two weeks ago when handling sheaves at the harvest, and it has now developed into poisoning. Please let this have your attention.
   Yours faithfully,
   H. Miller

***

140. Sept 14th 1911
Policy No 646210
Accident to Mary Fairgrieve
The L & L Insc Co
Dear Sir,
    I am in receipt of your letter of 12th inst. I regret having omitted to state Mary Fairgrieve's age, which is twenty-one years. She was building straw on the cart when the accident occurred, which I surely stated under head of the form.
    I enclose the form regarding Wm Inglis.
    Yours faithfully,
    H. Miller

***

144. Sept 27th 1911
Policy No 646210
The L & L Insce Co
Dear Sirs,
    Referring to the accident to Wm Inglis and to your letter of 16th inst. I beg to state that he has now returned to work, having started on Monday 25th inst. He was two weeks and two days off. The woman Mary Fairgrieve has not yet returned to work, but I expect she will do so before long.
    Yours faithfully,
    H. Miller

***

Accident to Mary Fairgrieve
Sept 30th 1911
The L & L Insurce Co
Dear Sir,
    I am in receipt of your letter of 29th inst with inquiry regarding duration of disablement of Mary Fairgrieve.
    I have asked Dr Caverhill who is attending her how long it may be before she will return to work and he says probably a week or two, but can say nothing definite.
    Yours faithfully,
    H. Miller

***

155. Oct 16th 1911
Policy No 646210
Accident to Mary Fairgrieve
The L & L Insurce Co
Dear Sirs,
 With regard to the above I beg to state that the whole family of which she is a member have left my employment today, or rather as from the 14th (Saturday), and have thereby broken their contract, being engaged for a year as from Whitsunday last.
 If a further claim for wages is made - and I have little doubt there will be - shall I pay this as I have been doing? Without prejudice to her however, my own private opinion is that there is now nothing the matter with her, but I say this for your own private information only.
 Please let me hear from you in course.
 Yours faithfully,
 H. Miller

***

163. Oct 26th 1911
The L & L Insurance Co
Accident to Mary Fairgrieve
Dear Sir,
 Referring to your letter of 18th inst, I wrote to Dr Caverhill, regarding the above, and I enclose his reply for your perusal. In view of what he says shall I pay her any further wages in name of compensation if she demands it? Of course, she left here on the 14th inst and I have heard nothing from her since.
 Yours faithfully,
 H. Miller

***

164. Oct 26th 1911
Dr Caverhill
Dear Sir,
   I am obliged for your reply to my letter, which confirms my opinion of the girl, Fairgrieve. I am informed that her address is 16 Park Road Tranent which I think will be correct.
   Yours faithfully,
   H. Miller

***

173. Nov 10th 1911
To Mary Fairgrieve -
   Please sign your name on the two enclosed papers where you see the red x and get somebody to sign their name as a witness where you see the blue x on the small paper, and return them to me at once.
   H. Miller

***

173. Nov 15th 1911
The London & L Ince Co
Dear Sirs,
   Referring to your letter of 8th Nov. regarding Mary (Marion) Fairgrieve, I herewith return the forms which I managed to get her to sign. I trust you will find the same in order.
   Yours faithfully,
   H. Miller

***

182. Dec 6th 1911
Miss Marion Fairgrieve
Madam
   I have your letter of 4th Dec and cannot understand what you want. You gave me a receipt for the money I paid you when you were off work here - namely £2.19.2, for six weeks all but half a day. You at the same time discharged me from all or any further obligation. The document is now in the Insurance Co's hands, and has been registered with the Sheriff, so please understand that I am not going to

communicate any further about it. I have only written this for your information, and not as an explanation why I did not send you any money.
Yours truly,
H. Miller

∗∗∗

John Hendrie
329. Jan 8th 1913
The London & Lancashire Insurance Co.
Policy 646219
Dear Sirs,
I beg to intimate that one of my horsemen met with an accident last night, receiving a kick from one of the horses. I cannot presently say what is the extent of the injury as I have not got the doctor's report. I do not think however it will be serious but will let you know in course.
Yours faithfully,
H. Miller

∗∗∗

This reports a horse related injury, probably a common occurrence, being the equivalent of mechanically related accidents today.

∗∗∗

Policy No 646219
Jan 22nd 1913
The L. & L. Ince. Co.
Dear Sirs,
I herewith enclose receipt forms of discharge in the case of the accident to John Hendrie, referred to in your letter of Jan 18th.
I trust you will find the same in order.
Yours faithfully,
H. Miller

∗∗∗

Tina Cook
346. May 17th 1913
The L & L Insurance Co.
Dear Sirs,
I beg to intimate that one of my workers - Tina Cook - met with an accident on

Wednesday last and will be obliged if you forward the necessary form that I may fill it up.
 Yours faithfully,
 H. Miller

***

Policy No 646219
May 24th 1913
The L & L Insurance Co.
Dear Sirs,
 I beg to acknowledge receipt of cheque for 6/8 in payment of claim in connection with an accident to Tina Cook.
 I regret to say that my grieve has met with an accident also, having got a rib fractured.
 If you will please send me a form, I will give you the particulars.
 Yours faithfully,
 H. Miller

***

William Anderson
William Anderson was still being recorded as grieve in the valuation role in 1919 so presumably made a good recovery and was a loyal employee.

***

347 Policy No 646219
May 30th 1913
The L & L I. Co. Ltd
Dear Sirs,
 I herewith enclose the inquiry form in connection with the accident to Wm Anderson. It was an overlook that it was not returned sooner. I will report to you in a week or two how he gets on.
 Yours faithfully,
 H. Miller

***

Policy No 646219
June 6th 1913
The L. & L. Ince. Co. Ltd.
Dear Sirs,
    Yours of 2nd inst. duly received, re accident to Wm Anderson. He is progressing all right, and is able partly to attend to his duties now.
    Yours faithfully,
    H. Miller

***

Philip McNulty
456. June 8th 1916
Policy No. 646219
The L. & L. Ince. Co. Ltd.
Dear Sirs,
    Referring to yours of 24th May re accident to Philip McNulty, his arm is better, and he would have returned to work on Monday last the 5th inst. but has been confined to the house since then with a bad cold.
    My total liability to him therefore is wages for three weeks less one day @ 26/- per wk. and he asks nothing more.
    Yours faithfully,
    H. Miller

***

These next two claims refer to property – damaged huts and fire-damaged barley crop and grass.

***

470. Feb 16th 1917
T. Honeyman Esq.
Dear Sir,
    Some time ago you got some information from me in connection with the huts erected on this farm - regarding the damages done.
    The huts are now being removed and as I have not yet made any claim I intend doing so now. Would you be good enough to give me any information that would be

helpful in this direction, as it is difficult to know what department to communicate with?

Anticipating your reply,
I am, Yours faithfully,
H. Miller

***

471. Feb 21st 1917
T. Honeyman Esq.
Dear Sir,

I am in receipt of your favour of 19th inst, for which I thank you, but I would feel obliged if you would state the basis of your valuation of £10.1.6. You surely do not mean this to represent the value of the barley crop, not to speak of the young grass that has been destroyed.

I will be glad to hear from you on this point before making up my claim.
Yours faithfully,
H. Miller

***

Matthew Jones
Policy No 6462219
517. Aug 30th 1919
The L. & L. Ince. Co. Ltd.
Dear Sirs,

Referring to yours of 15th inst., Matthew Jones returned to work on the 22nd Aug. He is able for his work although his finger is still tender.

He has informally made a claim for £10 for the loss of the part of the finger, which seems to me to be not unreasonable.

Yours faithfully
H. Miller

***

No 2
518 Sept 12th 1919
Policy No 646219
The L. & L. Ince. Co. Ltd.
Dear Sirs,

I duly received your communication of the 4th inst. regarding the compensation to Jones. I am sorry I cannot agree with you as to his incapacity, for there are some things that he will be distinctly the worse of the loss of his finger for. It will materially affect him for sowing either manure or seed, and I think on this ground alone he is entitled to what he asks. I may say that he had larger ideas of compensation to begin with, but I advised him to reconsider the matter and restrict the amount to £10.

I trust you will see your way to meet this claim, as I consider it is only justice toward the injured man.
Yours faithfully,
H. Miller

***

James Coyle
580. Nov 9th 1921
J. S. Proctor Esq.
Policy No 646219
Accident to James Coyle
Dear Sir,

The enclosed letter will so far speak for itself. The man was in my employment for about three months - Aug. Sept. & Oct. About the middle of Oct or thereabouts he racked himself lifting a too heavy weight. This was in course of his employment but was quite voluntary on his part and I may add unnecessary. He told me at the time he was feeling ill, and I urged him to go to the Dr. but I suppose his Irish reticence kept him from doing so, and I have no doubt but what he says in his letter is substantially correct. In these circumstances would you consider doing something for him, as it was only through his laxity at the time of the accident that there was no claim made.

I will be glad to have your observations on the matter.
Yours faithfully,
H. Miller

***

582. Nov 18th 1921
The L. & L. Ins. Co. Ltd.
Accident to James Coyle
Dear Sir,
 The accompanying form gives all the information that I can give, and of course you have the man's letter which I sent you.
 I may say that he got quite equal to £2 extra from me before he left, on account of the condition he was in, and I thought that would be the end of it. I do not think however that he will be difficult to settle with.
 Yours faithfully,
 H. Miller

***

J. S. Proctor Esq.
Policy No 646219
Accident to James Coyle
Dear Sir,
 Referring to my 595 Feb 22nd 1922 letter to you of Nov 9th last, and also that of Nov 18th when I sent you the particulars of the accident, would you be good enough to let me know if you have done anything in the matter, as I have had several woeful letters from Coyle in which he states he has heard nothing whatever from The Insurance Co.
 Yours faithfully,
 H. Miller

***

Brother George the Banker

A friend loves at all times and a brother is born for adversity.
– Proverbs 17:17

George Miller, Hugh's brother, was a banker in Ayr, having become a clerk in the Clydesdale Bank on leaving school and later manager of the branch in 1908. He was a well-known personality in the town, an elder in Trinity Church and supported many charitable organisations. He married Catherine Chalmers in 1909 and they had five children, one daughter dying in infancy.

George dealt with Hugh's annual accounts and insurance premiums. This series of letters contains snippets of family information, financial dealings that he entrusted to his brother and recurring comments about the weather. Correspondence suggests that Hugh was not always on top of financial affairs and perhaps needed a reliable brother. Valuation of crops, eg. turnips and potatoes still in the ground was difficult to estimate, but somehow the necessary annual balance sheet was completed between them. Regular payments of insurance premiums appear to have been made to George. Life Insurance premiums were paid in August and amounted to £46-18-9. The Workmen's Compensation Policy was due in November and crept up to £9-19-6 as the number of workers increased. A further premium of £12-12-11 was due in January.

***

21. Nov 20th 1910
Dear George,
   I herewith enclose Cheque for £6-18-9 in payment of premium of my wages insurance. As you will see, I have added 11/3 to the stated amount.

I got home all right on Saturday night and found things about normal. We have had some days of frost this week, but today has been fresh, and I hope it will be so for some time. I hear of a good fall of snow at Mauchline. I trust you are all well.
Yours affectly,
Hugh

***

27. Dec 6th 1910
Dear George,
I herewith send you a detail of my inventory income, expenditure etc, and will be glad if you make it up. I fear the result, however, and can only hope that I may not be insolvent. I have entered in the inventory only the portion or value of the potatoes that remains unpaid, and turnips the same.

There is no need to deduct anything from turnips for cake consumed, as this has not really yet taken place and will go into next year's account.

The compensations claim of £627 is included in the rent etc account.

I took the value of the engine on the basis of the old engine, as the new one is not payable until the beginning of the year. This accounts for the small valuation of that item.

I think I have given you all the details but if I have omitted anything that occurs to you, you might let me know.

We are having fresh weather and very short days.
Yours affectly,
Hugh

***

30. Dec 12th 1910
Dear George,
I have your letter of 9th inst. and am sorry to hear that you have been off duty, but hope that by this time you have quite got over the effects of your disposition.

Regarding your enquiries about my figures etc, as I did not include the new engine in my inventory, I did not include the amount in my creditor list. However, I will give you a note of it if you think it is necessary. It will benefit my balance to the extent of £35 as the landlord pays me this amount and makes me sole possessor of the engine. £1120 represents the value of the turnip crop for both last year and this.

If it is necessary for you to have my cash book I will send it to you, but in any case, I enclose a note of the totals on both sides if this is of any use to you. I will also detail the items under Rent etc. including all insurance and taxes.

Yours affectly,
Hugh

***

33. Dec 19th 1910
Dear George,

I am in receipt of your letter of 14th inst enclosing balance sheet. In the circumstances I am glad that things are no worse, but hope the result will be different if I am spared to see another balance sheet. In the meantime accept of my thanks for your trouble.

I hope you are now keeping better and able for your duties.

We have had very soft weather, and very dirty premises for the last fortnight or so, but we have had some drouth[1] today which is improving things.

I see that John Dobbie has crossed the bourne[2]. I always reckoned him as free from 'loop'[3] as anyone I had dealings with.

I expect to be at Mauchline after the New Year, and if I have time will look you up.

Yours affectly
Hugh

***

54. Feb 17th 1911
Dear George,

I heard from Bessie yesterday that you had been off duty again for some days, and though not back to the Bank you were feeling some better.

I am sorry that these attacks are making themselves so objectionably frequent, but hope that you have now got over this one and will not have a recurrence. May I ask what the Dr. said about it this time?

I trust that Cathie & Baby are well.

We have had quite a gale for the last two days but no rain. Tonight, however, is rather inclined to be wet.

I will be pleased to hear of your welfare when it is convenient.

Yours affectly,
Hugh

***

135. Sept 4th 1911
Dear George,
   I duly received your letter of 1st inst and had not heard of Uncle John and Auntie having celebrated their Golden Wedding. I can't say I feel particularly enthusiastic regarding a presentation, but if it is to be a family affair, I do not want to stand aloof from the others and so enclose £1 towards whatever you may fix upon.
   We are still having very dry weather, and everything is suffering. We finished harvest a week ago except a little bit of late stuff which we are finishing now. The crop is considerably less bulk than it should have been.
   I trust you are all well.
   Yours affectly,
   Hugh

***

179. Nov 24th 1911
Dear George,
   I herewith enclose Cheque for £9.12/- in payment of the premium of my wages insurance, being 2/- in excess of the stipulated amount.
   I trust that you are all keeping well and the family thriving. I once thought of being West for two days about this time, but I will not likely be this year now as far as I see at present.
   We have had a space of very broken weather lately, and the drains have got to work again that were idle for so long.
   I will be making up my balance sheet shortly, and will be glad of your help to do so, if you are not too busy.
   I am sending you a hare in the morning, and hope you will get it sometime tomorrow.
   Yours affectly,
   Hugh

***

185 & 186. Dec 9th 1911
Dear George,
   I should have written you last week acknowledging receipt of 18/-. I know how I made the first mistake of adding 2/- instead of 4/- to the wages premium, but I do not know what I can have been dreaming about when I wrote the cheque for £9

instead of £8. The consequences could however have been more serious.

I send herewith the details of my valuation, and will be glad if you can find time to make up the balance sheet. I think you will have all the information necessary, but if not you can let me know.

Jane and the two wee children went to Stewarton yesterday, so the house is a bit quiet.

The weather is just usual - sometimes wet and sometimes dry, but we managed to sow most of our wheat this week after waiting several weeks for an opportunity.

I trust that you are all well and the children thriving.

Yours affectly,

Hugh

***

188. Dec 13th 1911

Dear George,

I had your letter & enclosure this morning and herewith return the latter with the information you ask for. The bank interest may amount to £30 to £40, but I did not include it as I have stated that last year it was carried forward into this year.

I hope where things are balanced that I may be able to pay 20p a pound.

There will be some excitement in Ayr tomorrow over the sale of "The Baron"[4]. If it had been, or if I had been, nearer I would have helped to swell the crowd.

I trust you are all well.

Yours affectly,

Hugh

***

260 & 261. July 4th 1912

Dear George,

I had the renewal notice of my life insurance premiums yesterday and your note attached. I suppose the payment of these will be in time when you return, unless you are taking a very prolonged holiday. You seem to be seeking pastures new, and I hope you will have a good time and that Cathie and the children will be none the worse of going so far from home.

Things move on here much in the usual routine. We have had for the most part a sunless June with much more rain than was convenient at times. We would now welcome a spell of sunshine which would be beneficial for everything.

Crops are fairly good but some things have suffered for the want of sunshine.

We are not cutting hay which I would say barely is an average crop, as it was too late in getting the moisture. If prices only keep as good as they were last year for everything there will be a chance of getting the two ends together this year too.

We expect Mary and her children next week for a few days. She seems to be some better now, and I trust may continue so.

I am wondering what the issue will be after 15th July when the Insurance Act comes into force. By that time there will be a fair body of protesters, and I will be sorry if the protests do not accomplish the desired end. There will be some howling in any case.

Trusting that you are all well and that you will have a good holiday.
Yours affectly,
Hugh

***

320 & 321. Nov 30th 1912
Dear George,

I herewith enclose cheque in payment of the premium of my "Workmen's" Policy. My wage bill amounts to £40 more than the amount insured, so I have added the difference, making £8.18/- which I trust you will find in order.

I suppose you would have your share of the storm on Tuesday. We hadn't as much of it as we expected, but in the end, not so very much damage done. Some stooks badly ruffled and an old roof blown out is the most of the damage we have sustained.

I see from the papers you have had a good fall of snow and very severe frost - 21degrees. We have here no snow and sharp frost - yesterday I think 12 degrees, so the figures are reversed. I hope it does not last, as we are in a bad position for turnips for sheep not having new storage for them.

I have not yet had time to get my affairs weighed in the balances, but I hope they will not be found wanting, when they are weighed.

I trust you are all well as we are, for which I am thankful.
Yours affectly,
Hugh

***

324. Dec 21st 1912
Dear George,

I herewith enclose a statement of the past year's transactions along with the balance sheet of last year, and will be glad if you make it up as before. I have been long in getting this done - there are so many other things need attention.

I believe John is at Ferrygate tonight till Monday. It has been a wet day and evening or we might have exchanged a call somehow.

I expect to be in Ayrshire after the New Year, and if convenient for you I would stay Friday night Jan 3rd with you, but if not convenient, do not hesitate to say.

Jane left this morning so I am both father & mother, master & mistress, for the time being - no great job but will get through.

Yours affectly,
Hugh

***

375 & 376. Nov 29th 1913
Dear George,

The premium for my workmen's compsn. Policy is now due, and I herewith enclose cheque in payment of same, for £9.19.6, which I trust you will find in order.

Whatever else may come or go, the wages go on, and seem to go up for ever.

We have had very high winds of late, but very little rain. The land presently is like March, and we have great difficulty in getting any quantity of straw tramped into muck in the courts. We have seen it otherwise and it may happen again.

There has been a run of bad throats at Ferrygate, and Robert told me today that the Dr. said he would be a Dutchman, if it were not scarlet fever with little Mary. I hope he will have to change his nationality.

Our maid is away home with a bad throat too, which in a way may be a blessing in disguise, as it keeps my hand in the way of kindling the fire and milking the cow. All things considered however, I hope she will be back soon.

This was the sale day at Luffness Mains, and Allan Stevenson takes possession on Monday. Two of his brothers were there with him today.

David Bone has also taken possession at Markle, as Ayrshire is on the increase around us.

I trust you are all well.

Yours affectly,
Hugh

***

387. Dec 25th 1913
Dear George,

I have your letter, and with regard to my bank overdraft, I have simply put down a wrong set of figures, and did not test them before I enclosed the note to you.

The amount of overdraft is quite right, and you will see from the note where the mistake is. I am sorry it is not an omitted entry of £362.

There was a discrepancy of £8 or £9 crept into my cash that I was never able to trace but made an entry to balance. There is no discrepancy apart from this that I am aware of.

This is Xmas day[5], and our Irishmen are celebrating it by being off work, and I suppose, consuming as much whiskey as they can get on the outside of. At least this will be the case with some of them.

I trust you all keep well.

Yours affectly,

Hugh

The fire the other night was not at Fentonbarns but at Muirfield.

H. M.

***

408 & 409. Aug 7th 1914
Dear George,

I meant to have written you a few days ago, enclosing cheque for my Insurance premium, which however was not done. I do so now enclosing cheque for £46.18.9.

I suppose you will all be back from your holiday and I trust you are none the worse but the better of it.

Of course the one theme at present is the war. It is deplorable that the destruction of life and property accompanied with all the hardships of unemployment and the sorrow of desolate homes, should still be the final means of adjusting differences among the nations. But I suppose we need not wonder so very much at the state of affairs which only verifies Christ's words, that "Nation shall rise against nation and kingdom against kingdom". It is well to know that the Lord reigneth and that He can make even the wrath of man to praise Him.

We began cutting oats yesterday, and I expect we will get straight ahead in the course of a day or two.

We heard from Bessie that Jim[6] had been asked to go out for home defence. I was saying that she would be glad in any case that he had not got away to Service.

I trust you are all well and I am glad to say we are.

Yours affectly,

Hugh

***

423 & 424. Dec 26th 1914

Dear George,

I am sending you a statement of my affairs, and I will be glad if you will make up my balance sheet as before. I cannot get the final account balanced by over £86. I do not understand this as both my cash and bank a/cs balance all right. The strap is not far through the buckle this year, but I have allowed 10% for depreciation, and allowed nothing for straw and I do not think I have overvalued the stock and crop.

I suppose you will be busy with your balance now till the end of the year.

We have had some frost this week, with about the worst roads for two days I almost ever saw. A little rain fell and immediately froze making everywhere almost like a curling rink.

This is a new piece of history that Bessie is making[7]. It is all very interesting and I trust may be very satisfactory. Have you met your new brother-in-law yet? I would like to see him soon.

We expect Mr & Mrs Arthur tomorrow for a few days.

I trust you are all well and with the Season's Greetings,

Yours affectly,

Hugh

***

458. July 26th 1916

Dear George,

I had your letter some time ago with the Insurance notices enclosed. We also had a card from Cathie from Dalmellington. I hope you have all had a good holiday.

We have had real summer weather here for a week or ten days, thunder going about at times, but we have so far escaped any cloud burst.

We are now cutting hay in the tramp rick[8] and we want dry weather still.

Uncle Robert has been in these parts for a week or two, but is going home soon. I think he is the better of the change, but he is a lonely old man.

I herewith enclose cheque for £46.18.9 in payment of premiums, which I trust you will find in order.
I trust you all keep well.
Yours affectly,
H. Miller
<u>I forgot.</u>

***

Finance, Bank Managers and Accountants

A wise person should have money in their head, but not in their heart.
– Jonathan Swift 1667–1745

Farming, like any business, requires financial accounts to be kept, income to be declared and taxes paid. Hugh Miller's venture at West Fortune was no exception. The previous chapter has demonstrated that Hugh relied on the financial support and advice of his brother George but following his move east he also required relationships with local bankers. Early in the 20th Century local banking revolved around relationships and in particular, with the bank manager. These letters give us a glimpse of Hugh Miller's interactions with the accountants and financiers he was involved with and suggest a man who could get easily exasperated.

One of the central characters was Mr. R M McKechnie, the manager of the Clydesdale Bank in North Berwick. The Clydesdale was formed in Glasgow but opened for business in both Glasgow and Edinburgh in May 1838. The bank steadily made acquisitions until being sold itself to Midland Bank in 1920 although it continued to operate independently.

The 1911 census records Robert M McKechnie being aged 56, single and living with his sister and two servants. His address appears to be Westgate and the house was noted to have nine rooms with windows.

Each single letter requesting a Cheque to be deposited and stating the amount seems a laborious process but ensured the lodger knew how much was being deposited into his account. Several of these one line letters have been omitted from this collection.

The rent paid for the farm of West Fortune was £982-15/- (from the tax information for 1920) and a bank overdraft was taken out on 29th May 1920 for the purchase of the farm.

***

25. Dec 5th 1910
R.M.McKechnie Esq
Dear Sir,
 I herewith enclose cheque for £100 which please place to the credit of my account.
 Yours faithfully,
 H. Miller

***

64. Mar 15th 1911
R M McKechnie Esq
 Dear Sir,
 I issued a cheque in Edinburgh today for £346 which overdraws my account. It will be practically squared however, in the course of a day or two. I trust that I have not caused you annoyance in having taken this liberty.
 Yours faithfully,
 H. Miller

***

87. May 4th 1911
Dear John,
 I have seen McKechnie and he says the matter of the overdraft will be all right.
 We are getting turnip put in under ideal conditions, and so far, a braird will be secured.
 We had a good smart shower on Wednesday afternoon, but this is the only measurable quantity of rain we have had for a fortnight or so. Excuse the hurried note as I must be hence.
 Trust you are all well.
 Yours affectly,
 H. Miller

Former Clydesdale Bank.

169. Nov 10th 1911
R M McKechnie Esq
Dear Sir,
    Will you be good enough to allow me to exceed the guarantee of my overdraft by £200 for perhaps two months? I hoped to have seen you today but am sorry I could not get to No. Berwick.
    Thanking you in anticipation,
    Yours faithfully,
    H. Miller

***

451. Mar 29th 1916
Messrs Mungo Gray & Co.
Dear Sirs,
    I received your cheque in payment of a/c enclosed, which I return herewith discharged. There was a slight error however in the writing of the amount on the cheque which is as follows - "One hundred & fifty and five". The figures for the amount were all right.
    I paid in the money today and said I would let you know of the mistake. Will you please put the matter right at the bank as I thought it was hardly worth while returning the cheque.
    Yours faithfully,
    H. Miller

***

467. Nov 15th 1916
J.B.Small Esq.[1]
Dear Sir,
    Did you find a mistake in your cash today? I think I am £2 short.
    My transaction in the Bank was as follows -
    Mungo Gray & Co's cheque £102
    Wm.Kay & Sons'" 123. 4/-
    Lieutenant Fairniechough's " £5.
    I paid in £225 and if my memory serves me right - for I was in a hurry - you gave me £3.2.9 cash.

Of course, if your cash is correct, the mistake will be mine.
Yours faithfully,
H. Miller

***

470. Feb 14th 1917
R.M. McKechnie Esq.
Dear Sir,
　I herewith enclose cheque for £100 which I wish put into the War Loan[2]. Will you be good enough to negotiate this for me as I am not too well acquaint with the procedure.
　Yours faithfully,
　H. Miller

***

490. Feb 20th 1918
Dear Mr Leys,
　Your letter of 15th inst. is before me, and regarding the proposed Life Policy, I think with all deference to my brother's advice I will have the one payable at death or age 60 - premium £76.0.10.
　I have not yet had time to see the Dr. but hope to do so as soon as possible.
　Yours faithfully,
　H. Miller

***

515. Aug 19th 1919
R.M. McKechnie Esq.
Dear Sir,
　I have been thinking for some time that it would be more convenient for me to have my Bank Account in Edinburgh as the most of my business is done there and I am always in on the Wednesdays.
　I have spoken to Mr Inglis of the High St. branch and I would be glad if you would arrange to have my account transferred there as early as convenient.
　Yours faithfully,
　H. Miller

***

In 1919 he decided that he was in Edinburgh more regularly than North Berwick as he travelled to the Wednesday Gorgie Market and transferred his account to the Clydesdale Bank sited at 30 North Bridge. The total in his account to be transferred was £472. 2. 8., approximately equivalent to the purchasing power of £25,000 today.

The firm of G.K. Johnston & Smillie were Chartered Accountants with offices at 21 Albany Street, Edinburgh

***

538. Dec 29th 1920
Messrs. G.K.Johnston & Smillie,
Dear Sirs,
    Further to our conversation today I now enclose the other income tax form. The rent of the farm is £982. 15/-. This does not include £3. 3/- which I annually paid to the proprietor for insurance on the buildings, before I bought the farm, and which I do not think I should be charged on now. The shooting is valued at £40. There will be a deduction to make for Bank interest which I have paid, and I will send the certificate of this to you in a day or two, as I have not yet received it.
    Yours faithfully,
    H. Miller
    <u>Value of cottages £37</u>
    H.M.

***

542. Jan 29th 1921
Dear Mr Johnstone,
    I am in receipt of your letter of 28th inst. with enclosures for which I thank you. I now enclose the receipts for the income tax I paid last year. I had no other income last year than what my returns showed, which is the same as the current year except what I am charged under schedule A, and I do not understand why the Inspector of Taxes is suspicious of me concealing information from him, when he has got a correct return.
    I entered into an arrangement with the Bank for an overdraft when I paid for the farm. I became owner of the farm on May 29th 1920, and had no money borrowed except from the Bank.
    I do not think there is any further information I can give you, but I may call round on Wed. morning about 10 o'clock, and see how matters stand.
    Yours faithfully,
    H. Miller

***

566. July 11th 1921
G.K. Johnstone Esq.
<u>Income Tax Return</u>
Dear Sir,
 I have now received from the Bank the certificate of the amount of interest payable by me for the year ending Apr 5th 1921, which is £388.10.5, and which I herewith enclose.
 The other details are as follows -
From 5% War Stock £5
From 5 3/4 % Exchqr. Bonds £5. 15
Interest on Deposit Receipt £69 . 5. 8
These will complete my return.
Yours faithfully,
H. Miller

***

583. Jan 7th 1922
Messrs Johnston & Smillie,
Dear Sir,
 I have your letter of 6th inst. with enclosure, which I have signed.
 The amount of the subsidy which I received was £522 but I think there should be set against this for the present - the fact that I have paid £361. 13. 6 of Income Tax which I am not due.
 My work horses at the beginning of the year numbered 20, at the end of the year - 21;
 1 died, 1 destroyed, 1 sold, & 4 bought in (including 3 young horses unbroken).
 I enclose last year's balance sheet, but am not willing that the assessor should have access to all the figures there, as he has nothing to do with the profit of last year. You will see from that balance sheet that I have cut down the valuation of my horses to what they were in pre-war days, which I think I am entitled to do. I have no liking for a fictitious valuation.
 Yours faithfully,
 H. Miller

***

589 & 590. Jan 23rd 1922
Messrs Johnston & Smillie C.A.
Farm Accounts
Dear Sirs,

I return herewith the letter to you from the Inspector of Taxes dated Jan 20th 1922, which you sent me for perusal. With regard to the remarks contained in that letter, I beg to give you the following information :-

I hereby certify that the accounts are a true and correct copy of the transactions, not only as disclosed by my books, but of the actual transactions pertaining to the farm for the year. As you are aware, you have not seen or audited my books. I have no objection to submitting the books to you, but I understood you to say that a Taxpayer was not bound to go to the expense of having his books audited.

I keep a cash Book & a Ledger, as well as a Book recording the position with Debtors and Creditors and the result of the whole transactions are correctly reflected in the Statement of Accounts which I sent you. I just keep the one Bank Book which of course is kept for business purposes.

Implements - The following is the allocation of items of Implements:-
(a) Loose Tools £50
(b) Ordinary Farm Machy. £700
(c) Larger do. Tractors etc. £150
(d) Fixed do. Mill etc. £300

There were bought during the year the following:-
4 Carts   £ 192
1 Pot. Riddle   £ 1. 12. 6
1 Plow   £ 3. 10
                 ————
                 £ 197. 2. 6

and there were sold some old plows etc. amounting to:
                 £ 22. 10. 6
                 £ 174.12

This gives the sum of £174. 12 which appears in the accounts.

The farm is arable. The acreage is 464 - & 35ac of this is pasture. It was the same at the beginning and end of the year.

In addition to this there are about 80 ac. of admiralty land in crop. This was so at the beginning and end of year.
Yours faithfully,
H. Miller

***

591. Feb 1st 1922
Messrs Johnston & Smillie C.A.
Dear Sirs,
With reference to your letter of 30th Jan. and also enclosure from the Inspector of Taxes, regarding growing crop at the beginning & the end of the year. I beg to state that at the beginning of the year, turnips & mangold were valued at £915, and at the end of the year £710. These are all the growing crops, wheat & young grass being taken in both instances at the cost of the seed sown.
The drop in valuations is accounted for in a large decrease in quantity as well as the slump in prices.
Yours faithfully,
H. Miller

***

607. Oct 18th 1923
The Public Works Loan Board
Dear Sirs,
Would you please give me the following information under "The Agrlr. Credits Act".
1. Can a loan be arranged for any number of years less than sixty.
2. What would be the annual payment.
3. If the borrower wished to pay off the loan earlier than the agreed on date, what would be the sum payable at ten, twenty & thirty years for £12,000.
I will be glad to hear from you at an early date.
Yours faithfully,
H. Miller

***

It is difficult to see the implications of this enquiry to The Public Works Loan Board as accounts indicate that this was an arrangement to provide finance to local authorities particularly for housing and town planning.

***

613. Jan 13th 1925
Dear Mr Hope,
   I thank you for yours of 10th inst. with cheque enclosed for £10.5.8 in payment of the taxes on the shootings levied on the occupier. This squares up shooting season 1923 to 1924.
   The same taxes for season 1924 to 1925 amount to a total of £8.19/-.
   If convenient it would be better to have this brought up to date.
   Yours faithfully,
   Hugh Miller

***

632 & 633. Apr 23rd 1927
Dear Mr. Johnston,
   I have your letter of 22nd inst. regarding the valuation of my potato crop. Evidently Mr. Hare wishes to charge me with income tax whether I have any income or not. Fortunately I am now nearly through with my potatoes and can give you the sums I have so far realised for them.
   My actual sales have amounted to £533.15/- and I consider I have 30 tons of ware left which

   at present is worth   £ 150
   Then I would use for seed 20 tons @ £3 = £ 60
                                      —————

   making a total of ————-   £ 743.15
   This makes a loss of ——————   £ 516.5 on the valuation of the crop at Nov 28th.
   If Mr. Hare imagines I am keeping down the valuation for the purpose of showing a loss then I can only conclude that there is some twist in his mental capacity. If he is not satisfied with this statement I will ask the special commissioners for their decision on the matter.
   With reference to the 1925 valuation of £1100 for potatoes - the realisation of that crop was £1157.15/- apart from what my farm people got as their perquisites.
   I enclose the Bank certificate for interest.
   Yours faithfully,
   Hugh Miller

***

The Arbiter

Arbitration is justice blended with charity
– Nachman of Breslov 1772–1810

When the lease on a farm ends, a squaring up is always required between landlord and tenant or purchaser. This can be controversial, and most leases today have an arbitration clause to help manage a resolution and avoid the need to go to court. Throughout a tenancy there are likely to be regular inspections by agents of the landlord and a rolling inventory is undertaken, recording everything from the state of fences and hedges through to the quality of the soil and condition of farm buildings. At the end of a lease there is usually a schedule of dilapidations drawn up and this will be put up against a claim the tenant may make in respect of any improvements made to the property. This may be complicated and is regulated by statute.

Hugh Miller put himself forward as an arbiter in farm disputes. Some of these must have been by invitation as a neutral assessor when the value of farms was disputed. He obviously became experienced in such disputes, and his involvement in a case as arbiter in 1931 was with the firm of Dundas & Wilson, which became the leading law firm in Scotland later in the 20th century.

There are letters dealing with arbitration at Upper Bolton (near Haddington), Ruchlaw Mains (by Stenton), Wintonhill (Pencaitland), Whitekirk (near North Berwick), and Preston Mains (East Linton). The later group of letters appears to be supporting a friend's son in a farming venture at Horncliffe Mains near Berwick. It would seem that Horncliffe Mains had been acquired by a Mr Meikle, another Ayrshire farmer who had previously put in a bid for Markle Mains near East Linton. This farm, however, was acquired by a David Bone, also from Ayrshire, in Nov 1913, and so it was a few years later that Mr Meikle bought Horncliffe. It appears that Jack was his son. Hugh had the experience to deal with the challenge of seeking resolution with minimum expense and without involving lawyers. He was aware of an arbiter having to be appointed by 'the Board' if the parties could not agree and was also knowledgeable about the Agricultural Holdings Act although the matter of the engine was eventually laid aside. Hugh represented the landlord at the arbitration (a claim concerning dung was involved) and he was not impressed by the outcome but encouraged Jack to make the best of it. All seemed to be Pro Bono - the final letter suggesting that sharing a meal of salmon would be appreciated!

***

Horncliffe Mains

The village of Horncliffe lies just south of the River Tweed in Northumbria, 5 miles Southwest of Berwick-upon-Tweed. The discussions appear to have started in May 1921, but the deal was not settled until March 1922.

***

551. May 9th 1921

Dear Jack,

I have both of your letters and I do not think you should vex yourself by asking everybody's opinion about the arbitration at Horncliffe. Mr Wood may be all right, but I would like a man who is decided in his own opinion. After all, Mr Pringle of Branton was recommended by an outsider before ever Davidson offered his name to me.

I think it is likely I will take a run to Berwick on Saturday and try if possible, to arrange matters then.

Yours faithfully,

H. Miller

***

552. May 14th 1921

Dear Jack,

I found Davidson rather stiff regarding the appointment of an oversman[1], and after trying him every way with Wood, and after he refused, I offered to toss for Wood & Pringle. However, he said that he would not, and I told him that I would go to the Board and ask for the appointment of an arbiter. He just assented to this, and for a little time I left him to think the matter over.

The awkward thing about it is that the Board would have appointed a man in the district, who would not have been merely oversman but sole arbiter. Upon

further consideration and after further inquiry about Pringle, I accepted him, and in the meantime have arranged next Saturday morning for the valuation. You might send me the lease as there are one or two things I want to look at again. Davidson is having the submission prepared and is going to send it to me and then I will forward it to you for revision.
    Yours faithfully,
    H. Miller

***

555. May 25th 1921
Wm Pringle Esq.
<u>Horncliffe Mains</u>
Dear Sir,
    Your favour of 21st inst. with submission enclosed, I only received last night.
    I would like to point out that there are two items in the submission which the lease does not bind the incoming tenant to take over, (viz) the oil engine & the grist mill[2].
    I have no doubt but Mr. Meikle will be willing to purchase these from Mr. Embleton if the price can be agreed up, but I think it is only business that they should be deleted from the submission.
    I hope to meet you at Horncliffe Mains on Saturday first when I hope we shall be able to arrange matters. 10.30am will suit me quite well.
    Yours faithfully,
    H. Miller
    <u>Submission enclosed</u>

***

557. May 31st 1921
Dear Jack,
    I have your letter of 28th inst. and am a little surprised that Embleton has sold the engine already. Of course, knowing that it was not bound to be taken at valuation he would no doubt have an alternative arrangement made for the disposal of it before Saturday. I think in the end however you will not stand to lose much on that head.
    I have no doubt but the fences are giving them some thought, and I think I was right in refusing Davidson's proposal on Saturday. Nothing would have pleased them better and it was quite evident that Davidson was both sorry and angry. He was like

a bear outside.

They are taking a great interest in the saving of expenses by their proposals, but it is not difficult to see what is behind these.

I hope you have had sufficient rain now for crop requirements. We have had none too much.

Yours faithfully,
H. Miller

***

558. June 1st 1921
W. Pringle Esq.
Dear Sir,

Referring to our meeting at Horncliffe Mains on Saturday last, I wish to lay before you one or two facts regarding the mill. A new mill such as the one in question can be got for a little over £400, and the agents state that there is to be a reduction of 25% on the present price, as no one will buy mills at the current figure. Surely this fact cannot be ignored in arriving at the value of the machine, and considering that it has done at least seven or eight years' work, I am firmly convinced that I made a very generous offer.

Yours faithfully,
H. Miller

***

559. June 11th 1921
Dear Jack,

Yours of 9th inst. is before me. I have not heard anything at all about the mill since that day I was at Horncliffe Mains. If there had been anyone there examining it, you surely would have seen or heard of them.

Regarding Embleton's claim, I do not think it would serve any good purpose - but the opposite - to ask for it. I think however you should get your claim formulated and have it in readiness to be lodged before the two months are up. Perhaps they are waiting to see your claim before lodging theirs. The 12th of July at 12 o'clock will be the latest date for lodging.

I have been wondering if you should not make a claim for £50 for the state in which the pasture was left. It was swept absolutely bare, and the lease binds the tenant not to have more than the usual head of stock on the pastures during - is it

the last three months of the tenancy? I don't know how much pasture there is, but you should I think claim £1 per ac anyhow.
 Yours faithfully,
 H. Miller

***

560. June 16th 1921
Dear Jack,
 I have yours of 14th inst. with draft of your claim enclosed. I have looked over it and you will see the altered and added figures I have put in. I have the conviction that we will have to ask a bit more than we expect to get, as this may be the only way in which we will get fair treatment.
 I think you should now get your claim made out, but you might leave the figures out for the present, to see if you get Embleton's claim.
 It would have been all the better if you could have had your claim typed and have at least one spare copy.
 Yours faithfully,
 H. Miller

***

561. July 1st 1921
Dear Jack,
 There is a little matter with reference to the removal of the engine which I wish to lay before you.
 Section 20 of the Agrl. H. Act says
 IV "The tenant shall not remove any fixtures or building without giving one month's previous notice in writing to the landlord of his intention to remove it" ……
..and here follows the procedure to be followed.
 Now I think if I were in your place, I would let Embleton know what the law is, and if you were still anxious to take over the engine - failing an agreement between you - you could get the Board to appoint an arbiter, as I would not on any consideration accept of Davidson.
 I am merely putting the matter before you, but I think it would be a good thing to bring them to their senses
 It is still very dry here, but good hay-making weather.
 Yours faithfully,
 H. Miller

***

564. July 2nd 1921
Dear Jack,
 Further to our telephone conversation this evening, I do not think you should take Embleton's threat to remove the engine lying down.
 We did not refuse to take the engine but only refused to have it included in the submission with the fixtures that the lease bound you to take.
 My advice for the present would be for you to write to Embleton, and object to him removing the engine until Section 20 of the Agrl. H. Act is complied with.
 There might then be a possibility of dealing with him, but if not, your position will be no worse.
 Yours faithfully,
 H. Miller

***

567. July 11th 1921
Dear Jack,
 I duly received yours of 7th inst. with Embleton's claim enclosed. I would like to look into it for a day or two and will return it then to you.
 The vouchers will be returned to Davidson when you have finished with them.
 I don't think you can do anything else than apply to the Board for an arbiter, and then keep as much as possible out of Davidson's hands. The Act says that the Board will appoint an arbiter "on the application in writing of either of the parties", so that the procedure is quite plain.
 Yours faithfully,
 H. Miller

***

568. July 11th 1921
Dear Jack,
 I have now gone over your claim and adjusted it as I would have done if I was arbiter. I think you will be able to follow the notifications I have made. It will be an indication to whoever is appointed arbiter, what our opinion is.
 The £8.11.7 is deducted on the basis of compound cake & oats being put in at too high a rate. I cannot find a voucher for the 5 tons compound cake in the last year although nos. 5 & 6 for lamb food & bran do not seem to be entered at all. Then there are no vouchers or proof of the oats & beans - homegrown I suppose - having been

consumed on the farm. This will require to be produced.

My figures of course are based on the quantities being correct, and I consider I would be allowing ample at this amount.

Yours faithfully,
H. Miller

***

584. Jan 16th 1922
Dear Jack,

I had your letter this morning, and in any case, I meant to write you. I have had notice of the appointment of an arbiter - Noel Villiers - Estates Offices - Wooler, but I do not know anything about him.

I think it would be as well to get a move on as soon as possible and get something done. I note the points you mention in your letter regarding the extra acreage ploughed for white crop. I think however when the outgoing tenant's a/c is presented to you that it will be quite easily seen and proved whether or not he has exceeded his rights, and if so - by how much. I think you should insist on getting his statement of acreage as soon as possible, so that it may be laid before the arbiter oversman when necessary.

I hardly think it is worth your while coming here as we can exchange notes when we meet, but if you are along in any case, I will be glad to see you. I have a copy of the "claim" - indeed I suppose the original, and you can get it when you wish it, but I will retain it for the present.

Will be glad to hear how things go.
Yours faithfully,
H. Miller

***

586. Jan 19th 1922
W. Pringle Esq.
Horncliffe Mains
Dear Sir,

I have your letter of 16th inst. with enclosure.

There is a discrepancy with regard to field No 49. The acreage of this field was given as 20.927 on the valuation day, and you have put it down as 25.449. This 5 should evidently be a 0 as your summations are all right taking the field at 20.449 acres. Then I make out the harvesting to be £321. 5 taking 128 ½ acres @ 50/- per acre.

I agree generally with the statement on the understanding of course that the harvesting costs & the price of the grain have yet to be determined.
The other matters are quite in order.
Yours faithfully,
H. Miller

***

588. Jan 20th 1922
Dear Jack,
I have your letter of 18th inst. and I think you would be quite right to have Smith's help in the hearing by the arbiter.
Pringle sent me for my approval a statement of the acreage & quantities of the grain crop, also the amounts agreed upon for ploughing etc. I accepted of the statement generally with one or two corrections, subject to certain points to be discussed at the final settlement.
I was surprised to see the amount charged for the threshing machine viz. £229. 17. 6. This sum is put down without comment. I am glad Davidson had the sense not to take my offer that day we inspected it.
You will be getting this a/c from Pringle immediately, so I need not go into any further details. He deducts harvesting at 52/- per ac. But of course, that will be adjusted along with acreage, price, etc. at the final award.
Yours faithfully,
H. Miller

***

592. Feb 4th 1922
T.C. Smith Esq.
<u>Horncliffe Mains Arbitration</u>
Dear Sir,
I have now prepared a revised statement of the above claim. I think you will be able to understand it with my notes of explanation. I have set out in these figures, what I consider would be a fair award to both sides.
The matter of £100 in the counterclaim that you referred to today in our telephone conversation, I suppose will be the £100 I put down as an estimate for clearing the hedge sides all over the farm, as the hedges are so overgrown that the fields have not been cultivated as they should have been, and the uncultivated parts have in consequence become foul. This is not good husbandry on an arable farm.

The case of a grazing farm would be quite different as far as the growth of the hedges is concerned.

I enclose also a letter from Messrs Gray & Taylor showing the decrease in price of manure for this year. I do not think this will be required as it will be accepted by all concerned that there is a substantial drop in values. You are however better to have it.

Yours faithfully,
H. Miller

***

593. Feb 20th 1922
Dear Jack,
I have yours of 17th inst. with Pringle's statement enclosed. I note that what you state regarding the amount of crop that Embleton left. This will come up at the final settlement - I forget when this takes place.

I am exceedingly disappointed with the barley field that you refer to. I thought it should have come out about 5 qrs. in any case. However, you will see how the crop turns out on the whole.

I was disappointed with the manner in which Smith conducted the case on Thursday. If I had thought that he was not going to reply to some of Pieray's (?) allegations, I would have interrupted & protested at the time myself - even at the risk of a breach of etiquette. I felt bad that he had got away with all he said without a word of contradiction. The matter is now in the melting pot, and we will have to wait & see what comes out of it.

We have a cover of snow today, and if you have the same it will not be very suitable for Villiers making his inspection.

Yours faithfully,
H. Miller

***

599. Mar 30th 1922
Dear Mr Meikle,
I received the enclosed award from Jack this morning, and he asked me to send it on to you.

I am a bit disappointed with Villier's findings, as these seem very one-sided. I think he has distinctly erred in items 4 & 5 of the counter claims. In No 4 he admits liability by awarding £20 which does nothing like represent the damage sustained. In

No 5 he allows nothing, although the outgoing tenant's failure to lead out the dung was a distinct breach of contract. If these two items had been dealt with on the same lines as the outgoing tenant's claim, the findings would have been nearer equity.

I suppose the only thing to do now, is to pay and look as pleasant as possible.
Yours faithfully,
H. Miller

***

600. Mar 30th 1922
Dear Jack,
I had yours of 29th inst. this morning with Villier's award enclosed, which I have now sent on to your father.

I am worst pleased of all with his award or rather findings in Nos.4 & 5 of the counter claim. In No.4 he admits liability by the outgoing tenant, but £20 does not represent the damage done. In No.5 he condones a distinct breach of contract by the outgoing tenant through his failure to lead out the dung. The matter however is a fixture now and I hope you will be able to forget about it. The only thing to do is to pay & try & look pleasant.

I am not to charge you anything as witness in this affair, but sometime if you could get hold of a small salmon, we would feast to the memory of Noel Villiers!
Yours faithfully,
H. Miller

***

Life at Drem Station

Trains are wonderful.... To travel by train is to see nature and human beings, towns and churches and rivers, in fact, to see life.
– Agatha Christie 1890–1976

The North British Railway Company (formed in 1842) opened the line from Edinburgh to Berwick in 1846. A series of landslips between Drem and Berwick resulted in horse drawn coaches being used between Dunbar, North Berwick and Dirleton, but royal assent was given for a branch line running from Drem to North Berwick and in 1849 this opened with 4 trains daily to Williamstone, slightly short of North Berwick. Passengers were conveyed to the town by horse drawn carriages. The original plan was for the terminus to be at the harbour with an embankment and a new sea wall 6 metres high in front of Forth Street, but this was rejected and the station built near the old Abbey. This opened in 1850 along with a platform at Dirleton (although the contractors were still disputing costs in 1857.). As an economy, a single line was laid to North Berwick with a single platform for both passengers and goods – manure, coal and livestock arriving and fish, potatoes, grain and guano from the Bass Rock being exported.

A horse drawn rail service using a Dandy Car (horse drawn) was used, again for economy, in the winter of 1856-57 but as 3rd Class passengers sat outside exposed to the elements this was soon abandoned. It gives the line the right to claim it is the only branch in Great Britain to have used 4 different means of power: horse, steam, diesel and electric.

The visit of the future King Edward VII in 1859 to North Berwick placed it on the map as a golfing and seaside holiday destination, and its importance was such that Drem remained a request stop for London trains for 100 years. My father, Hugh Miller's son-in-law, took advantage of this arrangement when attending meetings in London in the 1950's.

174   *A Farmer in East Lothian*

From 1868 all southbound trains were designated Up Trains (to London) and northbound were Down Trains. The branch line train to North Berwick was regarded as southbound (from Edinburgh) and therefore, an Up Train.

The branch line increased Drem's standing, and the fact of it being appointed a post town and mail no longer having to be sent to Berwick (taking 3 days), added to the station's importance. Mail was first transported by train in the 1830's and soon rail-side apparatus was introduced so that the Travelling Post Office did not have to stop for drop off and pick up. The leather pouches were robust and weighed around 20lbs when empty, then filled with 30lbs of mail. This meant it was challenging to attach a full bag to the hook which was swung out into position for the arriving train, being caught in a net attached to the carriage. An equivalent bag would be offloaded into a net on the ground. There were 245 of these mail collectors in the country in 1913, the last one being decommissioned in 1971.

Mail bag apparatus. (photo credit with thanks to The Postal Museum)

Drem Station was a stone-built single storey building with two waiting rooms on each platform. One was demolished in 1984, but British Rail was required to rebuild it in similar form being Grade B-listed. This was the station around which much of West Fortune's life revolved, from essential deliveries to transporting produce and livestock as well as personal travel. This selection of letters sketches some of the activities that must have impacted the life of the Station Master.

***

34. Dec 17th 1910
R Thomson Esq
Dear Sir,
 I am in receipt of your letter of 15th inst. It was lintseed cake you were to send, as it is now just finished. The 2 tons of Bombay should be at the station on Monday.
 I got the 8 cattle all right.
 Yours faithfully,
 H. Miller

***

46. Feb 10th 1911
West Fortune, Drem, East Lothian
Feb 10th 1911
Messrs Jas Donald & Co.
Dear Sirs,
 You might please send the following addressed to me at Drem Station, for goods train, at your earliest convenience.
 4 travellers[1] & 4 <u>strong</u> cow bindings, 2 bolts for travlrs for a trevis[2] 6" thick, also half a dozen straight cart horse bits.
 I think I got the like from you before. I want just an ordinary size. If you have not got them do not trouble about them.
 Yours faithfully,
 H. Miller

***

77. Apr 14th 1911
Messrs Vivers & Sons
Dear Sirs,
 I have seen my brother and he wants some turnip seed too. You might send to me at Drem Station 160lbs X L All and 120 lbs Gale's Champion, and I will arrange

with him what he wants. We are having some odd fine days, but more barren ones, and things are very dry, but it has suited the seedtime.
 Yours faithfully,
 H. Miller

***

425. Jan 30th 1915
Wm Jackson Esq.
Dear Sir,
 I beg to call your attention to the matter of the distribution of sacks at Drem Station.
 While appreciating the difficulty there is at the present time of supplying the public with the necessary number of sacks, it seems unfair that one person should receive practically a monopoly of them. It is within my knowledge that one man has got upwards of 1000 of N. B. Ry. Sacks this week - specially consigned to himself - and while I have had 300 on order for more than a fortnight, I have not got one.
 As this matter is very urgent I trust you will be able to give it your immediate consideration.
 Yours faithfully,
 H. Miller

***

473. Mar 8th 1917
Messrs Guttridge & Co.
Dear Sirs,
 The lost heads & plucks have never turned up, and the Ry. Co. state that they were delivered to you. I enclose their letter to Messrs Dewar & Davidson, also the latter's letter to me for your perusal, which will show the position they take up. I will be glad if you sift the matter out as far as possible.
 I hope to send you 45 sheep heads & plucks for Monday's sale. Hope you get a good trade.
 Yours faithfully,
 H. Miller

***

477. Apr 21st 1917
Messrs Guttridge & Co.
Dear Sirs,
 I have delayed writing you in the hope that I would have heard from you regarding the 80 (?) heads and plucks that went missing about Feb 5th last. On inquiry here I learn that the Ry. Co. can prove delivery to you of these goods. That information must be either right or wrong, and I will be pleased to hear what position you take up regarding it, so that I may know how to proceed regarding their recovery.
 Yours faithfully,
 H. Miller

***

487. Dec 17th 1917
Messrs Guttridge & Co.
Dear Sirs,
 I duly received your favour of 12th inst. re the missing heads and plucks. As the Ry. Co. state that they have your signature for delivery, I do not think I should stand to lose anything, but in the circumstances, I will accept of £5 in settlement of my claim.
 I trust this will meet with your approval.
 Yours faithfully,
 H. Miller

***

622. Sept. 19th 1925
Mr Edington (L.& N.E.Ry.Co.)
Dear Sir,
 I have your demand to pay 2/2 on account of my son travelling without his season ticket on a date in July last.
 The circumstances have already been fully explained, and as there was no defrauding of the Ry.Co. by the ticket being used by anyone else, I am not going to pay what I do not owe.
 There is another matter that I wish to call your attention to. A waggon of lambs railed at St Boswells on Thursday afternoon last were not delivered to me at Drem till 12 o'clock next day. I consider they are 2/- per head the worse of the long and

unnecessary confinement in the waggon. This will work out to a total of £4.16. And I will be glad to hear from you on the matter.

Yours faithfully,
Hugh Miller

***

Hugh's reasoning over the non-carrying of a season ticket by Hugh (jnr) being balanced by the non-delivery of the lambs is an unusual argument.

The Impact of the 1914-1918 War

In peace, sons bury their fathers. In war, fathers bury their sons.
  – Herodotus c.484BC–c.420BC

***

452. Apr 24th 1916
Col. Main
Dear Sir,
   Referring to our conversation on the phone today regarding the two men - Alex. Sanderson & Thomas Ingles - in my employment, I beg to remind you as requested, that in our opinion they are both unfit for military service, so that you may accordingly have them marked off the register!
   Alex Sanderson
   No. on group card 26
   No. of group 13

   Thomas Ingles
   No. on group card 116
   No. of group 1

   I am,
   Yours faithfully,
   H. Miller

***

457. July 24th 1916
C.O. Beaumont
Dear Sir,
　　Perhaps you will pardon me taking the liberty of asking if it would be agreeable to you that a service should be held in the hall at East Fortune on a Sunday evening. If so, I would be glad to arrange for the same.
　　In suggesting this I have no other object than the welfare of the men.
　　If you care I would be pleased to call on you at your convenience and talk the matter over.
　　Yours faithfully,
　　H. Miller

***

459. Aug 9th 1916
C.O. Waston
Dear Sir,
　　There is a man Frank Anderson whose address I subjoin, concerning whom I write to ask for a month's leave for the harvest. His father is in my employment, and I would consider it a great favour if you can consent to him getting off. I would not require his services for the harvest till nearly the end of August.
　　Yours faithfully,
　　H. Miller
　　Address referred to -
　　7078 Pr. F. J. Anderson
　　195th Brigade Sigl. Sec. R. E.
　　Terling Camp, Terling, Essex

***

461. Aug 29th 1916
Lt. Col. Wemyss.
Sir,
　　I herewith enclose letter from Mr Glendinning, requesting that two of his former employees, who have been called up, should be sent to him for the harvest. He omitted to mention this when he sent in his application form.

If you find it possible to send Mr Glendinning these two men, it would no doubt be a great convenience as well as a great favour to him.
Yours faithfully,
H. Miller

***

462. Sept 21st 1916
The O.C.R.E.
Dear Sir,
With reference to my communication with Lieut. Cullen regarding a supply of water for the War Department Hutments at West Fortune - I am prepared to supply water at the rate of 2/- (two shillings) per 1000 (thousand) gallons as shall be registered by a reliable meter belonging to you, the water to be pumped by an engine of twenty horse power.
Yours faithfully,
H. Miller

***

465. Nov 10th 1916
Wm Bruce Esq.
Release of Soldiers for Agrl. Work
Dear Sir,
I have your letter of 7th inst. with enclosures referring to Mr Bone's application. I do not think there is much to report after reading over his form of inquiry. He was however rather late in getting his harvest finished, which considerably delayed his potato lifting and other work.
I know of no farm around this district that is not in arrears with the season's work, and wheat sowing will in consequence be at a disadvantage.
If possible, I think you should consider this application favourably.
Yours faithfully,
H. Miller

***

472
List of Workers on West Fortune
  Males
  Wm Anderson - Grieve   Age 52
  Peter McGauchrane - Cattleman   " 65
  Jamie Duncan - Shepherd   " 43
  Charles Campbell - 1st Ploughman " 30
  John McGauchrane 2nd Ploughman " 26
  George Anderson Ploughman   " 49
  Robt. Logan Ploughman   " 21
  George Anderson (Jr.) Ploughman   " 20
  John Logan Ploughman   " 18
  Robert Steele - orra boy   " 14

  Females
  Maggie Anderson   Age 20
  Chrissie Anderson   " 16
  Mrs. Steele   " 36
  Maggie Walker   " 63
  Lizzie McGauchrane }
  Katie Anderson   } Girls of 15 years
  Mary Logan   }
  February 26th 1917 Hugh Miller

                     ***

481. June 19th 1917
Lt Col Main,
Dear Sir,
    John McGauchrane & John Logan both in my employment have received notice to attend at Haddington on Monday next, "as definite date for them undertaking military service must now be fixed".
    I herewith enclose the particulars of my male employees, and you will observe that I have one horseman less than I had at May 28th.

In any case I see there is a new order from the War Office that no more men are to be taken from farms without the consent of the Agl. Extive. Conters. I will likely see you on Friday about the matter.
Yours faithfully,
H. Miller

***

485. Nov 15th 1917
A. Butter Esq.[1]
Dear Sir,
I hereby offer for the two fields on Muirhouses that are to let, the sum of fifty pounds Stg. (£50) for one year as from Martinmas first according to the condition set forth in your letter of 9th inst.
(Signed)
Hugh Miller

***

486. Nov 21st 1917
A. Butter Esq.
Dear Sir,
Referring to our conversation on the phone this afternoon, regarding the fields at Muirhouses - if I take the one I may as well take the other - unless you wish to give one to some one else. If you care I would stand in up to £80 rather than miss them, allowing about 4 acres off for the wireless and the road - this would be equal to 53p per ac. for 30ac.
If you wish me to send you a formal offer for this amount you can please let me know.
Yours faithfully,
H. Miller

***

496. June 25th 1918
A. Butter Esq.
Dear Sir,
Referring to the stack stands which I purchased from you at Muirhouses, there were thirty altogether and three of them I think were quite useless as stands. The remainder had been in use and up till last year had been quite serviceable, but sometime last summer the pillars were all pulled from under them, and the bars

being rusted in their sockets, a good deal of damage was done by the breakage of parts.

I considered that it would be possible to erect only about two thirds of the total number - the remainder being scrap. By the time I got possession of them, there were a good many parts missing which it is impossible to replace at the present time.

I quite agree that had the stands been handed over to an incoming tenant without displacing them they would have had a different value.

Yours faithfully,
H. Miller

***

503. Aug 22nd 1918
The O.C. 3rd Scottish Co. N. C. C. East Linton
Dear Sir,

As I am in a fix for harvest labour I am wondering if you could do anything to help me out of a difficulty. I have over 300 acres of grain to harvest and could do with six practical men. If you can possibly meet me in the emergency, I would esteem it a great favour. As the matter is urgent, I would be glad to hear from you at your earliest convenience. I may say that I have had four boys sent to me from Glencorse, but am sorry they know nothing about the work, and are not like picking it up.

My farm is about four miles from your camp.

Yours faithfully,
H. Miller

***

504. Oct 9th 1918
A. Butter Esq
Dear Sir,

In reply to your letter of 2nd inst. regarding the cultivation of land on East Fortune Airship Station, I agree to continue this for Crop 1919 on the same terms & conditions as arranged for this season.

With reference to the two northmost fields on Muirhouses, I have found these fields disappointing in their return. This coupled with the fact that I am unexpectedly being charged income tax on the double rental makes this land very expensive to hold.

However, I am willing to continue to cultivate the two fields at a suitable rent, and considering that there is a considerable area deducted by the wireless station & the sand pit, I think £60 (sixty pounds) fairly represents their value.

I will be glad to hear from you at your convenience.

Yours faithfully,

H. Miller

***

509 & 510. Jan 3rd 1919

J. Lorne McLeod Esq.

Dear Sir,

With reference to The Ministry of Labour forms E. D. 405, these do not appear very suitable for a farmer's requirements, but I herewith annex the number of my employees before the war - viz. 15 men, 1 boy & 4 women & presently, 9 regular men, 3 soldiers, 1 boy, 5 regular women & 3 warworkers.

I have however at present 80 ac. more land than I had before the war.

I require all the hands I have and could well employ other two or three men if I had accommodation.

Farmers in East Lothian are in a dilemma at present regarding demobilisation. We do not know whether to expect the young men back in the spring or not. Our hiring takes place at the beginning of Feb., and we do not know how to arrange. We will naturally seek to hire our full complement of men in Feb. and there is a great probability of many of these young men not finding employment on the same farms as their parents when they return. If you can render any light to solve this problem, I am confident you will do so.

I have already applied for two young men to be demobilised but have heard nothing of my application. I attach their names and addresses and will be glad of your assistance to get them returned to the land.

Yours faithfully,

H. Miller

The two names referred to are:

No. 3225521 L/CPL George Gillan 8th Royal Scots C. Coy. No 12 Platoon B.E.F. France

No 44270 Pvt. Robert Gillan 18 Scottish Rifles Attached to 145 Coy. A.S.C. B.E.F. France

These men are both plowmen and their work awaits them whenever they come home. H.M.

***

525. Jan 3rd 1920
Dear Miss McDonald,
 I regret to learn that the work in connection with the "Land Army" is likely to be given up. As one of the first in East Lothian to cooperate with this movement, I know the boon it has been both to myself and to others, in enabling the work of the farm to be carried through in times of difficulty. These difficult times seem to be always with us - and I fondly hope that something may be done to continue in some form this most useful organisation.
 With the compliments of the season,
 Yours faithfully,
 H. Miller

***

534. Sept 4th 1920
A. Butter Esq.
Dear Sir,
 I have your communication with reference to the cultivation of Muirhouses land for which I thank you.
 I am willing to continue the occupation of all the land that I at present occupy, but with reference to the aerodrome portion, I would like to point out that continuous white cropping is not good management, and yet the expense of green cropping & cleaning is prohibitive, where it is held on such short tenure.
 The two North fields I have had under a rotation of crops.
 I may look in on Wed. and talk the matter over.
 Yours faithfully,
 H. Miller

***

554. May 20th 1921
A. Butter Esq.
Dear Sir,
 Further to our conversation on Wednesday last regarding the house known as Merryhatton near East Fortune - I notice that the house is standing vacant, and as I am in need of temporary accommodation, I would be glad to know if you would let

it to me. I think a rate of 7/6 per month would be a valuation similar to others in the district.

In the event of the Air Ministry requiring the house at any time, I guarantee there will be no difficulty in their acquiring it.

Yours faithfully,
H. Miller

***

603. June 29th 1922
The Controller, D.B.IC., Earls Court Exhibtn. London.
East Fortune Aerodrome
Dear Sir,

I am in want of some material such as will be for disposal at the above aerodrome. I am quite close at hand and have seen the following, Viz.

Item 204   Lockers 2' x 2' x18" (Total stock 147)
"   161 Trestles for bed boards - 26
"   89 Tables - folding damaged 6' x 2 ½' x 2 ½" total 19
"   90   "   tops 6' x 2 ½'   " 15
"   91   "   "   4' x 2 ½'   "   2

I could take 20 of the lockers, and the total of the other lots referred to.

My reason for writing you is that I employ a large number of seasonal workers for potato gathering, with the consequent necessity of providing accommodation for them. I understood the sale at the aerodrome was to take place earlier, and I delayed fixing up till now.

I would be glad to know if you can offer me these items, and on what terms.

Yours faithfully,
H. Miller

***

604. Aug 2nd 1922
A. Butter Esq.
Dear Sir,

As the season advances, it is desirable that I should have some idea regarding the continuation of the tenancy of the two North fields on Muirhouses. They are sown out for temporary grazing after harvest, and as the fences require a considerable expenditure, I would be glad to know if the Air Ministry could consider granting a lease of at least five years, or as an alternative, if they were willing to sell, would they entertain an offer from me, as I can hardly be expected to do permanent fencing under the present conditions.

There are also considerations regarding the future of these fields that makes it desirable there should be something of a more permanent nature in the tenure. I would be glad to have your observations on the matter.

Yours faithfully,
H. Miller

***

605. Aug 2nd 1922
A. Butter Esq.
Dear Sir,

Herewith I append a note of the manures applied to the land which I hold from the Air Ministry for this season's crop -

	Tons	cwts	
To the two North fields on Muirhouses - - - - -	4	10	
Aerodrome land - - - — - - - - - - - - - - - - - -	16	15	
A total of -	21	5	of compound grain manure.

Yours faithfully,
H. Miller

***

606. Sept 25th 1923
The Secretary B.O.A.S. East Fortune (Muirhouses)
Dear Sir,

As I understand there is a probability of small holdings being formed on the above lands, my object in writing you is to ask if you would be willing to sell me the small field of 8.163 ac. No 188 O.S. I bought my farm some time ago and have occupied the above field for six years, and my reason for asking you to sell it is on account of the difficulty of getting crops driven off my land which has a considerable hang toward the North.

The acquisition of this strip of land would enable me to get access to the road at any point on the East side of my farm.

I trust you will be able to entertain this proposal, and will be glad to hear from you thereanent[2].

Yours faithfully,
H. Miller

***

608. Feb 1st 1924
Chas. Wetherall Esq. East Fortune
Dear Sir,

I have your favour of 30th ult. accepting of my offer of £130 for the land at East Fortune, for which I thank you.

I agree to remove from the lands at 1st Nov. next with the reservation of right to enter the lands to thresh any crop which may be unthreshed at that date. I trust this is satisfactory to you.

Regarding the small field of 8.163 acres No. 188 on the O.S., I would be glad to know if you are now in a position to negotiate a sale.

Yours faithfully,
H. Miller

***

611. Oct 25th 1924
No 26573A.
Chas Wetherall Esq. East Fortune
Dear Sir,

I have your letter of 24th inst. re the grazing of the seeds on the above lands.

The fencing between Mr Scott & myself is a difficulty, but to simplify matters I have agreed with him to offer for my piece of land, less a portion of 8 or 9 acres to the south of Muirhouses old steading, and he has agreed to include this in his offer, as it will take only about half the fencing under this arrangement.

For the portion now referred to, I offer the sum of £17 Stg. (seventeen pounds) as from Oct 18th curt. till Nov. 21st next.

As it will take some time to get the fencing done, as also to procure nets, I would be obliged if you would phone me on receipt of this, whether or not my offer is acceptable.

Yours faithfully,
H. Miller

***

612. Nov 19th 1924
The Secty. B.O.A.S. East Fortune
Dear Sir,
　　Further to my conversation with Mr. P.A. McWilliam today regarding the grazing on 22 acres of the above land for next season terminating at Martinmas 1925, I hereby offer the sum of £66 (Sixty-six pounds Stg.).
　　The situation of the two fields with the road between makes it rather an awkward grazing, but having had possession of the land and as it lies more conveniently to me than to anyone else, I can see my way to work it.
　　I understand that the land will be fenced in time for stock in the spring and that water will be supplied.
　　Yours faithfully,
　　Hugh Miller

***

640. Aug 10th 1928
B.O.A.S. East Fortune
Dear Sirs,
　　Referring to your letter of 13th inst. I have now seen the representative of the Water Committee and have agreed to pay £1 per annum to them when a connection with their water pipe is made.
　　Yours faithfully,
　　Hugh Miller

***

RAF Drem and RAF East Fortune

West Fenton Aerodrome was established in 1916, later renamed Gullane Aerodrome, and in 1939, RAF Drem. Originally the Royal Flying Corps operated there, and a Training Depot Station opened. In 1939 the grass strip was resurfaced and Spitfire from Drem were involved in a defensive sortie when the Luftwaffe made a first attack on warships in the Firth of Forth that October. In 1940 the Drem Lighting System for night landings was developed locally. The station was handed over to the Admiralty in 1945 and renamed HMS Nighthawk, but decommissioned shortly afterwards. Although Luftwaffe threats were relatively limited in the area, defence was necessary and fighter or night-fighter squadrons were often based at Drem for short periods either for rest, or to train in use of new aircraft. Its motto was: 'Exit Hunc Lumen' – Light has departed from this place.

The motto of East Fortune was 'Fortune Favours the Bold', and it was designated a Royal Naval Service Station in 1916 to combat the anticipated threat of Zeppelins. Airships flew from East Fortune to carry out fleet spotting and submarine hunting. After the launch of the RAF in 1918, the Torpedo Aeroplane Training School was opened at East Fortune which was by then the largest military aerodrome in Scotland. In 1920 the airfield was closed, hangars and airfield buildings demolished, but the domestic buildings were sold for use as a Tuberculosis Sanatorium, to which my father, William Murray, went in 1928 as medical assistant initially for 6 months but extended to 3 years. Initially he stayed with his Chief, Professor Charles Cameron, in the original farmhouse, East Fortune House, which became our family home in the late 1940s when my father returned as Medical Superintendent of the hospital.

The Sanatorium was evacuated to Bangour, Broxburn during WW2, later returning to East Fortune. In 1939 the RAF reactivated the site as a satellite airfield for RAF Drem and it was later developed into a night-fighter training unit, giving newly qualified pilots, wireless operators, air-gunners and navigators specific experience in night fighting. The focus was on Beaufort, Blenheim and Mosquito aircraft. East Fortune was also an emergency diversion airfield for RAF Bomber Command. It was available for heavy aircraft returning from raids if adverse weather prevented them from landing at their base. The main runway was once again put to use in 1961 when work was being done on the runway at Turnhouse, but the site is now a part of the well-visited National Museum of Flight.

The most famous event in the early years of the Air Station at East Fortune was the launch of the R34 Airship on 2nd July 1919 on its record-breaking return journey across the Atlantic. Although Hugh made no mention of the occasion in his letters, my mother, Betty, spoke of being present at the launch, presumably with other members of the family. The massive airship was 643 feet in length – more than the height of North Berwick Law, but affectionately known as 'Tiny'. Five engines were fitted in the ship which had a capacity of almost 2 million cubic feet of hydrogen gas enabling a lift of 59 tons. The fuel capacity was 6000 gallons, and 112 lbs of mail were loaded for delivery to the US, including letters from the King and Prime Minister to the US President.

The airship was gassed up, fuelled and ready for take-off and with favourable conditions launched before the 2.00am deadline on 2nd July.

Twelve hours into the flight, the discovery of 2 stowaways was made. William Ballantyne had been on the 30 man crew, but had then been removed from the list. Determined not to miss out, he boarded surreptitiously accompanied by the crew's mascot, a tabby kitten called Whoopsie. They hid in the darkness until the smell of gas made him nauseous and they had to emerge. They could not be offloaded so William was put to work as a cook and also hand pumping petrol into the tanks. Tiny completed her record breaking flight at Long Island, New York, after 108 hours flying time and carrying fuel for about 2 more hours. In the three days spent in the States, the crew were lavishly entertained before the airship made a rapid return to the UK in 77 hours, but to Pulham in Norfolk and not to East Fortune as planned. The airship came to an ignominious end at its moorings in a severe gale in Yorkshire a short time later.

East Fortune House.

R34 Airship. (photo credit with thanks to The Airship Heritage Trust)

Mission Outreach

"Some want to live within the sound of church or chapel bell; I want to run a rescue shop within a yard of hell."
– C.T. Studd (1860-1931)

Two American gentlemen, Dwight L.Moody and Ira D.Sankey travelled to Scotland in 1874 to revitalise Christian mission. One development was the Tent Hall on Glasgow Green, hosting relief work and providing 1000 breakfasts daily in addition to Bible meetings. Developing from this, The Faith Mission, founded in 1886 by John George Govan, focussed on Christian ministry in rural areas and pilgrims, as the workers were called, conducted missions and held annual conventions in Edinburgh and Bangor. The Mission Hall in Mauchline was started to explain the Bible and serve all. Hugh Miller became involved there and continued his support after moving east. Preaching from the Bible was important to Hugh, and he established a Sunday evening service in the barn loft at West Fortune, attended by up to 40 family and workers for almost half a century.

Hugh had several good friends in the Brethren Church, including Mr Garriock, and Hugh considered joining them, but Jane had more affinity with the Faith Mission and dissuaded him. They attended Abbey Church in North Berwick, initially travelling by pony and trap, but he declined the invitation to become an elder or to speak at meetings there. He was unimpressed by the minister in Athelstaneford in the early years but latterly shared support and encouragement with Rev. Downie Thomson and his wife.

A Man in Morocco
We know that Hugh served on the Council of the Southern Morocco Mission, a Christian organisation aiming to establish a church in Morocco. In addition

to his formal role his sister, Mary, had married Cuthbert Nairn and lived in Marrakesh. One letter suggests that Hugh travelled to visit them, but it is uncertain if he accomplished his goal to travel from Gibraltar to Casablanca.

***

631. Nov 8th 1927
Messrs T. Cook & Son Ltd.
Dear Sir,
When I booked with you on Jan 25th last from London to Casablanca, I was assured that I would get a direct connection at Gibraltar by the "Bland Line". I failed to get this connection and did not use the outward portion of my ticket between Gibraltar and Casablanca.
I will be obliged therefore if you will let me have a refund of that portion of my ticket which was unused and which I herewith enclose.
Yours faithfully,
Hugh Miller

***

Cuthbert Nairn was another Ayrshire farmer and after committing his life to God as a young man left farming and travelled to Morocco as a missionary. He arrived at Mogador on 10th January 1889 accompanied by his sister Jessie. After studying Arabic they moved to Marrakesh where there were few Europeans and they witnessed various uprisings. In 1895 the Misses McArthurs from Rothesay travelled out to join them. Cuthbert travelled to the coast to escort them to Marrakesh. There is, however, a harrowing account that on reaching the River Nafis, it was in spate. The horse carrying Marie McArthur stumbled and she was drowned. Cuthbert was also thrown into the river reaching the bank downstream. The bedraggled party entered Marrakesh that night but had to return to the coast for burial as no Europeans were permitted burial within the city.

Later that year Cuthbert visited Scotland and during this time married Mary Miller. Returning to Marrakesh, he set up a dispensary and worked there demonstrating care for the physical and spiritual health of the local people. A contemporary writer notes that 'Nothing was ever a trouble to him. Not only did he carry on his medical work often beyond his strength, but his patience with the great crowds seemed inexhaustible. He would get out of bed in the middle of the night to relieve the sufferers.' The author acknowledges, 'He was greatly helped by Mrs Nairn; their home was a haven of rest for many where love was poured out wholeheartedly.'

On 9th November 1944 he was crossing the road from their home to the dispensary when he was stabbed in the back by a local man and died. The Bible verse he had read that morning was Philippians 1:29 - For it has been granted to you on behalf of Christ not only to believe in him but also to suffer for him (New International Version – Cuthbert Nairn probably read in Arabic).[1]

The family friendship continued into the next generation with sons Jim Miller and Bryce Nairn. On the left is John Hannah of Girvan Mains Farm.

The following letters are fuller and more personal giving a glimpse of the man when he was not farming.

***

20. Nov 24th 1910

Suggested conditions under which Mauchline School Board may have the use of the Mission Hall.

That the said Board pay for the use of the Hall at the rate of five shillings per week.

That they accept all responsibility concerning damage to the Hall and its furnishings, and the general conduct of the children.

That they undertake to keep the Hall clean and put seats etc into their usual arrangement as often as required.

H.M.

***

29. Dec 9th 1910

Dear Mr Richmond,

We had the notice the other day of Mr Nairn having crossed the bourne. While sorry that he had to go by the way he went, I can be glad that he has indeed got to the end of the road. Life's battle fought, life's victory won, he thus has gone within the veil. 'hid from the sight of those who follow - till the day dawn'. I suppose you will now be thinking of returning to Morocco, but I hope we may run across you before you go. In any case, I hope to be in Mauchline for the 8th & 9th of Jan and may run across you then. If you are to be this direction, however, we will be pleased to see you.

With kind remembrances to those who feel their hands empty, but sorrow not as those who have no hope.

I am yours faithfully,

H. Miller

***

73. Apr 4th 1911

Dear Minnie,

Your letter has reached me this morning with heavy tidings, and I cannot help sending you a line or two.

Your dear Mother has had a good long battle to fight - and one thing is certain, that is it was fought patiently - and now that the victory is hers, I am sure you will not grudge her the rest and the honour and the joy that was awaiting her. But oh the parting! - for your father and the rest of you I will not try to express what I feel. The land that is afar off comes very near at such a time as this, and the reality of so many of our loved ones dwelling there in the presence of the Lord, makes earth a paltry place.

The beautiful life which has just closed will continue to wield its influence, and your mother's memory is indeed a precious treasure.

Through the tears of sorrow may you all be able to trace the bow of promise "I will be with thee in trouble".

Our thoughts and our sympathy are with all who compose the sorrowing circle.
Yours affectly,
H. Miller
Jane will write you before long. H.M.

**

81 & 82. Apr 22nd 1911
Dear Mr Munsie,
   I had your interesting "newsy" letter yesterday, and was glad to hear of your visit to Mauchline and the progress of the work. I am going there tonight for the weekend, so thought I would just send you a line before I go.
   Mrs Miller and all the children except Jim were in Ayrshire this week and came home last night. She had a report that was said to have arisen or at least come from the land of the Setting Sun that the Kelvinhaugh Mission friends were going to West Fortune again this year. Well - that may be so - but you & we would have been likely to know something about it if it had been arranged.
   The fact is, I have refrained from saying "trip" as long as possible in the hope that the trail of the serpent over last year's one might in course of time be obliterated. I hope this has had its fulfilment and that things are all running smoothly with you now. I do not think I need to say that if you have any thought of coming back again, we will be very pleased to put what we have at your disposal. But Mrs. M. is due to write Miss Munsie and arrange for you coming for a few days when you will be able to tell us what the programme is to be.
   We have had very high winds for a week but not as much rain as damp even the surface.
   We will have a lot to talk about when we meet, so "I will not with ink and pen write unto thee".
   Kind regards.
   Yours faithfully,
   H. Miller

**

88. May 6th 1911
Mr Andrew Reid,
My Dear Sir,
   I was passing through Glasgow ten days ago and called at the hospital to see you, but you were asleep at the time, and as your nurse told me that you were

weaker, however much I would have liked to speak to you, I thought it would be unkind to awake you. I am sorry that your strength is so quickly going, but I trust that in the midst of your weakness, you find that the everlasting arms are underneath you. You have been called upon to go by a way of much & sore suffering, but it is well to know that having committed your sins, your self, your all to a most gracious Saviour, the night of suffering will be followed by the dawn of a bright, bright morning in the happy land that you have been accustomed to hear about all your life, where there shall be no more pain.

It is not likely that I will have the opportunity of seeing you again in this world, but I look forward to meeting you some day in the other world, in the city where the Lamb is the light. And may the Good Shepherd's rod and staff be your comfort and support in passing through the valley of the shadow of death. With your soul anchored on the blessed fact that the blood of Jesus Christ, God's Son, cleanseth us from all sin, peace, satisfaction, Heaven & Home are our possession, in reality or in prospect.

Now "Goodbye" till the day dawn and the shadows flee away.

Your old master and friend,

H. Miller

***

90. May 9th 1911

Dear Mr Munsie,

I had your three postcards yesterday - one announcing Andrew Reid's death. Of course, it did not cause surprise, and it was not desirable that his life of suffering and weakness should be prolonged. It was very graciously said of the Master, "the bruised reed shall he not break, nor quench the smoking flax", and we can rely on the Judge of all the earth doing right.

I would like to thank you for all the interest you have taken in him on my account as that of others. The Lord Himself will see to the reward. "In as much as ye have done it" etc.

I am sorry my message was too late, but till I got your P.C. last week, I did not think of him going so quickly,

I trust you are having good meetings and "signs following".

We look forward to seeing you next month when you can arrange it.

Kind regards to Miss Munsie and yourself.

Yours faithfully,

H. Miller

***

111 & 112. July 6th 1911
Dear Mr Garriock,
 I have heard from Mauchline that you intend taking a cycle run "somewhere" on the Fair Saturday which I suppose will be the 15th inst. and I write this to say how very pleased Mrs Miller & I would be, if you cared to journey eastwards, to put you up on moderate terms for the weekend.
 We have a little meeting on the farm on Sunday night that we would be glad of your help for, and if you were inclined to go over to No. Berwick on the Sunday afternoon, there is a meeting on the shore for young and old where a goodly number gathers, and where your help would be valued. I saw Robert last night, and as he has some charge of this he would like to know soon if you can arrange to come. We are within twenty miles.
 If you have a friend with you, it will be all right.
 Now I hope for the sake of auld lang syne - and other things - you will be able to come.
 Yours faithfully,
 H. Miller

***

Mr Garriock must have been an early cyclist as bicycles were not in general use until the 1920's.

***

134. Sept 5th 1911
Dear Mr Fulton (a series of 3 letters)
 If it would not be asking too much of you, would you be good enough to a purchase a portable organ for me. It is for use in connection with a little meeting we have started on the farm on Sunday nights. If you had happened to know of a second-hand one, that would have done well enough, but if not, you could go from £3 to £4 and I suppose that would cover the cost of a new one.
 Pardon me taking this liberty but I remembered that you were a Dr of music in days gone by.

143. Sept 26th 1911
If you have not yet come across any other organ than those you mentioned in your letter, please do not incur any more trouble, but send me on the better one of the two to Drem Stn.
We are still having very dry weather and vegetation of all kinds has suffered much. I am afraid that my "fortune" is where it has always been - somewhere in the great unknown dim and distant future, and I believe there is a big crowd of us trying to elbow our way thither.

152. Oct 12th 1911
I received the organ nearly a week ago, and it is pronounced very satisfactory. Allow me to thank you for your attention and trouble in the purchasing of it, and also to say that we would be delighted to see you for a weekend and give you the privilege of presiding at it and in the pulpit as well.
Yours faithfully,
H. Miller

***

157 Oct. 19th 1911
Dear Mr Geddes,
I herewith enclose £2[2] which you can put to the funds of the S.M.M.
I am glad to know that the buckle is meeting the strap, with a little bit to spare, which state of affairs is different from what we have seen.
You will be thinking of extending your boundaries if things continue so favourable.
Yours faithfully,
H. Miller

***

165. Oct 27th 1911
Dear Mr Arthur,
I had your kind letter the other morning. Glad to hear you are all well. Sorry to learn that some people's education - or otherwise the sanctification of their <u>sixth</u> sense - is such a tedious business. Of course, we are not privileged in all circumstances just to give such free utterance to our "think" for which a man cannot be put to the gallows, but it is genuine fit that the crowd is so gullible.
We will be glad to see you for the 24th of Dec and if Mrs. Arthur could come

with you, it would increase the pleasure, without I trust diminishing yours.
You might let me know if we will consider this fixed.
Trust you are all well.
Yours faithfully,
H. Miller

**

175 & 178. Nov 18th 1911
Dear Mrs Travis,

I have kept a letter of yours lying on my desk where I would see it and be reminded of my purpose to write you. I suppose however I need not waste time, ink and paper, and fill up a letter with an apology for not writing, which by the way, is a very frequent occurrence. I did not think however till I consulted my letter book that I have not written you since - I don't think I'll say it.

I had your letter of 15th June, and the summer has been and gone since then. You were asking about the drought. Well, things looked very serious about the time you wrote but on June 24th we had a regular wet day, which saved things from disaster.

The months however passed with a persistence in dry weather, and while crops have done amazingly well in the circumstances, some things have suffered a lot. We are all the better of being reminded of our dependence on Him who feeds the ravens.

Just about the time I received your letter we had started a little meeting on the farm on the Sunday evenings. I think about the 10th of June was the first one. We did not know how the invitations would be responded to, but it has on the whole been better than our expectations. There is small facility for getting a meeting place in the village - about a mile off, and absolutely no encouragement but the opposite, on the part of the E.C. minister, who is the only one in the place. Hence the reason we meet under our own vine and under our own fig tree. We may not be beyond the bounds of his displeasure, but we are at least beyond the bounds of his jurisdiction. The last few Sunday nights have been wet and stormy and the number has been small, but there are always some who need the Gospel. We sometimes have a stranger but often we are just ourselves.

We are looking forward to having Mr & Mrs Arthur at Xmas for the weekend when we hope to have his help for the Sunday night. We have just been continuing from week to week as long as the people are willing to come.

Our two eldest children are still going to North Berwick school, while Betty - the third - goes to the village near. Our wee boy is still at home.

George has got a brother for his boy at 7 yrs so the number is slowly increasing.

How are you keeping yourself and also how are all your friends? I hope you have been able to enjoy the beautiful summer, and still fit to visit your old friend Miss Thomson, who seems to be to you - and you to her - a well of water.

I wanted Jane to write you this letter, but she said I was so much better at it, which I question very much. I will have to be drawing to a close, but I annex the outline of what I was telling the folks the other Sunday night.

Kind regards, Yours sincerely,

H. Miller

I may not have room here and so will take another half sheet. Hope you will understand it. "How shall we escape"! HM

***

197 & 198. Dec 25th 1911

Dear Mrs Travis,

I duly received your last kind letter, and we were glad to know that you are keeping so well & fit. Christmas has again come round and in a few days more, the sands of another year will have run out, another year of mercies new every morning and His faithfulness every night. We are so apt to take our Father's gifts as a matter of course that we need to pull ourselves to account at times and render to Him his right. It is a great privilege to know Him, a greater privilege to serve Him, but the greatest of all to what we look forward to - that of being ever with Him in His presence whence we shall go no more out but the present is ours for service and He is worthy of the best that we can give, for our time here is but a span.

"The time for sowin' seed, it is wearin' wearin' dune,
And the time for winnin' souls will be ower vera sune.
Then let a' be active if a fruitfu' sheaf we'd bring
Tae adorn the royal table in the palace of the King."

We had Mr Arthur with us over the week-end and he took the meeting last night. Mrs A. did not come. He is one of our old tried, trusted and true friends who year by year are turning fewer. His address last night was on Matt 16:26 "What shall it profit a man etc."

Here were his points:

1) A priceless treasure - The soul.

2) A poor equivalent - The world.
3) A possible calamity - It may be lost.
4) A pointed question - What shall a man give in exchange for his soul.
He gave us a very telling address and we leave the issue with the Lord.
With our kind regards and best wishes, and the complits. of the season,
I am yours faithfully,
H. Miller

***

216 & 217. 8th Feb 1912
Dear Mr Munsie,

It seems a long time since I saw you, and I often wish we had more opportunities of exchanging notes. The last we heard of your on-goings was from Miss Munsie, and since we heard of the 'clearance' at your hall of the undesirable element I have intended writing to congratulate you on the simplicity of its accomplishment. The Devil is both wise and cunning but occasionally he misses his point through attempting too much. I have no doubt however that you will have some further attention from him again. He does not readily take a rebuff.

Well, I hope things are moving along peacefully and satisfactorily with you and that you are having signs following the preaching of the Word. I hear that Miss Thomson is going to Mauchline for a Mission again sometime this month. I hope they will have a fruitful mission. I was there for a weekend at the beginning of the year, and was also at the children's Annual Social. I heard Mr Baird preach on the Sunday and thought that he was growing in years if not in grace and wisdom.

Our own little meeting continues in the loft with more or less interest. We have an average attendance of perhaps twenty five or thirty and sometimes over forty which is quite encouraging. Mr Gordon – the minister – preached his farewell sermon on Sunday last. He has at last managed to make a change by a majority of two. He goes this week to Aberdeen. I don't know what kind of man may fill his place, but for the most part there is not much regret at his departure.

The Spring will soon come round again, and we will look forward to seeing you as before.

Kind regards to Miss Munsie.
Yours faithfully,
H. Miller

***

257 & 258. July 3rd 1912
Dear Miss Nimmo,
   I received your letter this morning, and also one from Mr McKerrow. It was with deep regret that I learned of his circumstances and the burdens that presently weigh so heavily upon him, but you have set me a heavy task when you have asked him to call on me for counsel. I feel the gravity of the situation, but at the moment, could not offer a solution of the difficulty. It would be so different to have a talk over the matter.
   I did not know that John McN. had gone to the labour colony but am glad to hear of his well-doing. To me however it is too visionary to think of him coming back and being of any use in Mauchline. He will never be safe there. And then I did think that it was premature on George's part setting up business for himself, adding to his father's responsibilities and also increasing his worries. A Job's comforter you will say! - but the facts are just as well to be laid bare. However, that is no solution of the difficulty.
   It certainly would be a great pity to sell his house and business if this can be avoided. It seems to me that it would be better first of all to sell George's business if this can be done without much loss of capital, and let him come home for a time and relieve his father, and then perhaps find a situation.
   I think I will write Mr McK. to this effect, or better still if he would just come through here for a few days change and we would talk the matter over. He might be the better of it.
   Yours faithfully,
   H. Miller

***

364. Sept 26th 1913
Dear Mr Geddes,
   If nothing prevents me, I hope to be at the meeting on Wed. evening next, and will have pleasure in accepting of Pastor & Mrs. Findlay's invitation to tea at Cranston's at 5.30.
   I trust you are all well, and that the addition of triplets to your family is not proving a burden greater than you are able to bear.
   Yours faithfully,
   H. Miller

***

381 & 382. Dec 8th 1913
Dear Mr Arthur,
I sent you a P. C. this afternoon asking if you got my letter, and now I have yours tonight. I regret very much that you cannot come, and am exceedingly sorry for the cause. You will surely now have had enough rough experience with boating in connection to the Horse Isle[3]. I am glad the result was not worse.

I trust the rest and the proper treatment will put the disorder right, and we will look forward to you coming sometime later on. Keep a weekend open when it suits you and let me know.

I always felt that an allowance should be made for colour in the report of the Glasgow Mission. Glad to hear however that it is not all "paint". That stuff is easily made up and costs some folks little.

I was looking forward to you being here to give me a Sunday. I am left very much to myself as far as the preaching is concerned and while I value the privilege, I am always glad to give place to another. There are one or two in North Berwick who come over occasionally, and afterwards I am angry at myself for having asked them. I daresay this will coincide with some of your own experiences.

We are having the most interesting meetings this winter that we have had, and with the assurance that the Lord has promised to bless His word, we have the conviction that our labour is not in vain in the Lord.

If you had any scraps that you thought might be of use to me, I would be glad to have them, but mind, I can't go, with Saul's armour.

I will be glad to hear from how you get along.
Yours faithfully,
H. Miller

***

384 & 385. Dec 17th 1913
Dear Mrs Travis,
It is a long time since I wrote you, and I have often had a guilty conscience for my sin of omission, but I need not fill half a letter with an apology for not writing, so please forgive the past.

I hardly know where to begin, but am wondering how you are keeping. I have heard of you from Bessie but not for some time now. I hope you are still "feckfu"[4] and able to get about as you did formerly.

We have had a very mild winter here so far, with no rain to speak of for two or three months. The days are now very short, and our children don't see their home in daylight as they are left in the morning before it is light and not home till after dark, at least the two oldest ones. Janie is travelling to Edinburgh this year, and Jim goes as before to North Berwick, and Betty goes to the village school near us, and only our "Benjamin" is at home through the day. He will have to trot off next year.

Our little meeting on the farm on Sunday evenings is still going on, and we are perhaps having the most encouraging meetings this winter that we have had. The desperate need of a simple, blunt Gospel is most apparent all around us. The cloak of self-righteousness is in many cases double thick and heavily lined, and with the parish church person to brush it down once a week, the wearers are wonderfully well pleased with themselves. Perhaps you will sometimes remember us at the throne of grace.

I will enclose a note of what I was telling them in the meeting last night.

If you can be bothered writing, we will be pleased to hear from you.

Jane sends her love and hopes you keep well.

Yours most sincerely,

H. Miller

***

Dear John

There is a friend that sticks closer than a brother.
– Proverbs 18:24

Hugh obviously borrowed from both John Hannah, his brother-in-law, and from Bessie, his sister, explaining his regular sending of cheques until his debt was repayed.

***

10. Oct 24th 1910
Dear John,
    I am in receipt of your letter of 21st inst and will perhaps see you some time in the near future about the two machines. We have a few days potato lifting yet, however, and the weather is not very suitable for the work. We would have almost finished had the weather not broken down. I sold the balance of the high field to McArthur at £20 - he to lift them and I have since sold the rest to the Co-op at the same price with £1 up or down but I lift them. Of course, I do not lift them from the pits. This is a bit of private information. It may be that I have made a poor deal, it may be otherwise.
    We have got the engine and pump started and doing quite satisfactorily, but the other machine has not been started yet as some of the work is not completed. I expect the engineer back some day soon to see the mill going and try what the engine can do.
    We have over 60 cattle in the courts, and it will not be long till we are quite filled up. Store cattle[1] are now easier bought.
    We had Uncle Robert and Aunt Bessie for a week. They went to Ferrygate today. They are both quite well - for them. Wynne Crosby was at Ferrygate for the weekend and was here for a little this afternoon, so they come and go.
    I trust you are all well.
    Yours affectly,
    H. Miller

***

18. Nov 22nd 1910
Dear John,
I herewith enclose Cheque for £46-13-4 in payment of interest - £37-13-4 and of potato riddle and cake breaker[2] - £9 as agreed upon. I do not suppose the ry. carr. on the cake breaker will exceed £1, and so you can send it on at your convenience. I got home on Saturday night about six o'clock and was quite cordially received. I found the friends all well that I came across in my wanderings.

I bought two geldings[3] - two-year-olds - at Ayr on Thursday. Robert is taking one of them.

We have at last got a start to the shed and if the weather would be open the mason shapes at getting through expeditiously. We're having frost these days presently it looks like holding.

Trust you all keep well.
Yours affectly,
Hugh

***

35. Jan 4th 1911
Dear John,
I expect to be at Mauchline over the weekend and also Monday night which is the annual social meeting for the young folks there. I might be in Ayr for a short time on Tuesday and if you are there, I may run across you.

We are having a turn of splendid winter weather, a touch of frost in the morning sometimes and the ploughed fields like seed-time.

We were able to let the horses hold the new year in their new quarters and I think they will be quite comfortable. The shed is practically ready for the slates but there is much 'redding up'[4] to do.

Trust you are all well and have got safely over the season's festivities so far, and with the compliments of the same,

I am yours affectly,
H. Miller

***

36. Jan 12th 1911
Dear John,
I herewith enclose my balance sheet as at Nov 28th last for your perusal. The

result is not as good as I would have liked but neither is as bad as if it had been worse.

We had a wet day yesterday, the first for several weeks and a good stiff blow from the Norwest at night, and this morning the frost is gripping.

I had about half an hour to spare in Glasgow on Tuesday and managed to call at No 17. Auntie was telling me that Aunt Marion has had a relapse and the Dr holds out little hope of her recovery.

I trust you are all well.
Yours affectly,
H. Miller

***

55 & 56. Feb 21st 1911
Dear John,

It seems a long time since I heard much of your ongoings, so I think we might have an exchange of notes.

You have had great floods in Ayrshire I see and hear. We were at Castlemains yesterday and met in with Matthew Howie & his brother from Gullane. He was saying that he they had the worst flood ever he knew of on the place. We have not had as much rain as wet the lee side of the plough furrow. Indeed, the land would now work down all the better of what it has got. The month of June, however, is usually the time we could take some of your superfluous moisture, or all of it for that matter.

I suppose that you will have a good many potatoes planted, and the conditions would be good before the storm. We have not done anything yet but if next week permits in point of weather, we will make a start. I think Robert will be half through.

Mrs Fischer is at Ferrygate, and they were all over here today. She seems quite well, and her shadow does not grow less.

I saw Mr Guild last Wed and was asking him how the "Baron" was to be apportioned this time. He said, "I am afraid that we are to lose". The decision is long of being issued. He said he saw you at the Stallion Show. I intended once to be there but could not make it convenient when the time came.

The potato market has surprised the most sanguine of wiseacres[5]. Ours are all away but the seed. The price has ruled around 52/6 for practically the whole season.

I expect John Crawford on Thursday to try and make a deal. I trust you are all well as we are here.
Yours affectly,
H. Miller

***

70 (& 71). Mar 27th 1911
Dear John,
I don't know that I have anything interesting to communicate, but if I write something I will have the chance of hearing from you.

We had a change of weather, and seeding operations were suspended for about a week, previous to the middle of last week. Since then, we have been getting on. Tomorrow will see the oats all sown. I have double sown 50 acres of Waverley[6], which has put me a little bit behind some of my smart neighbours. We will still have 70 acres of barley to sow, but if the weather is good, it will soon work in.

We had our friend Thomson today and have sent him a waggon of cattle. He will have to get them reduced now, as we have still over 80. He says that he is not to have a shirt off them this time.[7]

The black mare has gone terribly lame on the bad leg for a week or two. I don't know whether she will come safely to the foaling or not. I sent a horse to J. Crawford ten days ago, and had a letter from him that he arrived hardly able to walk - like a founder. He thought it might be from his stomach and was to let me know how he got on. I have not heard from him since.

Potatoes are going now and look like paying the holders.

I see Auchenbrain has crossed the bourne. He will be missed in his circle.

I trust you are all well. Janie has been off school for a week, having got cold in one of her eyes. She is getting all right now.

We had Uncle Robert for 10 days doing some small jobs in the house.
Yours affectly,
H. Miller

***

96 (&97). May 25th 1911
Dear John,
I herewith enclose cheque for £30 in payment of interest for the past half year.

We are having very drouthy weather for the past few days, and everybody is agreed that a good wet day would be welcome. The turnip braird was secured where sown before the last rain that we had, but the young plants have had a rather trying time for these few days. Potatoes have been growing fairly well, but I hear that you cannot read the drills in the Girvan district, which is a long way in advance of anything here.

The black mare had quite a nice colt foal yesterday morning and I hope it may do well.

"Sam Black" is now very nearly all right I believe, and will likely be able for a full season's work. Guild says he has his suspicion that the hurt was wilfully inflicted by someone who came a good long way to do it, but I have no idea of anything further than that. The whole thing is a conundrum. This young horse is travelling in the county here.

I am expecting him (Mr G.) some day to look round the place. He has not been here since the beginning of Nov. and of course has not yet seen all his property.

I was asking him on the rent day if he would make the structural alteration in the barn if I was to put in a mill. He did not however say yes or no.

Monday will see a good many flittings on the road, and so we will have some new brooms for a time.

I trust you are all well.

Yours affectly,

H. Miller

***

102 (&103). June 9th 1911
Dear John,

I had your letter of the 3rd inst. with all your news. I had heard from the "Co." people that you were starting a motor car. My worst fear is that you will now not go out and in among your poor friends as before. However, I will keep in view getting a run in it sometime, but my chance of this would be improved if you take a run through here and stay for a day or two.

We have had no measurable quantity of rain yet. Last night there was a slight shower that laid the dust, but no more. Things are suffering in many cases and the weak spots are showing all over. Small turnips are having a hard time. Anything that has caught the ground well down is not so bad. We will be more than half singled this week, but I do not know when the last of the other half may be at that stage.

Potatoes are holding their own but not making much progress - that is early ones, but late ones are growing well. I see Jackson has started at Strand.

I am wondering if you know of a pony that would suit me even if it were temporarily. I had the misfortune the night before last of a fall and one knee is fairly badly broken. It was my first experience of the kind, but neither Jane nor I was out of our seat. Of course, the pony was on its knees and did not come down altogether. If you hear of anything that would be like suitable you might let me know.

The bottom has now gone out of the fat cattle trade, and the end is worse than the beginning. We have a waggon left still, but will be clearing out on Monday.

Trust you are all well.

Yours affectly,

H. Miller

***

108 & 109. June 29th 1911

Dear John,

I had your letter of 26th inst. Also, the photograph per same post, for which accept thanks.

We have had a good wetting now and things are improved. Last Saturday was one of the wettest days I have seen since coming here. There was a high wind also which left its mark, but things are wonderfully straightened up again.

I sold about 18 acres of Epicures to Campbell before the rain came and I believe I was wrong, but it can't be helped now. I expect to get £20 for them. There was a hard bit in the field that had suffered considerably with the drouth, and but for this they would have been more. They are growing well since the rain came. The Co. started digging at Ferrygate fully a week ago.

The late crop is looking well. We are getting through with hay cutting, having about 80 acres in the coil. We have still 15 acres to cut. The crop is variable, some fields very light, and others surprisingly heavy.

I got a pony shortly after writing to you last but it is very ill with cold this week and is taking a lot of nursing.

I suppose you will be in full work with potato digging, at least the supply can hardly cope with the demand in this district.

Saturday is the Show at Haddington, and this means a general holiday again this week.

I trust you all keep well.

Yours affectly,

H. Miller

***

114 & 115. July 10th 1911
Dear John,
 We have again had a spell of very hot weather, and things in general could do with a wetting. We had a slight shower last night, but it came to no quantity of rain. Crop prospects, however, are very different from what they were three weeks ago. Straw crop has stretched amazingly, and while there may be a shortage, it will not be nearly as serious by any means as it once looked. The hay crop although under average, has not been making a high price at the sales - £3.2/- to £3.5/- out of the small rick.

 Late potatoes in general are very good, and I don't think in this crop we are below the average. I expect the diggers this next week. I think they will finish at Ferrygate in a day or two. The trade has been not very good for a week, but the merchants are quite optimistic about it. I hope their optimism will become a reality.

 I had Guild here last Saturday, and managed to get some things arranged but he can talk a long while without getting to the point if he so wills it. He has practically agreed to the alterations in the barn, if I decide to put in a mill. I am thinking of having this done, but it should have been in hand a month ago. If the weather continues as hot as we have had it, there will be harvest in July in some fields quite close to us.

 It is a long time since you were here. Could you not take a motor run for a day or two and bring Phemie with you? We would be glad if you could do this. Bertie has been here since the beginning of the week.

 I trust you are all well.
 Yours affectly,
 H. Miller

***

210 & 211. Jan 25th 1912
Dear John,
 I did not take W Todd's pony as the other one has been sent here as a life-renter. It is needing some rest however before it is asked to do much.

 We are having very changeable weather, from touches of frost to hail and snow showers, reverting back to rain with dry intervals.

 We have at last got our road rolled, and for the time being the surface is much improved. It was done today, and the weather conditions do not demand the use of the water cart.

This is our hiring time and there is considerable dissatisfaction on the part of the men at the prospect of being required to pay 4d per wk. It is evident there will be a good lot of ill feeling between employer and employed when it comes to the tax-collecting.

The Co-Op has not touched the potatoes yet. I suppose they will be waiting for a big profit.

I trust that you are all well.

Yours affectly,

Hugh

***

224 & 225. Mar 21st 1912

Dear John,

I duly received your letter of 12th inst. and thanks for the information regarding the turnips.

You seem to have made slow progress with planting and you will not now have a very early finish. The succeeding weather however has much to do with results. We have not had much rain since "the flood" that morning you were here. There have been showers but nothing to wet the land seriously. We have been sowing oats and barley and have the big half of the potatoes planted. If the weather is favourable now, we will have an early finish to the seedtime.

The Co-Op started to turn over the potatoes this week. They are taking very few away, so they seem to have hope of the trade yet. The strike however will upset all calculations if it drags on from week to week.

We will soon all be kept in motion by Act of Parliament, however. At present it means a day of twelve hours to go to Edinburgh, so it is a consideration to go from home.

I trust you are all well. I suppose Phemie will be home again.

Yours affectly,

H. Miller

***

240 & 241. May 22nd 1912

Dear John,

I herewith enclose cheque of £30 in payment of interest due for the past half year. I am sorry that it is not for the capital, but we live in hope.

We have had fine growing weather with nice showers occasionally for a week past. The turnip braird is practically secured and other things in general are looking well.

I hear that potatoes are far forward with you and that a very early start is expected to be made with digging. The portion of the old crop that is left, will more or less cripple the trade. There are a good many on hand in this county still.

Tuesday will bring about the annual "jaunt" of the agricultural community here.

We have a good few changes, and I almost begin to cease hoping that the future will be any better than the past. In some directions the men here are past reformation. A total exodus and then an importation of blacks might be a solution of the problem but that would be too drastic for Lloyd George.

I trust that you are all well. There are cases of scarlet fever here and there in the parish and we will be quite pleased if it does not call at our door.

Yours affectly,
H. Miller

***

266 & 267. July 16th 1912
Dear John,

I had yours of the 5th inst. in due course. I went to Cupar on Wednesday and saw what was to be seen and heard what was to be heard regarding the Insurance Act. I do not know how the country will struggle out of the muddle that it has been thrust into. Instead of being passive resisters I think we should all be active resisters regarding some of the unreasonable things that are asked of us. If it 'must be' it must be, but never with good grace.

We are lifting potatoes and we expect to be finished this week. It took me a struggle to make £20 for them, but I expect there will be a fair margin for the Co. considering the market they are having. We have a very good cover of late potatoes, but this is not the case everywhere.

We are in the midst of ricking hay but there is a thick "haar"[8] today, which has stopped the work.

Mary and her children are here, so we have a "snod"[9] little family about us when they are all gathered together.

Trust you are all well,
Yours affectly,
H. Miller

***

289 & 290. Sept 20th 1912
Dear John,
   I had your letter yesterday with Willie Todd's enclosed. I feel very sorry for him. The prospect of the enjoyment of health is certainly far from bright.
   As to feeding his cast ewes, I think it would be a mistake to force them on in the meantime, unless of course he has to be quit of them in a given time. February and March or around that time is considered the best time to sell ewes, at least so say Middlemas and my neighbour Laird Thomson, so if he starts to feed them now, he will have a long keep on them till that time. He might be better to hold his hand for two months yet before giving them much hand feed. It is usually Bombay cotton cake and Pea Bran that Middlemas uses here for all his sheep, but the cotton cake has gone to a big price.
   We are having very fine weather, and hope that there will be more to follow.
   We will have another full day's leading tomorrow and it will take us tight to finish.
   We have a good fair bulk - but not a stack to the acre. East Lothian will have to be content to follow Ayrshire afar off. Good samples of barley are making 37/- & 38/- per qr. So if prices hold there will be a chance that this crop will pay its way.
   We had Phemie's letter this morning. Sorry to hear about Maggie Craig. You will have heard that Uncle John of Holmes is very ill too. We will be very pleased to see Phemie when she can come.
   Trust you are all well,
   Yours affectly,
   H. Miller

***

302 & 303. Oct 23rd 1912
Dear John,
   If nothing prevents me, I expect to be at the horse sale at Ayr next Thursday, and if it is convenient for you, I would go to you in the afternoon. I will try to be on my best behaviour seeing you are now in some degree a representative of the law. I noticed your name in the honoured list the other day.
   We have still four or five days digging of potatoes which I could fain run away from.

The weather is fairly broken and the land a "plouter"[10].
Trust you are all well.
Yours affectly,
H. Miller

***

316 & 317. Nov 26th 1912
Dear John,
I herewith enclose cheque for £26.10/- in payment of interest now due. I have deducted £3.10/- which I am charged by the income tax authorities.

I have not heard of a customer for the two-year old, but I do not think your one will need to go a-begging.

We are having fine weather - a little blowy but the land is dry, and conditions are very favourable for wheat sowing. Indeed, the land is whitening on the top these days behind the harrows.

The Co-Op people have started to lift the potatoes and intend going on through them. The market is not coming away as was expected. Today's price is around £3.

You may have heard that Burns has got Hatton Mains, so the potato merchants are forging ahead. David Bow of Dunbar has bought Abbey Mains for £17,000. The rent is £850 but it would make £1000 if put on the market, I think, today.

I trust you are all well.
Yours affectly,
H. Miller

***

348 & 349. June 4th 1913
Dear John,
I had intended for some time to write you asking for your welfare, but time slipped past, and this was not accomplished, and now you have forestalled me with your letter of 31st May.

The season is a little later here than it was last year, but the country is generally looking well. There has been no lack of moisture, but personally speaking, there has been none too much.

We finished turnip sowing nearly three weeks ago, and we are now ready to begin singling. There will still be a good few to come in places.

Your Italian is costing you 6' per bushel less than it cost us here for our sow-out. As for barley I do not think I could give you much information regarding a catch crop. I would think however, that our standard kinds here would be too late to get a crop that would thresh. If you were thinking of trying some foreign, I have a bag or two of Goldthorpe[11] left that you could have to try alongside.

We had a few changes at the term, but I do not hear of so much agitation amongst servants as there was a month or two ago. Farmers themselves are inclined to discuss this <u>coming</u> half-holiday or at least some modified form of it. We are truly living at a great pace, and we are not at top speed yet.

I was thinking of being through at the conference of the S Chamber on the 20th of June if nothing prevents me. Would you not manage to give us a look up before that? You will soon have forgotten the way.

I have been in the house and in bed part of two days with a sore throat, which is a little better tonight. Betty & Hugh have had whooping-cough for a week or two. Betty is over the worst, but Hugh takes bad turns yet. He will soon be through the worst too, however.

Our neighbour Mr Lee died on Sunday morning last, and was buried today in Newcastle. This will doubtless make changes at Congalton.

Sorry to hear your gardener has got beyond the bounds of hope.

I trust you all keep well and that the whooping-cough will long stay far from your door.

Yours affectly,
H. Miller

***

357 & 358. Aug 28th 1913
Dear John,

I see from the Herald, under "Ayrshire Coast Notes", that the drought of 1913 has now broken up. This may be the case as far as the Ayrshire coast is concerned but it is certainly not yet taken place here. We had a shower last Thursday night, that looked like the beginning of a break in the weather, but since that the clouds have rolled away, and there is at present no appearance of rain.

We finished cutting on Tuesday night last and have begun to stack. Barley and wheat have cut up perhaps beyond expectations but oats as was foreseen are very poor. There was a sale of barley made yesterday in Edinburgh market at 34/-, so the trade for it looks all right to begin with.

I think late potatoes around here will be the smallest crops seen for a long time, and the same can be said of turnips, which in many cases look as if they will have to be used more as medicine than food. In the midst of it all however, we have much to be thankful for.

Jane & the children except Janie have been at Stewarton for about a week. We are hoping to see them home on Saturday. I suppose you will be gathering your wanderers home sometime soon now too. We had Uncle Robert & Aunt Bessie for ten days, and the latter seemed the better of the change. They both move very slowly now.

I never heard another word from Guild about Wm Kerr's son. I don't know what arrangement he made.

I trust you all keep well.
Yours faithfully,
H. Miller

***

361. Sept 13th 1913
Dear John,

I had your letter of yesterday, this morning, and later in the day I got the box of tomatoes and grapes for which accept our thanks.

We will be pleased to see you next week, and I will no doubt do my best to keep you right among the shorthorns. Of course, we will expect you to stay Thursday night as well.

The weather broke down yesterday morning and has been as unlike harvesting as you want it. This has been a soaking day. We have still 50 acres of barley out, and it will take some drying after today.

I trust you are all well.
Yours affectly,
H. Miller

***

366. Sept 29th 1913
Dear John,

In the Scotsman of Saturday, Congalton is advertised to let with entry at Martinmas 1913, so if there are still some Ayrshire men on the hunt for a farm, it would be quite a desirable place, I would say much more so than Markle. It is returned in the year book at about £500, and is 300 acres in extent. We got our harvest finished last Thursday, and both before & since we have had very poor harvest weather - such as you could carry a candle about outside

Mr Simpson got a sudden call. He went to bed on Friday after Congalton sale, and on Sunday morning became unconscious, and died on Wed night.
(Unsigned)

***

369 & 370. Nov 12th 1913
Dear John,
I herewith enclose cheque for £26.10/- in payment of interest due at this time, being £30 less £3.10/- of income tax. I am sorry I cannot conveniently reduce the capital at present, but I live in hope of doing so.

I saw my friend Guild yesterday, as it was rent day. He gave me a lot of information with a few extra adjectives added. It is quite true he has lost the factorship and he had to pay his own rent to the new factors yesterday. It so happens however that he remains factor for West Fortune only, this place being left to Lady Mary and he being one of the trustees. The young man seems to be like many more - in desperation for money, and he blames Guild for certain terms of his father's will, passing everything that he possibly could to Lady M.

There are many changes taking place at Luffness. Luffness Mains, the home farm is to be let at once, so that will be another sudden in going. There is some fair good land on it, but much of is very stiff[12], and it is very badly overrun with game, which in conjunction with the woods is a menace to cropping.

David Bone has now taken possession at Markle, and he will not require to go begging for a job for some time to come. I would much rather tackle West Fortune over again.

By the way, is Phemie not going to get that jaunt carried out? We have been expecting to hear of her coming.

I hope to send the potatoes tomorrow, and if they do not suit you, you can gift them.

I trust you are all well.
Yours affectly,
H. Miller

***

395 & 396. Feb 20th 1914
Dear John,
I am sending you some iris bulbs, but am not quite sure of the pretty one that you wanted. There are two kinds growing in the clump so I will put in some of both,

and you will be sure to have the right one.

The weather keeps favourable for being on the land. We are planting a few Golden Wonders today & tomorrow and mean to plant Epicures next week. I suppose you have had some mixed weather which would interfere with your planting operations.

I was sorry to hear from Phemie the other day that your arm is still troubling you. I hope you will get it put right before you leave for America.

I had Purdie Sommerville round last week. I sold him the colt at £140. I wanted more but was unwilling to let go the bird in the hand. He is to remain with me till the Spring. You will know that Sommerville has sold Scotland Yet to the Aberdeen people.

What are the faults of Scotland's Victor? I only had a broadside look at him that day at the show. James Weir says he is the best horse ever was at Sandilands.

I don't expect to have a foal of any kind this year. I could have done fine with a full brother of the last one.

Trust you are all well.

Yours faithfully,

H. Miller

***

400. Mar 17th 1914

Dear John,

I suppose if your former arrangements still hold you will be thinking of getting your bag packed to cross the water.

I hope you have had a turn of better weather and that your planting is now well advanced. We have had rather broken weather for ten days and plowing being about finished we have been getting little done on the land, and even now only the very driest is in anything like condition.

I do hope your arm is better now, and that the others are all well, and that you will have a safe and prosperous voyage.

Yours affectly,

H. Miller

***

John Hannah appears on the passenger list (carrying over1000) of the *Lusitania*, on her trans-Atlantic trip from Liverpool to New York in 1914. The *Lusitania* held the Blue Riband for the fastest Atlantic crossing in 1908 and was briefly the largest passenger ship in the world until the *Mauretania* was built a few months later. The *Lusitania* was sunk by a German torpedo boat off the coast of Ireland in 1915, killing over 1000 passengers and crew.

***

415 & 416. Oct 16th 1914
Dear John,
 I received the horses all right on Tuesday afternoon. I think they might have been here in the morning, but they were evidently delayed. The four year old horse will be the dearest of the bargain, at least he looks like that at present. I took the brown colt that Robert bought, as he thought he could do well enough without him.
 I have not arranged with Middlemass for the cattle turnips. He seemed to want out of them this year, or to make his own terms. I am communicating with Thomson, and he would take them, but will want his own terms too.
 If I don't arrange with him, I was thinking of trying them myself on credit with Swans. Do you think I should?
 Turnips are scarce and I want to tramp course as much straw as possible, and by supplementing the turnips with cut hay I think this could be managed.
 We had a little rain last Monday night which laid the dust in the potato field, but that was about the extent of it.
 I enclose cheque for £138 in payment of the horses, which I think is correct.
 Yours affectly,
 H.Miller

***

417 & 418. Oct 21st 1914
Dear John,
 I had your letter of 18th inst. yesterday, and I thank you for your offer to accommodate me regarding the cattle. I feel however more than sufficiently indebted to you already, and am reluctant to accept of your kindness. In any case I do not expect that I would have the cattle realised in March, and inconvenience would probably arise thereby. Swan would charge 5%.
 I expected Thomson yesterday or today to see the turnips, but he wrote me saying he had taken another lot, and would not take any more at present. I have an idea he wanted to be coaxed. Middlemass kept me hanging on till he thought I would lay them at his feet, and I had in the meantime arranged about the sheep turnips. Of course, the combination that has the sheep turnips is not exactly the

same as that which had the cattle ones. As far as I can see, I am now pretty well shut up to putting the cattle in myself.

It just occurred to me that if you would be in Edinburgh any day soon you might come out for a night, or if that is not convenient, I would try to meet you, and talk the matter over.

I trust you are all well.
Yours affectly,
H. Miller

***

439 & 440. Sept 24th 1915
Dear John,
I have received yours of 23rd inst. with cheque enclosed for £1000, for which accept of my thanks. I enclose receipt for the same which I hope you will find in order - if not - I will correct it, but I think these are much the same as the terms were last year.

The new income tax will impose a burden which should be shouldered without complaint. We may well pay in money when so many are paying in blood.

We have just finished harvest today except an odd few acres. The weather has been very slow this week.

There is quite a little excitement in the district here, over a new aeroplane station which is being formed on East Fortune. Fully a week ago some officers arrived and took possession without saying they wanted it. They have taken 500 acres, and already we are being treated to daily displays of one or two machines. They say a branch railway is to be run into the ground, and extensive shedding to be erected.

This will be a new target for the Zeppelins when the Germans are able to locate it.

I am sorry Phemie is not gaining strength more quickly, but trust she will continue in the right direction. I might be through at Ayr colt show on the 8th of Oct. and if so, I would be pleased to look you up if quite convenient for you.

Yours affectly,
H. Miller

***

449 & 450. Feb 22nd 1916
Dear John,
I got home last week all right, and got the pictures safely conveyed as well. We

have now got them hung up, and the large one recalls many tender memories. We both thank you for parting with it, and while we do not need the picture to remind us of Phemie, yet to look on it brings very vividly to our minds the dear life that has gone, and particularly her last visit here when she spoke about the pictures. We often speak of the happy time we had then, and I have no doubt that "Within the veil we'll clearly see, That all on earth had need to be, To bring us safely home"

May the Lord Himself make His grace to abound to you and yours.

We are having cold blustery weather, with occasional showers of small hail. The land however is drying now and should soon be fit for working. Indeed, I think Ferrygate will have made a start.

The Jersey cow calved yesterday - a bull calf - and a very weakly one. I do not suppose you wanted it unless it was a heifer.

J. Thomson is getting some sheep next week at 1/- per ? They had a very bad time for two or three weeks, but are doing a little better now that the land is drying.

I trust you all keep well.

Yours affectly,

H. Miller

***

454 & 455. May 12th 1916
Dear John,

I herewith enclose cheque for £1030.13/- in repayment of loan of £1000, £30 interest due at this term, and 13/- which I think should pay the commission. They charged me 12/6 on the last draft for £1000 which I sent you, and the charge was the same when I cashed the last cheque you sent me for £1000. I used to think the commission was less on a draft than on a cheque, but I have evidently been mistaken.

I trust you will find this in order.

The land is drying up a little yesterday & today, but this afternoon broke down again, & tonight looks as if it could rain without much effort. We will soon have had a year of wetter weather than the west.

We will look forward to seeing you and Elma on the 27th. Would you not bring some of the boys with you? We would like if you could, and it would be a nice day's outing for them. We will expect you as early as you can come, but Jane says we will make dinner-time to suit.

I will send the horse by the 7.30 train on Monday morning. Thanks for the use of him and I hope he will not be the worse of his change of air.
I trust you all keep well.
Yours faithfully,
H. Miller

***

479 & 480. May 11th 1917
Dear John,
I herewith enclose cheque for £510.6.9 in payment of loan of £500.
Bertie thinks he will be sent to France before long.
They are still planting potatoes at Kinnears and I have no turnips sown.
We got the turnips almost finished yesterday except a few endrigs[13], and we have had as much rain as braird the new ? them, and it is still inclining to rain today.
Campbell was saying to me on Wed that he would buy my potatoes next Wed. I bantered him that I did not think he would be able to buy them. Should they be worth £50? I don't think he will give me this as he will have bought Ferrygate at easier terms, I think.
We were sorry to learn from Bessie that Miss Young has had a relapse. She does not look like getting quickly over her illness.
I trust the children are all keeping well.
Yours affectly,
H. Miller

***

497 & 498. July 1st 1918
Dear John,
I am sending you herewith for your observations my balance sheet of my cattle transactions for the past season. An ounce of fact is worth a ton of theory, and I think some folks would be all the better of knowing some of the facts concerning cattle feeding, and what controlled prices mean. I have allowed nothing for the dung, but have charged nothing for the straw, which may not please everybody, but as a commercial transaction I think it is about fair. The hay is both underestimated in quantity and undervalued. The quantity would easily be ten tons more and the price I got from the govt. amounted to £6 .2 .6. Turnips and mangolds would have been worth more than double the estimated cost of production, but I have allowed £2.6/- to go against any residual value of the manures used in growing these crops.

I was thinking if I could get another half dozen men to make up a similar balance sheet, and let these be published, it would ventilate an injustice that is already making itself felt in a decrease of production of food.

If you have any alterations to suggest I will be pleased if you will do so, as I want to be quite fair on both sides.

I quite forgot on Saturday evening before hanging up the phone to ask if you have fixed up with Miss Goer.

We are still having it very dry and strong winds are sore on everything.

I trust you are all well.

Yours faithfully,

H. Miller

***

522, 523 & 524. Nov 29th 1919

Dear John,

I have your letter of 27th inst. and note what you say regarding the fence between Drem[14] and Mungoswells. I think you should delay the fencing at least till there is an opportunity of meeting McDowall on the ground, as he suggests in his letter. Even although the Whitehill man has the Western portion for this year, you might be able to make terms with McDowall for his portion of it and then a temporary fence would serve the purpose for the coming grazing season. It will not likely strike McDowall that you would be willing to purchase his bit unless this fact is made known to him. I happened to see David Brown at the station this morning and he was speaking about the grazing. He says there is a good spring on the Drem portion - at present just a bog that he had to fence round when he had his horses in it before. A little work would make a good watering place of it, and if the.......?...... .McDowall's bit would be left without water. Everything considered I am convinced that a single ownership of that piece of land would be best.

However, if your mind is made up to have it divided, I would like if you would allow me to do anything I can in the way of supervising the erection of the fence - or anything else - in recognition of your kindness to me from time to time. There is only one local fencing contractor that I know of, and he can make quite a good job. In the meantime, I could ask him what fence such as you mention would cost per yd. For horses however I think it should have a barbed wire on the top in any case.

Then regarding the grazing, I hardly see that you can go past Brown & give it to Robert. Brown took an early opportunity of speaking about it, and I think your tenant has the best right to it. Brown will be disappointed if you put it past him.

I have had a good laugh over Campbell's letter. He has everything cut & dry, and almost suggests that he might be willing to let you the shooting on Drem, when he gets it in order. He certainly thinks he is in, & I am afraid you will require all the diplomacy you can muster if you want him out.

Janie thanks you for your kind invitation but she does not feel like going from home just now. Her face - I am glad to say - is some better but is a good bit from being right yet. I trust that a little time will put it right.

If you are to be at the Fat Stock Show, or the S.C. Conference next week we will be pleased to see you.

It is quite current in the public that Bertie has got Seggarsdean. I suppose Guild said so to someone on Wed., but as far as I know there is nothing official yet.

The weather is the chief lament at present. If we had a long drought, we are now having the rain

…………Ending illegible………

***

532. July 31st 1920
Dear John,

Your letter of 29th inst. was awaiting me on coming home last night from the S.C. trip, and I think I can give you a little information regarding the house in question. Drem people have had this house for at least twenty years, being included in their cottages. It happens to be in the block that Baillie the joiner bought when the property was sold. Drem people have it let at present to Mrs Hardy, and it seems that Baillie is trying to get the rent when he can. It seems to me that the responsible party is the seller, as he could not terminate the right of occupancy by your tenant during the currency of the lease. If he has any recourse at all, it surely must be to the Marquis of Linlithgow. I know Baillie very well and could talk the matter over with him if you wish.

We had quite a good time at the trip - also some evidence of the need of Prohibition.

Yours affectly,
H. Miller

***

Family Correspondence

Children of the same family, the same blood, with the same first associations and habits have some means of enjoyment in their power, which no subsequent connections can supply.
– Jane Austen (1775-1817)

Bessie
Bessie was Hugh's sister. She appears to have given him a financial loan and he paid interest twice yearly.

***

17. Nov 14th 1910
Dear Bessie,
　When writing some letters the other day you were on my mental list, but I have discovered that I did not put my intention into execution. I have been trying for some time to get a run westward but have not been able to get away. If nothing comes in my way this week, I am looking forward to see you all. Or the most of you. I will not be able to stay a night, much as I would have liked to, but if convenient I will take tea with you on Thursday afternoon and go up to Mauchline with the evening train. I am going to ask my dinner from George that day but if I do not get it, I may have a chance with you.
　Trust you are all well.
　I enclose cheque for £10 in payment for interest for half year.
　Yours affectly
　Hugh
　I expect to spend Wed night at Girvan. HM

***

308. Nov 8th 1912
Dear Bessie,
　I enclose cheque for £10 in payment of interest due at this term. I trust you will

be able to pay 20/- a pound and have something over.

Jane is at Stewarton tonight seeing her mother. They think she is keeping some better. Jane is coming back tomorrow.

We were at Ferrygate for a short time yesterday and saw Bertie. He does not look any the worse of his photographic experience. I was going to have said to you before I left, that we had ours taken on the quiet. You will see them by and bye.

I posted a letter to Auntie yesterday, but I don't know whether I've made "a kirk or a mill o't"[1]. Please let that little bit of information bide on the paper.

I trust you are all well.

Yours affectly,

Hugh

***

314 & 315. Nov 16th 1912

Dear Bessie,

I had your letter this morning, and you would have mine. I only wondered if you had got the cheque.

Well, you ask about Auntie, and thereby hangs a tale. You have had your finger in the pie, and you may as well know it all. It would be better however in some respects if you did not know it all, I mean for your own sake. I hope however you will not allow the matter to affect you unduly. I enclose a copy of my two letters, and also Auntie's letter in reply to my first one, for your own perusal and return. I want you to be frank enough to tell me what you think of my first letter, and if I well deserve all that I got in Auntie's reply. If I have gone about the matter clumsily, one thing is certain, I was making for the "end in view", which I am sorry I have sadly missed.

Read my first letter well before you read Auntie's one, and then read my second when you have read hers.

I have no doubt but you will have food for thought for at least one day when you get through these enclosures.

Trust you are all well.

Yours affectly,

Hugh

***

318 & 319. Nov 25th 1912

Dear Bessie,

I duly received your letter with the sorry enclosures and meant to write you before this but have not got it done.

I have not said, and have no intention of saying what I have felt since I received Auntie's letter. As for my manner of signing myself - as far as I can remember, I have signed myself in no other way to any Uncle or Aunt that I have written to. You say that "a welcome awaits me at No 17" I should make a point of calling at an early date. Well, I do not feel like doing this at present. My effort toward a reconciliation has been so decidedly spurned and thrown back in my face, that I will think twice before I try again. And beside this, the veneer of piety has almost given me the jaundice.

Auntie pleads innocence and ignorance of any misunderstanding, and as long as she does this in face of the fact she spoke to both Mary and you about it "in the good while ago", she is simply impossible.

I am sorry if other friendships will be in danger of being affected, but hope that these fears may not be realised. I trust too that you will try to forget as much of this as you can, and not bear about an unnecessary burden of vexation of spirit.

Please destroy this when you have read it, and you will perhaps forget about it the sooner.

Trust that you are all well.

Yours affectly,

Hugh

***

This misunderstanding appears to have been with Aunt Janet of the Holmes and refers to the following letters, but did not result in the desired reconciliation.

***

306 & 307. Nov 6th 1912

Dear Auntie,

I feel there has been a long silence between us, and if the spell is to be broken some one must take the initiative. I have neither intention nor desire to drag anything unpleasant out of the past, but I regret exceedingly that anything should have come into existence to mar our friendship.

I have little doubt that needless gossip, bearing abundant fruit each time it was told is largely accountable for misunderstandings that have grown into heart burnings. Now as far as I am concerned, I would be glad to see all the "little foxes" destroyed, that the vine of our friendship may flourish as before, and that all that has caused annoyance on either side will be forgotten. What I say for myself, I say for Jane as well.

I have taken upon myself the responsibility of writing you thus, in the hope that you will receive it in the spirit in which it is written. If so, the end I hope for, will be accomplished.

I trust both you and Uncle John keep well.
Kind regards,
Yours affectly,
Hugh Miller

***

312. Nov 12th 1912
Dear Auntie,

I have received your letter of yesterday, and will refrain from making any comment thereon, lest I should be further misunderstood. I only wish to say however that I had nothing but the best intention & hope in writing as I did, and am exceedingly sorry that the purpose I had in view has so miserably failed.

Yours affectly,
H. Miller

***

410 & 411. Aug 12th 1914
Dear Bessie,

I have been wondering how things are progressing as far as Jim is concerned. I know you will be having an anxious time, but I trust and pray that you will in the special circumstances have all the needed grace and strength. I was just thinking the other day that Jim is the first soldier of the Miller connection as far as I know, but before this present strife is finished it is difficult to say how many more of us may be added to that list.

"For Romans in Rome's trials, Spares neither land nor gold, Nor son nor wife, nor limb nor life, In the brave days of old."[2]

For myself I will be quite willing whenever the need arises to take my place in the defence of our dearly loved land.

There is evidently nothing being left to chance in this defence. They are digging trenches on a neighbouring farm to us, and I believe are going to mount machine guns that will sweep the whole of this valley if this extremity should arise.

When you can see your way to come, we will be glad to see you. You will be just as well in one place as another as far as Jim is concerned.

We are busy with harvest work, and the weather is good.

Tell George that none of our horses have been commandeered, although we had a visit of the officers on Saturday.

We will be glad to hear from you when convenient.

Jane is at Stewarton for a day or two this week, but I don't know whether she would get to see you or not.

Yours affectly,
Hugh

***

Uncles

***

75. Apr 12th 1911
Dear Uncle[3],

I feel I am under a double obligation to you as I have had two letters from you, so I will send a line tonight although it should be short. We were not much surprised to learn that Aunt Marion had gone home to her rest. We cannot grudge her what she has gained but our sympathy goes out to those of her circle who are left behind. I cannot but think of her life as having a beautiful sunset, to rise in another sphere with a light that shall not grow dim. <u>Then</u> shall be brought to pass the saying that is written - Death is swallowed up in victory. Oh death where is thy sting, oh grave where is thy victory?

I see Aunt Janet's sister, Mrs Granger, has also crossed the bourne this week.

You asked about Mr Stewart's meeting. Well, it was disappointing as far as numbers were concerned. There was nothing further arranged regarding another meeting.

We have been busy in the fields, but the good weather has been favourable for the seedtime. We finished sowing last week and will just about finish up potato planting this week. There is no prospect however of our being out of a job for a long time, and even then, I will be able to find something to do I have no doubt. (Surely that is Irish.)

We expect George & Cathie for the day on Friday. Then Jane and some of the children are going West next week, till about the end of it. Then I am due at Mauchline for Sunday the 23rd. and will likely see Ayr Show on the 25th & 26th and so the programme gets filled up and time is not allowed to be heavy on our hands.

Potatoes have now gone to £5 per ton here. A fine handy price and easily counted, for those that are fortunate enough to be holding some.

Aunt Bessie will be in Glasgow this week, but trust you both keep well.
Our kind regards,
Yours affectly,
H. Miller

***

83 & 84. May 1st 1911
Dear Uncle John,

I got your letter on coming home last Wednesday evening after a sojourn of a day or two in the West.

I was at Mauchline over the weekend, and was at Ayr Show on Tuesday & Wednesday. I was very nearly being your length on Wed. afternoon but recalled that it was Auntie's day at home and as I would have had a very short time, I thought it better not to disturb her if she had visitors. I was along at the cancer hospital to see Andrew Reid, but he was sleeping, and as he is a good deal worse, I did not ask the nurse to waken him. The poor man has suffered a lot, but he seems to be very patient in the midst of it all. I trust that for him there will be a light in the valley.

I am sending by the same post a parcel of turnip seed to Mr Gunson. Swedes are in very good time sown now. Indeed, they might grow too large sown so early, but of course that depends largely on the weather. I sent a little of two kinds, and you can experiment with them. I think however the "Bronze Top" is the finer of the two.

As duty calls me hence, I must close up.
Trust you both keep well.
Yours affectly,
H. Miller

***

100 (& 101). June 3rd 1911
Dear Uncle,

I was almost in the act of writing you the other day, but did not get it done, and now your letter has come to hand. Many thanks for your kind invitation to visit you at the convention. While it would be a great pleasure for me to be there, I am sorry that it is not possible for me to get away. What with extra hands employed at turnip singling etc, and the majority of our regular hands new this week, my presence here is more or less of a necessity. We had a good many changes at the term and I hope we may be "nae waur"[4] than before, which is not hoping too much.

We are feeling the drouth a good deal, and some things are suffering. Small turnip plants are having a trying time, and in some cases are rather growing down than up. We hope and trust that relief may be not far off. I daresay that we are all the better of being made to feel our dependence on Him who feeds the ravens.

I have not heard anything from Mr Stewart since that day you saw him here. We are thinking of having a meeting on the farm on Sunday week, when we expect Mr Munsie with us, and we hope there may be a fair response.

Things are moving along quite heartily at Mauchline when I was there, and I have heard nothing to the contrary since then.

Betty started school at Athelstaneford a month ago, and to our surprise and I may say comfort, is liking it quite well.

I trust that Aunt Bessie & Mrs Spence may have a good time at Crieff, and be the better of their change.

I see by the way that bee trouble has been rife over a wide area, and I was wondering how you have fared with your "gentry". They should be giving a good account of themselves this weather.

Kind regards.
Yours affectly,
H. Miller

***

161. Oct 23rd.1911
Dear Uncle,

I think I promised when you were here that I would send you a bag of potatoes at lifting time, so my promise has been fulfilled today, and I trust you will receive them all right. We finished lifting on Saturday and I was quite glad to see the departure of some of our "friends" that had been with us for longer or shorter.

We got exceptional weather being off only one half day all the time. The crop has turned out quite up to expectations, if not more.

We have now got our little organ installed and it is quite an acquisition to the meeting. The numbers keep up beyond our expectations, now that the darkness has set in at meeting time, so we continue from night to night or rather from week to week while the folks come.

The mill is now in a condition that we can thresh, and we will likely be having a trial of it tomorrow. It has been a "driech"[5] job in the end.

I hope you both keep well - also Mrs Spence.
Kind regards,
Yours affectly,
H. Miller

***

School correspondence and letters to other family members
Prior to 1893 there were 2 schools in North Berwick, the Parish School and the Burgh School, which united in 1868 and moved into what is now the Museum in School Road. In 1893 North Berwick High School started with 13 pupils and soon moved into their new premises in Law Road (now the Community Centre). In 1931 the High School and the Burgh School combined, retaining both the School Road and Law Road buildings until 1940 when secondary pupils moved to the current building closer to The Law.

***

189. Dec 15th 1911
Mr McIntosh
Dear Sir,
　　I beg to call your attention to the fact that a boy named Herbert Clark from the Marine Hotel, stabbed my boy on the leg today with an open knife. Tonight his leg is very sore, and he is quite lame when he walks. I can make great allowance for boyish pranks, but such hooliganism as using an open knife to the effusion of blood is rather serious. I request that you make inquiry regarding the matter, and unless there is an apology forthcoming, I will press the matter further.
　　Yours faithfully,
　　H. Miller

***

293 & 294. Sept 24th 1912
Miss Keith
Dear Madam,
　　I am loth to interfere with a teacher in what she considers to be her sphere form an official standpoint, but circumstances have arisen which I consider demands my interference.
　　My boy, Jim has been set the task of writing sixty lines of poetry as punishment for what seems on the face of it to have been a very paltry offence. He had this task about half accomplished when I discovered what he was doing, and as a protest

This photo was taken during the 1912-1913 session with Jim Miller third from the left in the back row. This would be in front of the Law Road building and presumably it is Mr Glover, the Rector, in the middle of the photo and the 2 members of staff may well have been Mr McIntosh and Miss Keith as mentioned in the letters.

against such a punishment I have assigned what he had written to the fire.

If there is a recurrence of a similar kind, I will not deal with it privately. I would be the last to forbid correction, but I claim to have some say as to how it is to be applied to my boy.

Please do not infer that Jim asked this of me, and if there is any further difficulty in the matter you must deal with me personally.

Yours faithfully,
H. Miller

★★★

531 July 22nd 1920
J. Alison Esq. M.A.
Dear Sir,

I have received your letter of 21st inst and am disappointed with its contents. I certainly did not understand that you made it a condition that my boy was to board with Mr Ford, and I do not think I can be blamed in concluding thus when there are no other housefuls of boys boarding in Edinburgh who attend George Watson's College.

I have arranged with Miss Imrie, Warrender Park Road, to board my boy, and will be sorry if you refuse to take him on this account. I trust that this arrangement and the explanation I have made may be quite satisfactory to you, and I will be glad to hear that the enrolment of the boy as a pupil will hold good.

Yours faithfully,
H. Miller

***

This refers to Hugh, the youngest of the family. Presumably when he went to Edinburgh he wore shoes, unlike Elshinford, where he carried his boots strung round his neck like the other children, putting them on when he neared home.

***

271. Aug 16th 1912
Dear George[6],

I had your note of 13th inst. and have sent a waggon of wheat straw today. I will arrange to have the six pigs killed on Monday and will send them on Tuesday morning. I think it was understood that they would be sent in their skins.

We are making a start with the binders today.

Yours faithfully,
H, Miller
West Fortune
Drem. 16-8-1912

Four waggons wheat straw railed to College Station, to your address as follows -

T. C. Q.[7]

Aug 13th	No 62393	2	-	-
" 13th	31398	1	18	2
" 13th	53226	2	1	2
" 14th	53138	2	0	1

H. Miller

***

275. Aug 23rd 1912
Dear George,
   Yours to hand with cheque enclosed for £32.11/- in payment of six pigs and waggon wheat straw, for which accept of thanks.
   I hope the pigs were none the worse of the delay. You would likely have said so if they were. Your father would be surprised at the weights. He said they would not be six Ayrshire stones. I suppose the weights you mention would be without skin. Is this so?
   I hope the children got safely to their destination along with David today.
   This afternoon has been out and out wet giving another set-back to the harvest.
   I hope Jim remembers the message I sent with him for you.
   Yours faithfully,
   H. Miller

***

281 & 282. Sept 6th 1912
Dear Uncle,
   I had your letter yesterday with your kind inquiries for me and mine. I am very well thank you. My side is still a little bit weak for "fechtin"[8], and while I have had a kind of excuse for not doing any heavy work for a week or two, I have never been very far removed from the seat of war.
   As you say the harvest has had its difficulties so far. We have been 3 weeks cutting 220 acres or thereby, that operation being finished today. Of course, wet weather protracted the work very much. Crops are bulky in the most of cases, and we now hope for dry weather to gather them in.
   We had some damage done to a field of wheat with Wednesday's wind. I never saw as much loss with "shake". I had between 20 & 30 acres to shear with the hook - barley - being so badly twisted that the machine would not work it. However, we are so far through and thankful for that. In the midst of all, there is satisfaction in knowing that there is an unerring, ruling, guiding hand, and promises that cannot be broken.
   I am sorry to hear that Aunt Bessie is not so well, but hope she will strengthen to her usual soon. If she was well enough to face the journey, we would be pleased to see you both before the days darken down again.

Jane is fairly well suited with a maid, but that "fairly" would be none the worse of a line under it.

I suppose you will be aware that C. Nairn is home. I know nothing more than that bare fact.

Thanking you for your kindly interest, and with kind regards in which Jane joins.

Yours affectly,
H. Miller

***

310 & 311. Nov 12th 1912
Dear Uncle,
Your letter of Oct 22nd. has been lying here on my desk, frequently giving my conscience a prick but now I seek to make amends.

We were sorry you were unable to visit the East country this back end but trust your visit will keep till another time.

Thanks for all your kind enquiries regarding our welfare.

The harvest was an abundant one of straw, and I am quite satisfied that the grain will not be deficient. We had to "shear" between 20 & 30 acres of barley that we could not manage with the machines.

The Co-Op people again have the potatoes, but these are disappointing because of disease. The month of August did the damage here. But for that, the crop would probably have been far too large in the country to insure a decent price per ton.

We finished lifting about ten days ago but there are still a good few here and there to take up.

Mr Thomson has not done cattle this year. He did not have them last year either. We have 85 in the courts now, so with these to keep in turnips, fodder & bedding, we know of a job for any odd time we have.

We are preparing to sow wheat tomorrow if the weather is dry. I mean to sow over 70 acres if we can manage it.

I was in Ayrshire the week before last, and plenty of harvest still out. It is heartless work now in the short dull days.

Our little meeting continues from week to week with as much encouragement as prevents us shutting the door. Is that optimism?

If we can manage to arrange it, Jane and I will be pleased to go to you for a day - perhaps a Saturday when the children would be at home.
Trusting you both keep well - also Mrs Spence.
Kind regards,
Yours affectly
H. Miller

***

373 & 374. Nov 26th 1913
Dear Uncle,
Your letter is before me and in order to put you in my debt I will just answer it. We were pleased to hear that you were both keeping well, and hope you will get comfortably through the dark winter days.

The farm that David Bone got is not the one you are thinking about. It is about three miles from here near East Linton. Then we are getting new neighbours at Congalton - the farm next to us on the way to North Berwick. Perhaps you noticed from the papers too that our old laird had died at Luffness, and this has made many changes there. Luffness Mains, the Home farm, has been let to another Ayrshire man, and so the colony extends.

You ask about the mushrooms. Well, they somehow forgot to grow and that was the result of the experiment.

Robert's arm is now about all right, but Elizabeth has been in bed for some days with a bad throat. Little Mary too is affected. James had his turn last week and is now running about. I hope they will all be well soon.

Dr Chapman was in Edinburgh on a Saturday afternoon recently, and Jane and I heard him. He is a wonderful evangelistic force. We look forward to hearing him again when he comes to Edinburgh.

We had Phemie and her little girl for two nights last week. They are all well at Girvan Mains.

Our little meeting still goes on, with as much encouragement as we have ever had. Between blindness, ignorance and self-righteousness, the need of a plain blunt gospel is great. We are glad to have a place in your remembrance as Sunday evening comes round.

We will be glad to hear of your welfare when you feel inclined to write.
Yours affectly,
H. Miller

***

427 & 428. Feb 15th 1915
Dear Uncle,
It is now a considerable time since we had an exchange of letters, but the fault is entirely on my part as I should have written you ere this. We have been hearing a little of you however from time to time, and I trust you are both in your usual again. We heard of Aunt Bessie's upset from Ferrygate, but the last we heard was that she had got over it.

Some of our connection are passing through deep waters. The death of the little boy at Fearn will be a sore grief to the father and mother, coming as it did so unexpectedly and so suddenly. This is one of the things in our earthly life that with our finite vision we are not able to see through. And now Uncle John seems to have come very near to the end of his journey. How different in his case - a shock of corn fully ripe. Earth is always poorer by the loss of men like Uncle John. But what can we say!

The horrors of war continue, and with increased armies there is the necessity for increased hospitals, and of course there will be an increased death roll.

The highest civilization that the world has ever known, has developed into a scientific system of taking human life in the most wholesale manner that the genius of man can invent. Oh, the horror of it!

We feel that we are again approaching the Springtime, and with a few dry days we will soon be thinking of getting out the potato boxes.

I sent a small bag of "Golden Wonder" potatoes to you today, and hope they may turn up all right in due course.

With kind regards to Aunt Bessie and remembrances to Mrs Spence,
Yours affectly,
H. Miller

***

464. Nov 1st 1916
Dear Uncle,
I had your letter the other morning and am glad you have accomplished the sale of your house. It will be one little burden off your mind and for the future will simplify your other arrangements.

Every step in life is part of an unknown road, but being in the company of the very best guide we have the satisfaction of knowing that He will lead us right. And we have the assurance that He will stay with us, for has He not said - "I will never leave thee nor forsake thee".

We have had broken weather. But have now got the late potato crop lifted. It is the smallest I have ever handled.

The war news from the East has been gloomy for the past week, and the end is not yet. May He who alone can - intervene.

Yours affectly,
H. Miller

***

614 & 615. Mar 16th 1925
Dear George,

I am in receipt of your letter of 13th inst. And we are sorry to hear of Grandfather having a cold, but hope he will soon be in his usual good health again. Your letter otherwise has given me much concern, and it is exceedingly unfortunate that you find yourselves so hampered financially, but I pointed out the position to you before and I am sorry I do not see my way any clearer to accede to your request than I did at that time. To be quite frank I hardly think it is business to ask anyone to become surety at the Bank in ignorance of the real state of affairs. Has it not occurred to you that it would be advisable in the circumstances to put your affairs in the accountant's hands, and get to know exactly how you stand? If things are as you say, you would be in a much better position to retain the confidence of your customers as well as the confidence of the Bank. Of course, this is your affair, but I am only suggesting what I would do myself in such circumstances. It would let you know exactly how & where you stand, and perhaps also show where the shortage has arisen.

If the shop is still doing as well as you indicated some time ago, would it not be advisable to drop the ham trade altogether, and devote all your energy to the bakery? I am exceedingly sorry to again refuse your request but there are several considerations which compel me to do so.

Kind regards,
Yours affectly,
H. Miller

***

Hugh declined his brother-in-law's request to stand surety. David and Robert (George's brothers) were supportive but, being church ministers, unlikely to be able to pay off debt. Their sister, Euphemia, appears to have received an inheritance and was able to offer some assistance.[9]

***

623. Nov 17th 1925
Dear George,

I have your letter of 16th inst. but have difficulty in understanding its contents.

Am I to understand that you wish me to come good for whatever you may offer to your creditors in order to effect a settlement? If so - I consider your request preposterous & cannot entertain it, as I have no idea what your liabilities & assets are.

I expect to be in Ayrshire this week, & if I have time I may be in Kilmarnock on Friday and will hear how you get on.

Yours faithfully,
H. Miller

***

624. Dec 23rd 1925
Henry Smith Esq. C.A.
Messrs D. Whiteford & Son Sequestration
Dear Sir,

In connection with the above, would you be good enough to send me a copy of the valuation list of furniture at Ashbank, Stewarton, and which I understand you have given the firm the option of buying back.

I shall then let you know immediately whether I am taking it over or not.

Yours faithfully,
Hugh Miller

***

625 & 626. Dec 26th 1925
Dear George,

I have today received a copy of the inventory and valuation of the furniture from the trustee. I will not do anything definite till I hear how the sale of the house goes.

David was telling me going home on Tuesday evening the position of affairs regarding the bill for £500 which he and Robert were let in to signing on the assurance that the £300 bill would thereby be cancelled. I think Robert & David have been very badly treated in this, and now as a 'quid pro quo' I want to ask you - if I buy the furniture at £109 - or such part of it as may be arranged - will you get Euphemia or her successors to guarantee the payment of the £500 bill when she becomes a beneficiary under the will of the late Captn. John Smith - our uncle?

I do not think I am asking anything unfair or unreasonable in this - for I do not think - to use a scriptural term you should be 'eased' and your two brothers 'burdened' with the payment of this amount. They may have to go on paying this off for years, and I do think they should have some guarantee that they will get their own back.

You might let me know what you think of this proposal.

I trust you are all well.

Yours sincerely,

H. Miller

***

Politics / Miscellany

Politics is not a game. It is an earnest business.
– Winston Churchill 1874-1965

***

253 & 254. June 24th 1912
Wm Middlemas Esq.
Dear Sir,
   Referring to the meeting on Friday and the manner in which it broke up, I am afraid it will be difficult to get a following sufficiently strong to resist the collection of the employee's contribution under the Insurance Act.
   Would it not be better to frame a conditional resolution, which would not be binding, until a given number had signed it, such as the following -
   "I hereby declare & bind myself to refuse to collect for the government, the employee's contribution under the National Insurance Act, on condition that (300, 400, 500) employers in the county of Haddington sign this resolution, and I hereby agree to a penalty of £10 for the breach of the foregoing resolution."
   I think it would not be difficult under this condition to get a large number of signatures, and the situation might be saved.
   This of course is only a suggestion, that if you think worthwhile, you can put before some of the others.
   I would have gone to Haddington today, but cannot get away, so send this if you should happen to be going to the market there.
   Yours faithfully,
   H. Miller

***

429. Feb 20th 1915
The Editor of The Kilmarnock Standard
Dear Sir,
On Friday last (12th curt.) I sent you a letter Express post - for publication in your issue of the 13th curt. if you received it in time.
Would you be good enough to let me know if you received that letter, and if so for what reason you have not published it, as I meant you to put it in this week, if it was too late for last week's issue.
Yours faithfully,
H. Miller

***

469. Jan 25th 1917
The Editor of the S. F.
Sir,
In your leading article of last week on "Bread v. Meat" quoting from "The Glasgow Herald", you make reference to the appalling waste of food stuff by the liquor traffic. It would no doubt be difficult to paint the picture with as dark a background as the reality, and the evidence of the need of reform is so overwhelming, that it seems almost unnecessary to make any suggestion, but if the Executive Food Production Committee which has been formed all over the country would take up this matter, and forthwith send to the Government a protest against this waste, it would at least like "Old Barbara Frietchie of Frederick Town"[1] show what side they were on, and incidentally might strengthen the hands of those who have a difficult and heavy task to deal with.
Yours faithfully,
H. Miller

***

500. July 10th 1918
A. McNeilage Esq.
Dear Sir,
I have been making up a balance sheet of my cattle feeding transactions for the past winter, and would not object to put it in your hands for publication anonymously - if you care. I think with facts before you for a text you could preach a powerful sermon on this vexed subject. Every man I speak to here seems afraid to open his mouth to his neighbour on his feeding results, but any information I have

got, I assure you is far from encouraging for this kind of food production for next year.

If you favour the idea, I quite believe I could get another one or two to submit their balance sheet as well.

Will be glad to hear from you.

Yours faithfully,

H. Miller

***

The following letter stands apart from the various others and there are no clues as to how a farmer was on personal terms with the High Sheriff of Fermanagh. Mr Carson was one of around 42 border loyalists kidnapped on 7th & 8th February 1922 by Irish Republican Army members based in Monaghan. They sought to hold them as hostages for the release of IRA prisoners. The kidnappings provoked outrage and after diplomatic intervention from Dublin, London and Belfast they were released.

In the journalistic style of the times 'The Scotsman' of Thursday February 9th, 1922, stated "The house of Mr Ivan Carson, High Sheriff for Fermanagh was attacked by men, who broke in the front door with hammers and axes. The Sheriff, when he appeared in the hall, was fired at by the intruders, who seized him and carrying him to a waiting motor, drove off."

A column in The Scotsman, dated Friday February 10th, 1922, states that further kidnappings had taken place on Wednesday night in the district of Rosslea, County Fermanagh, when four more men were conveyed on a horse cart to Clones where they were placed in a motor and taken to Ballbay to join the other captives. The article continues, "Mrs Carson, Killyreagh House, wife of Mr Ivan Carson, ex-High Sheriff of Fermanagh, who was kidnapped on Tuesday night, received yesterday a letter from her husband from an unknown address, stating that he was well, that his captors were looking after him all right, and that there was no cause for anxiety."

***

594. Feb 20th 1922

Dear Carson,

I had your letter of 6th inst. on Thursday the 9th inst. and the same morning your name was in the paper as having been kidnapped the day before. I am exceedingly sorry for the unfortunate circumstances in which you have been placed,

and I would have written you at once but did not know where you might be. I have been watching the paper each day for your name among the released but am sorry I have not yet found it. I hope however that you are now safely home, and that you will not be further molested. We here are much annoyed that the Loyalists of the North of Ireland should be subjected to such rough handling but hope that you will be able to hold your own. Promises from the government are not sufficient. We have a whole host of unfulfilled ones over here too.
With best wishes for your safety & welfare.
Yours faithfully,
H. Miller

***

644. Jan 29th 1930
Lord Beaverbrook,
Sir,
I am in receipt of your favour of 21st inst. and in reply I have only to state that I have no objection to the publication of anything I said in my former note to you, if you consider it will further the cause we aim at. Each week our markets here are sinking lower & lower - 10/6 per ton being quoted for good ware potatoes in some of the Fife markets. The case is desperate and yet a sympathetic(?) Government stands by with the means of help at their disposal and refuse to extend that help to us. I hope for the country's sake that they will not delay till we are past redemption point.
Yours faithfully,
Hugh Miller

***

Hugh Miller was Chairman of the Scottish Chamber of Agriculture and in November 1932 attended a meeting at Whitehall with the Minister of Agriculture to add his weight to the case for much needed support for Scottish agriculture. Under the heading 'Great Farm Deputation at Whitehall' it was reported that a proposal was made to restrict the import of foreign and dominion meat so that home livestock farmers could be assured of a reasonable return.[2]

***

Miscellaneous Correspondence

106. June 23rd 1911
East Lothian
Wm Alexander Esq
Dear Sir,
    Would you please send me a ten stone bag of oatmeal if you have any beside you. I have never taken to the Edinburgh stuff. There is a hardness and want of flavour about it that I don't like. We had a fine rain in the beginning of the week, but none too much for requirements. Mauchline should be looking well this season.
    We are in the midst of our haymaking.
    Yours faithfully,
    H. Miller

***

225. Apr 1st 1912
A Hendrie Esq.
Dear Sir,
    I am in receipt of your favour of 30th ult. intimating that I have been elected a member of Athelstaneford School Board, and have pleasure in accepting of the honour thus put upon me.
    Yours faithfully,
    H. Miller

***

Postal delivery
242 & 243. May 28th 1912
T G L Pennington Esq.
Dear Sir,
    We, the undersigned, beg to lay before you the fact that very considerable inconvenience has been caused to us by the new arrangement of the delivery of letters from Drem. Under the best conditions we are nearly an hour later than formerly in receiving our letters, and we find that this will seriously interfere with the transaction of urgent business.
    We place the matter before you in the confidence that it will receive immediate attention, and that our delivery of letters will be made at least no worse than it was before.
    We wanted also to request that an afternoon or evening delivery might be

arranged on this route which would only be granting us a service, similar to that enjoyed by others in the district at present.
Yours faithfully,
H. Miller
M. Skirving
P. & G. Lothian
Robert Sinclair
Joseph Lee

***

The other signatories occupied neighbouring farms: M. Skirving - *Muirton* ; Peter & George Lothian - *Prora* ; Robert Sinclair - *Drem* - gardener - tenant ; Joseph Lee - *Congalton* ; John Hope - *Kilduff* -tenant.

***

274. Aug 21st 1912
T G L Pennington Esq.
Dear Sir,
I am in receipt of your favour of 19th inst. and am pleased to learn that arrangements have been made for the improvement of the postal deliveries here. Allow me to thank you for your attention to this matter.
Yours faithfully,
H. Miller

***

328. Jan 7th 1913
Dear Mr Small[3],
I have your letter of 2nd inst. but have been from home for some days. Hence my delay in replying.
I am sorry however that I cannot accede to your request to be a speaker at the congregational meeting, and feel that this is quite outside of my sphere.
I trust you are all well again, and with the complts. of the season,
I am, Yours faithfully,
H. Miller

***

521. Nov 8th 1919
Dear Mr Small,
Your letter of 5th inst. was awaiting me on coming home last night.

Thank you for the kind expression of appreciation therein, and I also thank any others who think me worthy of taking office in the eldership of the church.

I cannot however see my way to accept the request you lay before me so please accept of my refusal to do so.

Yours faithfully,
H. Miller

***

Telephones
368. Proposed Exchange at Athelstaneford
Oct 31st 1913
C.M.
The Contract manager.
Dear Sir,

I have your favour of 30th inst. with enclosures which I have signed and herewith return.

I wish a wall instrument supplied with an extension bell, and trust the work will be proceeded with as soon as possible.

Yours faithfully,
H. Miller

***

The number was Athelstaneford 08 and as two spinster ladies at the Athelstaneford exchange had to connect a call it was understood that no conversation was private. The outside bell could be heard in the garden and byre at West Fortune.

Alexander Graham Bell, born in Edinburgh, is credited with inventing the telephone. His invention impressed the judges, including Lord Kelvin, at the Centennial Exposition in 1876 but telephones were not established in the UK until the turn of the century. It was 1930 before the majority of better-off homes had a telephone.

***

371 & 372. Nov 19th 1913
Dear Mr Stevenson,

I had a letter from Mr Hannah this morning, in which he stated that you had got Luffness Mains, and I congratulate you that Ayrshire is to the front again. Mr Hannah mentions that you wish to let the turnips and if I can be of any use to you in the matter I will gladly be so. I spoke to Middlemass today, who has my turnips, and asked him if he would care to have the turnips at Luffness Mains. He said he wasn't anxious, because of the price store cattle had gone to. He said however that if you got no one else, he would take the turnips, if he could make terms with you.

If it would further matter any, I would be pleased to see you here to arrange for you to meet Middlemass and you do not need to book for a night's lodging elsewhere.

Middlemass is always in Haddington on Friday, and in Edinburgh on Thursday, but could be seen by arrangement between these days.

If you want me to do anything you can let me know.

Yours faithfully,

H. Miller

***

397. Feb 23rd 1914
Dear Mr McGill,

I was in Kilmarnock one day recently and met a man with whom I had a little acquaintance, quite accidentally. He was saying he heard a man in the cross on the Friday before "blawin aff some big anes" regarding me. The words that were repeated were words that I spoke to you when you were here ……last summer, and as far as my memory serves me, I said these words to no one else. I suppose you will know what I refer to, but I would like to hear from you if you know anything about who gave currency to the statement that was made in the cross.

Yours faithfully,

H. Miller

***

431. June 21st 1915
Wm Gemmill Esq.
Dear Sir,

I duly received your letter of 10th inst, with reference to a situation for a young lady. I purposely delayed answering, on the chance that I might hear of something suitable, but so far have not been able to learn of anything. If, however I should hear of an opening that might be suitable I will be pleased to let you know.

Yours faithfully

H. Miller

***

453. May 8th 1916
Messrs Mackintosh & Bain,
Dear Sirs,
   Yours of 4th inst. duly received with Dividend warrant enclosed, which I have signed and herewith return.
   I am wondering how the affairs of my late uncle now stand, and also if the trustees of his estate are under any obligation to you. The reason I ask this is that I cannot remember having seen a note of your expenses, nor that these were discharged, and I would only like the matter made satisfactory for myself.
   I will be glad to hear from you at your convenience.
   Please note that my postal address is <u>Drem</u>, not <u>Luffness</u>.
   Yours faithfully,
   H. Miller

***

638. Dec 10th 1927
Messrs James Ross & Sons,
Dear Sirs,
   Referring to our phone conversation today I hereby confirm the order for a 1928 Model fourteen Hillman saloon car painted maroon, delivered here as early as possible in January, for £300 and my old Rover Car, this price to include a bulb horn fixed underneath the bonnet.
   We spoke of tipping headlights, but I am not quite sure if you meant to include them in the transaction. Please let me know about this and also the position of the tipping lever. Is it an obstruction for getting out and in the car?
   Yours faithfully,
   Hugh Miller

***

West Fortune Farmhouse and type of phone installed.

Family Tributes

Concluding this account of Hugh Miller it is fitting to include excerpts from tributes celebrating his 80th Birthday on 11th July 1952 and Hugh and Jane's Diamond Wedding Anniversary on 19th October 1956, at the Marine Hotel, North Berwick. There is also one unusually personal copy of a letter written to Jane in 1912. In spite of his denials he was wont to burst into rhyme on occasion. His gift of colourful description is evident here.

Jane Miller (Nee Whiteford).

***

325 & 326. Dec 24th 1912
My dear Jane,
    I am sending you a line or two,
    although I think there's nothing new,
    but still I hope you may be glad
    to hear that none of us is sad.
    but poetry is not in my line,
    so I will cease to try & rhyme
    and simply say, to see you home
    we will be glad the day you come.
    It seems that still this rhyme will clink
    as from my pen runs out the ink,
    but never mind howe'er it goes
    whether it's poetry or prose.
    Well, how are you getting on/ & how is Betty?
    I hope you are surviving all your knocking about. You will be at Mauchline when you get this. I sent Mary a pair of fowls this morning, and though in life they were ill, thrawn, temper-provoking beasts, I hope that now their nature will be changed. They were two that would have made a saint say "things", so there is some excuse for a poor sinner like me using kind of strong language.
    I was in Edinburgh today as the market was held today instead of tomorrow.
    I said to Robert that you had said they were all to come over on Sat. Was that right?
    We have not had much rain today but tonight the keyholes and the window seams are making all the music they can with the wind.
    I have to go to Edinburgh on Friday to the court but do not know how long I will be detained. If I am not all the longer I will get home with you.
    Kind regards to all the friends. Trust Mary is better.
    Your Own & Always,
    Hugh

***

These family verses mention a cloud looming over the family in 1922 which was never apparent throughout the letterbook. Hugh was diagnosed with a cancer causing such a significant lump on his shoulder that he required a specially tailored jacket. He was referred for surgery and is reported as announcing to the surgeons that they would pray before the operation commenced. Evidently he received a letter from one of the surgeons who had disagreed with the cancer diagnosis but rejoicing in the healing.

Back Row: Janie, Willie, Margrett, Betty Miller, Betty Murray, James, Hugh, Douglas, Jim. Middle Row: Jane & Hugh. Front Row: Helen, Jean, Alison Jane (Ally), Margaret.

***

From Betty Murray (daughter)
We thank you all for coming here
To honour him, by each held dear –
Now eighty years have passed away
Since he first saw the light of day.
*

A happy home, with parents wise
He learned the best in life to prize.
And there with brothers, sisters too,
From boy to man's estate he grew.
But bye and bye he left all these
And went to work at Grassmillees.

*One thing now lacked to crown his life;
The loving presence of a wife.
To Stewarton then he took his way,
He chose his bride, they named the day.
He never did a wiser thing
Than when to Jane he gave the ring.*

*

*His time at Grassmillees did close.
West Fortune was the farm he chose.
And there he laboured through the years,
In war and peace, mid joy and tears.
The good seed sown had taken root.
And harvest time brought forth much fruit.
We come to Nineteen Twenty Two –
A cloud on the horizon grew.
The tragedy struck each one dumb,
But by God's grace 'twas overcome.*

*

*So once again there came a day
When Hugh to namesake, Hugh, gave way.
At Congalton he's found a home,
And from it may he never roam.
For there with children's children round
His days with happiness are crowned.*

***

From Jim Miller (son)
*My Father's a man who's very well known,
For many long years he has ploughed and has sown.
Though eighty years old, he is hardy and strong,
And always is right and can never be wrong.*

*So now he's retired, he must kittle folk up,
Comparing the past with the present set up.*

*His sons struggle on and are doing their best,
Under his eagle eye they are never at rest.*

*

*Now on Wednesday to town he's determined to go,
Although he is ill or the roads blocked with snow.
He's a mind of his own and to speak is no use,
It is just like putting your head in a noose.*

*He seldom is ill or has anything wrong
But Jervis may some time come sailing long,
If medicine he gives him has got a bad taste
He just chucks it out and recovers in haste.*

*On ministers sometimes he may look with doubt,
For many there are we could do fine without,
So humbug and cant he can nowhere abide
But trusts in his Lord as his Saviour and Guide.*

***

From Hugh Miller (son)

*He was born at Shaw
In seventy twa,
He started work just a year or twa later.
There are very few men
That you or I ken
Could have done that excepting the pater.*

*He once was the worse
For defying his nurse
And through a wasp bike he went messin',
Soon after he felt
He should dae as he's telt
For he'd learned a gey severe lesson.*

*

He now needed a wife
To help him through life,
And he got one without any bother.
But he chose with great care,
For if I'd been there
I wouldn't have chosen another.

*

Now West Fortune was poor,
It was quite like a moor,
For Kirk Mackie had been a bit hazy.
But under his hand
It became better land
For he didn't have time to be lazy.

*

Then Congalton farm
Had suffered some harm,
So he thought he'd just take it as well.
Now he lives with his spouse
In that beautiful house,
And all things in the garden are swell.

*

Well, I've had my say
On this happy day
But I'd just like you now to recall,
That although we have laughed
And quite often chaffed,
He has really done well by us all.

***

Bill Murray (son-in-law)
With over forty years of faithful tending
Hugh Miller's been a leader of the band.
He's served with faith and labour never-ending
To sow, to reap and to refresh the land.

Long years of hardest work and honest dealing
Have earned him human thanks and worldly praise.
But he has aye aspired a higher ceiling,
His Lord's "Well done" at end of earthly days.

★★★

Reply from Hugh Miller (senior)
Three score and ten the Bible says
Sums up man's spell below,
And if four score be reached by some
These years but end in woe.

There is a maxim all have learned
When first we went to school.
We have the law of average,
Exceptions prove the rule.
*

Now Grandpa still is going strong,
At least that is what they say.
He does not feel the weight of years
Though four score's reached today.
*

Bet then addressed the evening's guest,
And how she did excel,
In happy mood she told the good –
The bad she did not tell.
*

Then sonny Jim to say his piece
Was next to take the floor,
The old man's eccentricities
He did not quite ignore.
*

He told of his peculiar ways
Determined, often thrawn.
Of doctor's bottles – market days,

"To Edinbro' are ye gaun?"

Then Hugh his contribution gave
With humour overflowing.
What he left out, to tell about
Would hardly be worth knowing.

*

A tribute I would like to pay
My wife before I close.
What she has been throughout the years
Her husband only knows.

***

Family gathering in Marine Hotel, North Berwick (including Dr & Mrs Heavenor, Abbey Church and Jane's two brothers James & David and their wives).

Taken at Congalton on the Sunday of the Diamond Wedding celebrations. Hugh Miller's Wolseley on the right of the photo.

Diamond Anniversary Tribute by Hugh & Betty
Dear Mother & Dad we're all very glad
That you asked us to come here to dine
In this lovely hotel – and you both look so swell
The pleasure for us is just fine.

There's a lot to be said when you're sixty years wed
Of the troubles and worries you've had,
But among your great joys you have two girls and boys
Who all love their Mother and Dad.

When Jane married Hugh there was plenty to do
But she did what she did with great zest;
No washers or driers, or electrical fires,
The Electricity Board was non est!

If children were ill or had a bad spill
Castor oil or carbolic did fine;
Wee homeo pills cured most of their ills
From a cold to a pain in the spine.

*

I expect you've all seen the note from the Queen.
I'm glad that her message came through.
Her great great granny did reign, when Hugh married Jane.
If she'd known she'd have sent one then too.

In the West Fortune hall there's a grandfather tall,
The right time he always has kept.
Mother heard every hour from twelve until four,
And after that usually slept.

Now I have not yet spoken of a very small token
To tell of our love all the time –
A grandmother clock It can tick but won't talk
And they tell me it fairly can chime.

***

Jane Miller died in February 1964 and Hugh in June 1967, aged 94 and still living at Congalton. They are both buried in Dirleton cemetery. Some Canadian friends had visited the Millers in 1966 and enclosed a note with their Christmas card describing the family as "one of the finest examples of what family can mean, and there is a grandfather who at 94 has 'nae pith'[1] and is afraid he is getting lazy!"

This collection has brought together a sample of Hugh Miller's recorded correspondence giving a glimpse into his life and the farming and social conditions of the early 20th Century. Some incidents and challenges appear familiar to us while others paint pictures of a very different way of living, but perhaps we spot vaguely familiar characters arising in our communications today.

Hugh Miller.

Congalton Farmhouse to which Hugh Miller 'retired'.

Explanatory Notes

Abbreviations of dates used in letters:
   inst = instant = this month
   curt = current = this month
   ult = ultimo = last month
   prox = proximo = next month

Money : £-s-d
   £ = libra = pounds (£1 = 20s)
   s = solidi = shillings (1s = 12d)
   d = denarii = pence

Measurement
   12 inches (12") = 1 foot (1')
   3 feet = 1 yard
   22 yds = 1 chain
   10 ch = 1 furlong
   8 furl = 1 mile

Area
   1 acre = 4840 square yards (approx. half a football pitch) = 4 roods
   1 rood = 40 perches or poles
   1 pole = 30 ¼ sq yds

Weight
   16 ounces (oz) = 1 pound (lb)
   14 lb = 1 stone
   8 st = 1 cwt (hundredweight)
   20 cwt = 2240lbs = 1 ton
   1 tonne (metric ton) = 1000kg = 2204.6lbs

Capacity
   20 fluid ounces = 1 pint
   4 gills = 1 pt

2 pts = 1 quart
4 quarts – 1 gallon
2 gallons = 1 peck
4 pecks = 1 bushel (8 gallons or 36.4l)
6 bushels = 1 boll
8 bushels = 1 quarter

A traditional bushel measure.

Chapter 2 History of Agriculture in East Lothian
1. Singling: thinning
2. Shawing: cutting off the tops
Chapter 3 The Manure Man
1. "Where There's Muck, There's Brass" The Market for Manure in the Industrial Revolution, Liam Brunt. Nuffield College, Oxford.
2. Demurrage: now confined to container shipping but refers to a charge payable on failure of delivery as agreed.

Chapter 4 Potatoes
1. Seed: for sowing of next year's crop.
2. Brock: small potatoes, remnants or rubbish.
3. Ware: potatoes for consumption (this is the same word used elsewhere for seaweed).
4. Rogued: removal of potatoes that do not appear healthy for use as seed.

Chapter 5 Grain, Hay and Straw
1. Fanners: series of revolving blades supplying air for winnowing or cleaning grain.

Chapter 6 Livestock and Keeping Them Fed
1. Mangold (or mangold-wurzel): an elongated beet, often yellow in colour, provided good cattle fodder as its roots reach deeper than turnips thus extracting extra vitamins.
2. Braird: first sprouting.
3. Shearling: first year before being shorn.
4. On break: portion of turnip field which was fenced off until grazing was completed. The fencing would then be moved.
5. Hoggets: sheep around 15 months before 2 permanent teeth have developed.
6. On cutter: being fed on turnips which have been harvested, cut by hand and tipped into troughs.
7. Finger and toe: clubroot which is difficult to eradicate. Crop rotation is vital, and some varieties are less susceptible to infection.
8. Weed: fever in milking cows.
9. Scour: diarrhoea in livestock.

Chapter 7 Horses
1. Shivers: a rare neuromuscular disorder, but a horse may also shiver to warm up.
2. Stocked/stocking up: Puffy fetlocks after a horse has been standing for a long time. This resolves and does not contribute to lameness.
3. Stifle: equivalent of the human knee joint in the hind limb.
4. Blistering: involves injecting or spreading a counter-irritant mixture of iodine and almond oil into the affected area, such as torn tendon fibres.
5. Spavin: arthritic disorder of the lower hock joint.
6. Stringhalt: jerking lameness.

7. Windsucker: gulping air which can lead to colic or ulcers.
Chapter 8 Miller's Mill
1. Luck's penny: a tip which went into the back pocket, not through the books.
Chapter 9 Farm Management
1. Stobs: stakes or posts.
2. Needless is situated near the foot of Athelstaneford Brae.
3. Paling: fencing with wooden cross bars.
4. Cotlands: common grazing land for the Cotlanders who lived in the village and marched (bordered) with West Fortune.
Chapter 10 Lawyers' Letters
1. Foggage: grass growing after hay is cut.
2. March fence: boundary between two farms.
3. Waygoing: departing.
4. Slump sum: lump sum.
Chapter 11 Employer's Insurance
1. References: History of the UK Government in https://www.gov.uk ; https://on this day.com ; Supplement to British Medical Journal Saturday January 12th 1907.
2. Reference: www.johngraycentre.org.
Chapter 12 Brother George the Banker
1. Drouth: drought.
2. Bourne: boundary or limit (also end of life).
3. Loop: trickery or wile.
4. The Baron of Buchlyvie was a prize-winning Clydesdale stallion sold by public auction in Ayr for 9500 guineas (over £1m today), an event attended by over 4000 people. This was a world record for the sale of a horse at the time. Auctions were conducted in guineas (1 guinea = 21 shillings) the seller receiving the set amount in pounds and the auctioneer receiving the extra shilling in the pound as commission.
5. It would only have been the Irish who were on holiday on 25th December. Christmas Day did not become a national holiday in Scotland until 1958 and Boxing Day in 1974.
6. Jim was the son of Hugh's sister, Bessie.
7. Bessie, had been married to George Osborne, farming near Fenwick for 7

years before being widowed in 1898. In 1915 she married another farmer, James Henderson, moving to Fife.
8. Tramp rick: a metal frame filled with hay and tramped down before being turned out as a rick.

Chapter 13 Finance, Bank Managers and Accountants
1. Mr Small appears to have been the banker in the Edinburgh Clydesdale
2. The War Loan in 1917 was the 3rd government initiative to increase financing of the conflict. The loans earned 5% interest. A Labour politician wrote later "No foreign conqueror could have devised a more complete robbery and enslavement of the British Nation". Reference: The Financiers and the Nation Thomas Johnston 1934.

Chapter 14 The Arbiter
1. Oversman: overseer or umpire.
2. Grist-mill: mill for grinding grain.

Chapter 15 Life at Drem Station
1. Traveller: ring sliding along a rope.
2. Trevis: something laid across as a bar.

Chapter 16 The Impact of the 1914 – 1918 War
1. Mr A Butter was the gentleman with whom Hugh Miller corresponded over the letting of land on East Fortune Airship Station, Muirhouses.
2. Thereanent: Scots for concerning the matter.

Chapter 17 Mission Outreach
1. Taken from a pamphlet published by Pickerine & Inglis 'A Biography of Cuthbert Nairn'.
2. £2 would be equivalent to £240 today.
3. Horse Island: uninhabited island in Firth of Clyde.
4. Feckfu': full of resource.

Chapter 18 Dear John
1. Store: livestock bought for fattening.
2. Cake breaker: used to break up slabs of linseed oil cake for livestock feed.
3. Gelding: castrated horse.
4. Redding up: tidying up.
5. Wiseacre: know all or wise guy.
6. Waverley: a variety of oats.
7. Having a shirt off the cattle: having a small profit margin.

8. Haar: sea mist.
9. Snod: neat or snug.
10. Plouter: wet, muddy & disagreeable.
11. Goldthorpe: wheat variety.
12. Stiff: difficult, unyielding.
13. Endrigs: ridges at the end of the field where the plough had turned to make the next furrow.
14. John Hannah had purchased Drem Farm for his son, George.

Chapter 19 Family Correspondence
1. 'Mak a kirk or a mill o' it': Scots proverb meaning 'The choice is yours'.
2. Quotation from Lord Macaulay's 'Horatius'.
3. Probably Uncle Robert married to Aunt Bessie.
4. Nae waur: no worse.
4. Driech: tedious.
6. To George Whiteford, Jane's brother.
7. T : tons C : hundredweight Q : quarters.
8. Fechtin: fighting.
9. David Whiteford (Sen) had a ham-curing business in Stewarton, Ayrshire. This business was taken over by his sons, George & James but was bankrupted years later. George was married and possibly emigrated to New Zealand with little further contact with family. James married Jeannie Mackie, but they had no family. An engagement ring belonging to Jeannie was identified from the inscription inside. As Jeannie had predeceased James, he must have given the ring to his sister, Jane. The ring has now been put to good use by one of Jane's great-great-grandchildren in New Zealand.

Chapter 20 Politics / Miscellany
1. Barbara Frietchie was made famous by John Whittier's poem about the American Civil War. It seems surprising that it should be quoted by an East Lothian farmer.
2. Aberdeen Press & Journal Friday November 11th 1932.
3. Mr Small was minister of Abbey Church, North Berwick.

Chapter 21 Personal Tributes
1. nae pith: no energy.

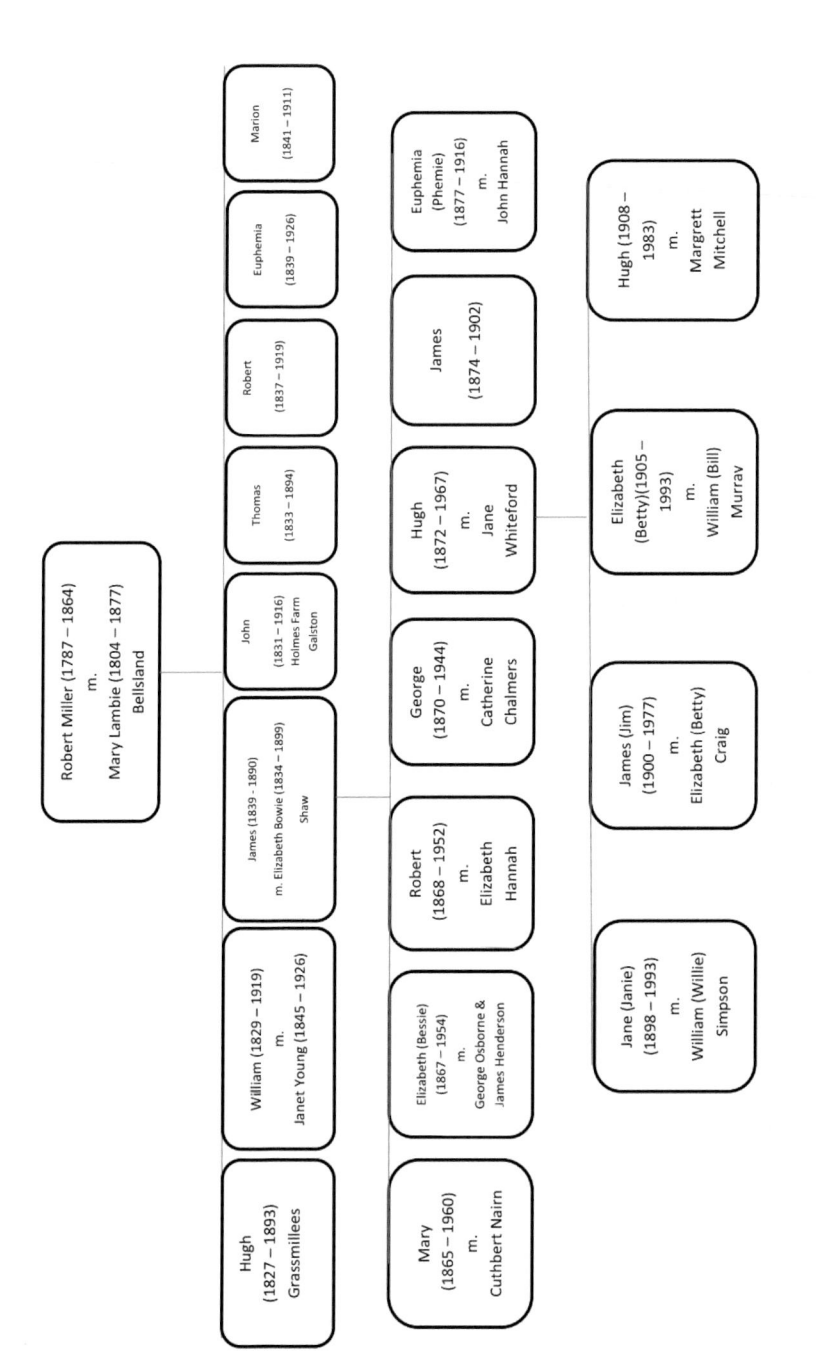

FamilyTree Part 1

- Robert Miller (1787 – 1864)
  m.
  Mary Lambie (1804 – 1877)
  Bellsland
  - Hugh (1827 – 1893) Grassmillees
  - William (1829 – 1919)
    m.
    Janet Young (1845 – 1926)
    - Mary (1865 – 1960)
      m.
      Cuthbert Nairn
    - Elizabeth (Bessie) (1867 – 1954)
      m.
      George Osborne & James Henderson
    - Robert (1868 – 1952)
      m.
      Elizabeth Hannah
      - Jane (Janie) (1898 – 1993)
        m.
        William (Willie) Simpson
      - James (Jim) (1900 – 1977)
        m.
        Elizabeth (Betty) Craig
      - Elizabeth (Betty)(1905 – 1993)
        m.
        William (Bill) Murray
      - Hugh (1908 – 1983)
        m.
        Margrett Mitchell
    - George (1870 – 1944)
      m.
      Catherine Chalmers
    - Hugh (1872 – 1967)
      m.
      Jane Whiteford
    - James (1874 – 1902)
    - Euphemia (Phemie) (1877 – 1916)
      m.
      John Hannah
  - James (1839 - 1890)
    m. Elizabeth Bowie (1834 – 1899) Shaw
    - John (1831 – 1916) Holmes Farm Galston
    - Thomas (1833 – 1894)
    - Robert (1837 – 1919)
    - Euphemia (1839 – 1926)
    - Marion (1841 – 1911)

Family Tree Part 2

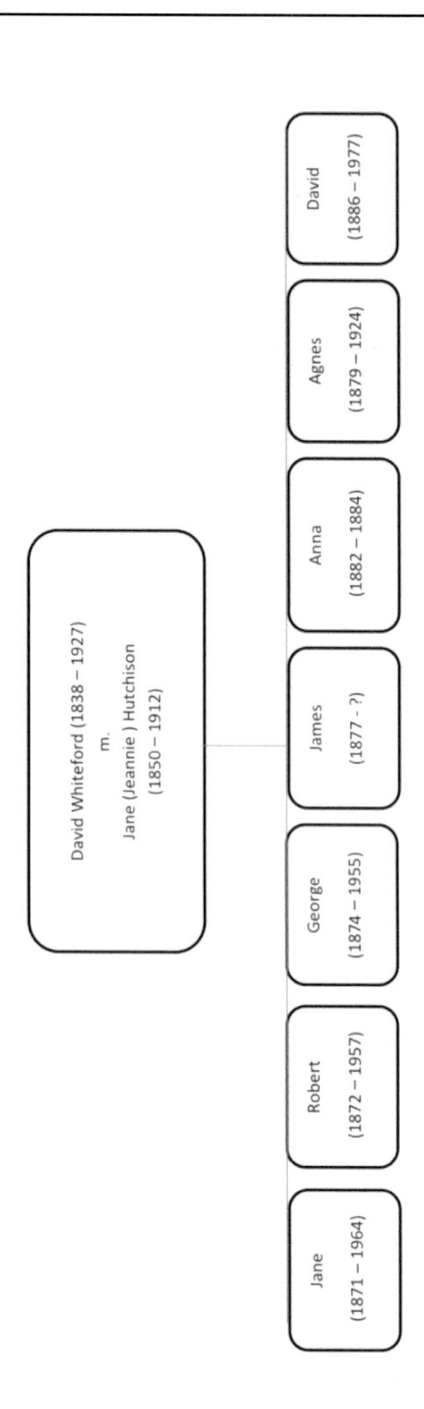

- David Whiteford (1838 – 1927)
  m.
  Jane (Jeannie) Hutchison (1850 – 1912)
  - Jane (1871 – 1964)
  - Robert (1872 – 1957)
  - George (1874 – 1955)
  - James (1877 - ?)
  - Anna (1882 – 1884)
  - Agnes (1879 – 1924)
  - David (1886 – 1977)